Acknowledgements

We would like to thank the following people for their assistance, support and patience in preparing this volume:

Dr David Picard of the Centre for Tourism and Cultural Change.

Andrea Murphy and Moira Page at Business Education Publishers Ltd.

Mrs Trellis from North Wales.

All of our contributors.

Contributors

John Beaumont-Kerridge: Luton Business School, University of Luton, UK.
E-mail: jbk@luton.ac.uk

Graham Brown: School of International Business, University of South Australia, Adelaide, Australia. E-mail: Graham.brown@unisa.edu.au

Deepak Chhabra: School of Health, Physical Education and Leisure Services, University of Northern Iowa, USA. E-mail: deepak.chhabra@uni.edu

Ralph Cousins: Paichai University, Korea.

Jonathan Edwards: School of Services Management, Bournemouth University, UK.
E-mail: jonedwards@bournemouth.ac.uk

José Escaleira: Viana do Castelo Polytechnic Institute, Portugal.
E-mail: jescaleira@estg.ipvc.pt

Hisham S. Gabr: Department of Architecture, Cairo University, Egypt.
E-mail: H.Gabr@link.net

Linley C. Hartmann: School of International Business, University of South Australia, Adelaide, Australia. Email: Linley.hartmann@unisa.edu.au

Gang Hoan Jeong: Paichai University, Korea.

Eleri Jones: Welsh School of Hospitality, Tourism and Leisure Management, University of Wales Institute, Cardiff, Wales. E-mail: ejones@uwic.ac.uk

Pandora Kay: School of Hospitality, Tourism and Marketing, Victoria University, Melbourne, Australia. E-mail: Pandora.Kay@vu.edu.au

Hoon Lee: Hanyang University, Korea.

Paula Alexandra Malta: Aveiro University, Portugal. E-mail: maltapmalta@egi.ua.pt

Peter Mason: Department of Tourism, Leisure and Sport Management, University of Luton, UK.
E-mail: peter.mason@luton.ac.uk

Miguel Moital: School of Services Management, Bournemouth University, UK.
E-mail: mmoital@bournemouth.ac.uk

Nigel Morgan: Welsh School of Hospitality, Tourism and Leisure Management, University of Wales Institute, Cardiff, Wales. E-mail: nmorgan@uwic.ac.uk

Keith Nurse: University of the West Indies, Institute of International Relations, Trinidad and Tobago. E-mail: keith_nurse772@hotmail.com

Maria Inês Pinho: Department of Arts and Humanities, Polytechnic Institute of Porto, Portugal. E-mail: inespinho@ese.ipp.pt

Melville Saayman: University of Potchefstroom, South Africa. E-mail: ontms@puknet.puk.ac.za

Galal Salem: Welsh School of Hospitality, Tourism and Leisure Management, University of Wales Institute, Cardiff, Wales. E-mail: gsalem@uwic.ac.uk

Lizl Steynberg: Pretoria Technikon, South Africa. E-mail: steynbergL@techpta.ac.za

Susanne Storm: University of Southern Denmark.

Jan Timmermann Pedersen: University of Southern Denmark.

Roger Vaughan: School of Services Management, Bournemouth University, UK.
E-mail: rvaughan@bournemouth.ac.uk

Richard Voase: Faculty of Social Science & Law, University of Lincoln, UK.
E-mail: rvoase@lincoln.ac.uk

Contents

Section 3
Impacts and Evaluations

Festivals and Tourism: Links and Developments

Philip Long, Mike Robinson and David Picard

Sheffield Hallam University, UK

Introduction

Festivals that celebrate, commemorate and perform aspects of local, regional and international cultures are a world-wide phenomenon that are receiving growing attention from the academic research community as well as from policy-makers and practitioners in the fields of tourism, the arts, and community development. This book is part of the on-going critical examination of festivals and particularly the various relationships they share with tourism. In these relationships, it could be said that festivals that celebrate various aspects of culture are the better established phenomena of the two, having long, long histories (Falassi, 1987). However, international tourism, as an important dimension of the wider concept of globalisation, has in many cases, shifted festivals from being relatively parochial and stable concerns with more or less localised audiences, to events that can attract global audiences, either as tourists, or via other forms of communicative media. Few festivals are resistant to at least some degree of tourist glare and the corresponding processes of change and adaptation that allows them to function with changing audiences, social objectives, and the new, often global, pressures upon them. In some instances, this has signalled the end of meaning for some festivals and even their discontinuance. In other instances, established festivals have changed and new festivals have emerged better designed to meet the needs and pressures of international tourists adopting a more reflexive approach that understands the realities of tourism (Ravenscroft and Matteucci, 2003).

In recent years there has been a clear increase in the number of festivals and events taking place across the world, though it is problematic to put an exact figure to this (Chako and Schaffer, 1993; Getz, 1997). Explanations for this proliferation of festivals vary in their emphasis. For some, the growth in the number of local festivals can be explained in part by an increasing, if not necessarily articulated, desire to re-assert local/community identities as part of an effort to combat a sense of cultural dislocation associated with processes of globalisation (Manning, 1983; Boissevain, 1996; De Bres and Davis, 2001; Quinn, 2003a). For others, and in contrast, a number of festivals, such as carnivals and melas, are themselves expressions of globalised and diasporic cultures and identities and are becoming more visible beyond the confines of their 'host' communities as a consequence of their external promotion by festival organisers, the media and tourism marketing agencies, contributing to the building of 'global festival themes'.

As well as being significant events in local communities' social calendars, festivals and events are also conceived and staged with the aim of attracting external audiences and particularly, valued tourist markets. In this sense, festivals have a dual role in being occasions for local participants, while also performing important and complex social, emotional and educational roles for tourist audiences. The interactions that take place between 'hosts and guests' in a festival setting are of growing interest to researchers as well as being a pragmatic concern for organisers and managers. Festivals are occasions by which a local community can legitimise, establish, display, or embellish its collective identity, and provide the tourist with the opportunity to temporarily confront and engage with aspects of 'otherness' expressed in the context of celebration.

Alongside the growth in the number of festivals, there has also been a general increase in the degree of professionalism in the occupations that are linked with festival planning, management, organisation and operations reflecting their social, political and, importantly, their economic roles. Indeed, heightened professionalism in the realm of cultural festivals and events indicates a more or less common recognition (or assertion) that festivals do make important contributions to tourism and economic development strategies, as well as providing a vehicle for community participation in regeneration programmes, a heightened sense of civic pride and an improved place image.

The significance of festivals can also be explained in the context of wider and complex cultural changes in the societies in which they are held and from which visitors come. In this sense, festivals may be seen as 'productions' and 'performances' that are emblematic, particularly of both the modern and post-modern world, but also pre-modern societies, reflecting social changes and continuities in the consumptive practices of leisure and tourism, as well as in relation to communities asserting and celebrating their distinctiveness and shared cultural traditions.

It is not surprising that over the years, festivals and events and their relationships with tourists and the tourism sector, have attracted increasing degrees of attention amongst researchers (see for instance: Getz, 1991; Saleh and Ryan, 1993; Watt, 1998; O'Sullivan and Jackson, 2002; Quinn, 2003b), as well as generating a proliferation of course programmes at various levels in festival and event studies and management (Formica, 1998). However, while this attention is justified, by some large measure there has emerged a rather mechanistic and unchallenging element in the literature, including uncritical, 'boosterist' accounts of how festivals 'should be done', and the utilisation of dominant 'westernised' models of practice (see, for example: Allen *et al*, 2002; Goldblatt, 2002). This literature, while making a relevant contribution to the development of the field of study and for practitioner use, offers little in terms of critical reflections on the complex relationships between for example, festivals, cultures, tourist and audience motivations and experiences, and particularly in non-western contexts.

This volume aims to contribute towards the development of these more critical perspectives in its collection of chapters that explore a number of key issues regarding the relationships between festivals and tourism. Relationships that impact upon festival and event organisers and local communities in a range of international settings, and policy, planning and management contexts. The chapters collected here also suggest some new research directions for the study of festivals and tourism.

As a book concerned with festivals and events, we are aware that this is an extremely broad field that is open to a range of possible definitions. However, we suggest that festivals may be delineated and classified in relation to their themes and social/public purposes. For example, they may be festivals that:

- perform important religious and sacred functions for participants;

- involve more or less elaborately staged ceremonial performances;

- celebrate anniversaries of notable figures and historical events;

- celebrate artistic and creative performances and achievements;

- centre on competitive 'traditional' events and sports;

- have a particular ethnic or 'exotic' dimension.

Typically, therefore festivals are conceived as 'cultural' where they are celebrations of 'characteristic' traditional and/or new art forms, customs, histories, peoples and places. However, they may also include festivals that perform elements of culture that are not necessarily a characteristic feature of local community life. Examples include festivals that are programmed with international arts and musical genres and that are created primarily to attract tourists, as well as catering for local audiences.

Festivals may also be categorised in relation to their scale and scope, locations and use of physical space. The scale and scope of cultural festivals ranges from, for example, World Fairs and European Cultural Capitals that attract international audiences numbering into the millions and widespread media attention. These 'mega-events' which often connect cultural events with major competitive sport tournaments, involve extensive and often controversial planning, programming and large budgets (Roche, 2000). At the other end of the spectrum are the huge number of, more or less, informal and localised village or neighbourhood celebrations, which may or may not attract tourists but are nevertheless significant for local communities. The nature of festival organisation and the extent to which they are managed professionally thus varies considerably, in part as a consequence of their scale and prominence.

Festivals provide opportunities for involvement in community life and celebrations, for the showcasing of local cultures, and for marking local associations with historical events, anniversaries, individuals and social/political achievements. However, the triumphalism and celebration that may be inherent in festival themes may be contested, controversial and exclusive to particular sections of a community and may or may not be welcoming of the tourist as an 'outsider'. A further function of a festival relates to its ability to involve, attract, even discourage, a diverse range of people including tourists. Festivals have always possessed the potential to mobilise political causes, perhaps aptly demonstrated by lesbian and gay pride festivals established in the United States and now replicated in the UK, Canada, Europe and Australia. As Kates and Belk (2001) indicate the festivals and parades celebrated on Lesbian and Gay Pride Day have defined audiences of lesbians and gays and seek to raise awareness of social injustices amongst wider publics, and yet they also increasingly seem to be playing to commercial tourism interests, in part to maintain their political message while under a threat of diluting it. Clearly the magnitude and make-up of the tourist audience relates to features of a festival such as the event's uniqueness, 'characteristic' or distinctive nature, its location and accessibility, its timing in relation to tourist seasons, the extent to which it is promoted to tourist markets and the involvement of the tourism industry.

With significant tourist audiences, some festivals have become big business events. Globalised, commodified festival forms that are linked with diasporic communities and art forms represent significant opportunities for commercialisation and sponsorship, reflecting the fashion ability of particular national and regional cultural expressions. Examples include the large number of festivals worldwide that are based on 'authentic' Irish and Caribbean themes and associations. These events have at times attracted major sponsorship and 'branding' by for example, the producers of alcoholic beverages such as Guinness and Red Stripe beer (with these companies themselves being parts of global corporations). The advertising of festivals and the festivalisation of advertising and product branding, for example in relation to St. Patrick's Day, and Caribbean/Latin American carnivals raises critical questions about the demands and requirements of commercial sponsors in a competitive funding environment. This injection of transnationality and globalisation to such festivals produces interesting questions for the researcher. Does direct and large scale commercialisation produce community discontent and a dislocation of social meanings, or does it lead to an invigoration of cultural expression? At the very least it generates change, new opportunities for exchange, conflict and social benefits (van Koningsbruggen, 1997). It certainly points to new challenges for the management and organisation of festivals and for the researcher.

There is a need for the refinement of methods for researching festivals and events and their tourism dimensions. There are problems associated with collecting data that are unsurprising given the short-term, large-scale and mobile nature of many festival populations, and consequent shortcomings in the quality and usefulness of the data collected. There may also be inherent biases in research commissioned by festival organisers themselves in seeking to 'prove' significant economic and social benefits that may be attributed unambiguously to their events.

Audiences, motivations, behaviour and marketing

Understanding the personal, shared, conflicting and social meanings and expectations that people attribute to their experiences of and participation in festivals and events, and their motivations for attendance are key concerns for researchers and festival organisers alike. These meanings may for example be conceived of as fulfilling (or failing to fulfil) perceived needs for a break from routine and 'everyday life', enlightenment and education, celebration, entertainment and novel experiences.

For the individual, festivals and events literally may be extraordinary occasions, providing unique, unanticipated and memorable experiences. In such cases, questions are raised about the richness and/or spirituality of the experience and the extent to which this may be compromised by 'over-managed' events that seek some illusory form of generic 'quality management' systems in their organisation. In contrast, the febrile atmosphere that surrounds some festivals may provide visitors with excuses for 'anti-social' behaviours that would not normally be tolerated in the visitor's home environment and that present particular management and regulatory challenges. Establishing and communicating what is acceptable and unacceptable behaviour at festivals, managing interactions with others and with the physical environment, and understanding the etiquette of events all represent challenges for policy makers, festival organisers, the tourism industry and participants.

The growth of tourist interest in festivals and events is in tune with now established market trends that suggest that as well as the ubiquitous search for 'pleasure' and enjoyment from the destination, there is increasing tourist demand for novel, exploratory, apparently 'authentic' (Getz, 1994), and participatory experiences through festivals (Crompton and McKay, 1997). Festival tourism thus links into more general tourist demands for adventure tourism (Swarbrooke et al. 2003), sport tourism, (Hinch and Higham, 2003), heritage tourism (Robinson et al, 2000) and cultural tourism in its broadest sense (Richards, 1996 & 2001; Smith 2003). From a supply-side perspective, attracting tourists to festivals and events against competing leisure options may also link directly with wider objectives such as arts marketers seeking to develop culturally diverse audiences, sports organisers seeking to encourage wider public participation in sport, or heritage agencies seeking to develop their education agendas. Certainly from the point of view of destination and promotion agencies seeking to expand tourist markets for economic gain, festivals have become highly significant. Of course the objectives of festival organisers and tourism agencies may not always be compatible. There are instances where festival organisers and social/cultural agencies may seek to promote access for audiences from disadvantaged sections of the local population, in contrast with the tourism industry's common desire to attract high spending middle class 'cultural tourists'.

Typologies of festival audiences and tourist markets may be identified in relation to, for example, their wants, needs, interests, gender, age, socio-economic class, ethnicity, group composition, extent of involvement in the festival, and the meanings that visitors attribute to the festival experience. The adaptation and application of generic marketing strategies and techniques such as market segmentation, targeting and analyses of visitor motivations is widespread both in management practice and in the festival management literature. However, the assumptions and methodologies that are associated with market segmentation studies may be insufficient as an approach to understanding the deeper picture of cultural change that underlies the motivations, expectations and experiences of festival audiences. Festival and event organisers and researchers alike may find more fruitful lines of enquiry in historical, anthropological and sociological perspectives on this subject (Picard, Robinson and Long, 2004).

Management and operations

The adaptation and application of management disciplines and their associated conceptual frameworks and approaches feature in much of the literature that has appeared on the subject of festivals and events and their connections with tourism. Festival and Event Management courses at universities and colleges are proliferating, as is the promotion of management focused short course programmes for festival practitioners. This interest in the planning and management of the strategic and operational dimensions of festivals is unsurprising given the competitive context in which they operate, the complex legal and regulatory frameworks they have to work within, the large budgets of some events, the allocation of public funding and private sector sponsorship monies to many festivals, and the consequent requirements for accountability and demonstrable returns on investments made.

Aspects of operational management that are critical for festival managers include programme planning, scheduling and logistical considerations, such as, for example, transport and accommodation requirements for artists and production staff. The infrastructural requirements for staging, audience management, health, safety and licensing in the context of the characteristics of particular festival sites also need to be given careful consideration. Operational management and risk assessment processes are thus important in the contexts of health and safety legislation and organisers' public liabilities and insurance cover.

Service quality management theory may also be applied to the study and practice of festivals. 'Quality' in this context, can, for example, be conceived in terms of a festival's business performance, the extent to which it fulfils its social responsibilities, and/or delivers to defined levels of consumer service. The quality of the tangible dimensions of a festival can also be assessed, for example in relation to the festival programme, the calibre of the artists and the facilities on site, while the quality of a festival organisation's responses to audience and community enquiries, concerns and recommendations might also be assessed. All in all, quality, however defined, relates to the administrative capacity of a festival, the levels of investment required, the degrees of support from key stakeholders and local communities, and the anticipated socio-economic legacy of the event.

For the majority of festival planners and managers, being able to demonstrate the economic value of festivals to politicians, funding bodies, potential sponsors and local communities has become increasingly important. This is not to deny the range of associated social benefits, but at the very least acknowledges that all festivals have a financial cost attached and this requires to be met. Various funding models exist depending on the nature of the festival, where it is located and the value particular societies and politicians place upon the idea of 'culture'; whether defined in a 'high arts' sense, in a more popular, inclusive way, or in the sense of communities and various ethnic groups. Clearly, there are diverse and dynamic approaches adopted, but as the number of festivals has increased so too has competition upon resources to fund them. Organisers have therefore to be ever more creative in the generating of funding sources and careful in the financial management of a festival. Attracting sponsorship to offset festival costs and to support programme elements is now a priority for many festival organisers. However, securing such funding needs to be balanced against the commercialisation that is inevitably associated with corporate support.

Increasingly, festival organisers are also being required by government agencies to provide some evidence of the economic impacts of their event in order to justify public funding in competition with other demands on the public purse. Such studies commonly emphasise the additional and positive economic impacts that are generated by the tourism that is attributable to festival attendance. Methods commonly employed include various income, spending and employment multiplier models, input-output analyses, calculations of value added, cost-benefit analyses, estimations of the spatial and social distribution of economic costs and benefits, and economic forecasting techniques applied to festivals.

Arguably, there is a tendency for at least some economic research on festivals to be uncritical and focused inwardly on individual case studies, with limited reference to experiences and methodologies employed elsewhere. There is also a tendency to assume, or even 'construct' positive economic outcomes and 'benefits', particularly in research commissioned by festival organisers as part of their case for continuing public funding. The short-term nature of festivals and events further complicates the accuracy of economic analyses and makes the attribution of economic benefits problematic. There are also difficulties of distinguishing festival visitors from residents, disaggregating their spending and defining 'appropriate' expenditure that is retained in the locality. Estimating the extent to which expenditure may be displaced from other local attractions and businesses during the duration of a festival is also problematic and organisers may not be forthcoming with revenue data from admissions and direct spending during an event. Thus, unambiguously attributing additional positive economic impacts to festivals and festival tourism is extremely difficult.

The pressures for professionalism and accountability entails that the organisational management and leadership dimensions of festivals have been given added importance. However, there seems to be a bi-polar split between on the one hand, highly professional planned and managed events that are well resourced, and on the other hand, a large number of relatively small festivals that are largely created and sustained through the efforts of individuals and small groups of volunteers. Now while a festival's grounding in the efforts of local individuals and networks can be a significant strength in maintaining local support and commitment, it may also be a weakness in terms of a festival's reliance on amateur organisers that may lack professional skills and experience. This is particularly important when considering basic health and safety issues. Managing risk and ensuring compliance with the law are vital considerations for festival and event managers in situations where large crowds in combination with a celebratory atmosphere, possibly involving the consumption of alcohol and drugs, inexperienced management and voluntary staff in particular settings and weather conditions combine to create dangerous conditions. Life threatening and dangerous behaviour may be integral to an event experience, and visitor behaviour, such as 'crowd surfing' and 'stage diving' at rock festivals and 'running the bulls' at Pamplona in Spain, have resulted in deaths and serious injuries. In this context there have been calls for policies, legislation and regulation and the establishment of legal liability to cover festival management.

Other risk avoidance strategies that may be pursued by festival organisers include attempts to avoid, reduce, diffuse and reallocate risk factors, as well as taking out insurances to cover anticipated risk scenarios. All of these approaches can be subjected to various evaluation methodologies that are adapted and applied in festival and event tourism in connection with their appropriateness (the match between event objectives and the needs of core stakeholders); effectiveness (the match with the festival's own objectives); and efficiency (in relation to costs) (Faulkner 1993; Mossberg, 1993).

Linked to the issue of risk management for the organisers of festivals are those of communication and media relationships. For increasingly risk concerned tourists, festivals must demonstrate safety at the very least, and should there be any accidents or health and safety scares, they should be able to handle the often intense spotlight of media attention so as not to compromise the future of the event. Working with the media has become yet another aspect of operational management of growing importance for festival organisers. Areas such as the selection of media outlets to work with, the design and drafting of press releases, text and visual images for marketing materials all require attention. The ways in which various audiences, including tourists, 'read' and respond to messages about cultural festivals relates directly to wider touristic aspects of destination image. Festivals, are in this sense an important way in which the prospective tourist shapes his or her image of a place at the stages of pre-visit, during a visit and post visit.

Festivals, policy and regeneration

Festivals and events are political matters. Indeed, they may be highly charged and contentious occasions when festival organisers and participants play out conflictual and/or consensual community, ethnic, local, regional or nationalistic agendas. Festivals provide opportunities and outlets for celebrations of multi-cultural communities and they *may* reinforce cross-cultural understanding, recognition and esteem. Conversely, they may emphasise local exceptionalism, exclusivity and superiority. As such, the political dimensions of festivals are of critical interest.

Policy studies provides various frameworks for the analysis of the extent and nature of local participation in, or opposition to, festival programmes, and the promotion of particular political interests and constituencies that may be explicit or implicit within a festival's cultural themes. Policy studies also directs attention to the institutional context within which festivals exist, are contested and develop as well as to the areas of public policy that impinge upon them (D'Angelo and Vesperini, 1998). For example, while festivals are most obviously affected and directed by explicit arts, cultural and tourism policies, they may also relate indirectly but significantly to social, education, health and regeneration affairs.

Festivals can also be conceived of as being part of the 'new' political economy of partnerships in urban and local governance that has emerged since the 1980s, most strongly in the United Kingdom, parts of Europe and North America. Partnerships and collaborations exist between the various interest groups or stakeholders that are involved with festival planning, management and performance, and with local artistic and resident constituencies and the tourism industry. However, 'partnerships' may be little more than nominal or be characterised more by conflict than the consensus and agreement suggested by the positive connotations of a 'partnership'. Collaborative relationships, partnerships and policy networks are complex and mixed in their depth and breadth and they have generally received limited attention with regard to festivals and cultural events (Long, 2000).

In terms of tourism development at the destination level, festivals and events provide new product and packaging opportunities for the private tourism sector in collaboration with festival organisers and destination marketing organisations. They may also support the generation of tourist demand during off-peak seasons and attract new 'niche' market segments drawn to those destinations that host special interest festivals. As such, festivals can broaden the tourist destination offer and supplement as well as celebrate more traditional and established, but perhaps declining attractions, venues and spaces. There is a risk though that these supposedly generic benefits are claimed without regard to specific local circumstances and resources. There may also be difficulties in persuading local electorates and politicians that public funding for festivals is defensible on economic and political grounds.

Festivals and events may also be used to contribute to the development of positive place images through the re-positioning of urban and rural areas in the public imagination as sites of creativity, innovation and tolerance. Festivals and cultural events play an increasingly important role in cities and regions that are seeking to transform their local economies and to obtain competitive advantages in tourism terms and for inward investment. In rural areas too festivals built around local food and beverages celebrate and present distinctive and quality products for tourist consumption. Such events are often linked by tourism and rural development agencies to the creation of trails and networks in support of the rural economy. There may though be a risk of over planning and managing such initiatives which may be best served by local idiosyncrasies and control.

In their programming, festivals typically allow for an emphasis to be placed on the unique characteristics of place, particularly with respect to cities, regions and countries bidding to host 'mega-events' where representations of locally unique 'characteristics' and attributes play a major part in competitive bidding processes. But while there are undoubtedly success stories, this transformative power of festivals may well be over exaggerated at times, although it is often difficult to disaggregate the impacts of festivals from wider promotional activities.

Major cultural celebrations such as the European Cultural Capitals programme can have significant and positive influences on physical developments, as well as more intangible considerations such as improved images of host cities and regions, quality of life, community participation and civic pride. It may also be argued that the competitive bidding processes to secure major cultural events may in themselves be a catalyst for partnerships to emerge, with a focus on social inclusion and regeneration. However, bidding processes are vulnerable to accusations relating to local politicians squandering scarce resources on speculative projects that do not address directly local development priorities.

Despite such criticisms, festivals nevertheless do provide a means for re-structuring, re-shaping and animating city spaces and new communities, for example in new town settings, or recently settled migrant populations. They provide opportunities for democratising and 'reclaiming' the idea of 'urban commons' in increasingly privatised city neighbourhoods. It may also be the case that urban development policies themselves are becoming 'festivalised' with cultural festival spaces being conceived as a contribution to an urban aesthetic streetscape as part of wider planning, architectural and design processes.

There is a risk though that such aestheticised festival spaces and forms may lead to 'sanitised' events with some communities made unwelcome and excluded from the programme and even cleared from the streets during its duration. In this vein, Atkinson and Laurier (1996) discuss the example of the Bristol International Festival of the Sea where they argue that 'traveller' communities were discouraged from participating in the event. Such exclusion may of course result in oppositional festivals being staged to coincide with the 'official' event. So called 'oppositional' or counter-cultural festivals and events also of course take place in rural settings, with 'free' rock festivals and raves continuing to outrage public decency and morality in the countryside. Some of these events, such as the Glastonbury Festival in England have become more or less mainstream and commercialised occasions, although they continue to attract controversy through the licentious behaviour and drug and alcohol consumption that tend to be a feature of such festivals.

The chapters

Through various international cases at various scales, the chapters in this book present issues relating to the development, planning, marketing, management, and various impacts of festivals and events with regard to tourism and tourists. The book is broadly divided into three sections

(Marketing and Markets; Planning, Management and Operations and; Impacts and Evaluations), however it is recognised that there are inevitable overlaps between all.

The performing arts are an important dimension of festivals. The latter can, in a short space of time, provide much needed income for artists and management companies, and importantly can raise the profile of performers and overcome issues of competition from new media and other leisure activities. Attracting tourists as part of wider efforts of audience development is one strategy for sustaining and reinvigorating the performing arts by generating much needed external income. This has long been the case in London, where overseas visitors account for 30% of all theatre tickets bought (Department of Media, Culture and Sport, 2002), though not surprising given London's position as one of the World's leading tourist destinations. Kay, in chapter 2 on cultural event tourism develops the important linkages between the performing arts sector, cultural events and tourism and focuses upon research undertaken in Australia and the Melbourne area in particular to highlight the need to define and research target markets in a structured and meaningful way. Through such a process Kay argues, the performing arts sector, in the context of cultural festivals and events, can harness significant potential from tourism by building new audiences.

Understanding tourists as an important sector of festival audiences is at the heart of an investigation by Mason and Beaumont-Kerridge (chapter 3) into the motivations of visitors attending the largest folk festival in Europe; the Sidmouth International Festival. As the authors note, understanding the tourist and their motivations has been a major theme for tourism research over many years. Importantly, they point out that such research should increasingly inform the organisers and managers of festivals and cultural events. This focus on audiences indicates the importance of adopting but also going beyond marketing theory and practice. In seeking to understand motivations and behaviour the researcher is drawn into the realm of social psychology to inform methods of approach and the conceptual frameworks for subsequent analysis.

The work of Mason and Beaumont-Kerridge involved the study of a cultural festival that has been established for nearly fifty years. However, festivals and events are being developed all the time and require ever more critical planning to establish themselves and, if the festival is seeking to attract tourists, clear understanding and measurement of the target market(s) is vital. Lee, Jeong and Cousins (chapter 4) articulate the need for strategic planning and develop a seven stage model based upon an analysis of the then new 2000 Science Festival held in Daejeon, South Korea. Their contribution also implies that more research attention is directed to the educational and social roles that festivals can play. The Daejeon Science Festival is now an annual event and attracts some 300,000 visitors.

Now, while there are apparently practicable and 'orthodox' ways to market and plan for festivals and events, Voase, in chapter 5, reminds us that these too are open to reflection and challenge. Standard approaches to segmenting the market by difference he argues, overlooks the realities that festival visitors are bound by the commonalities of their senses and sensibilities as well; effectively a selective approach rather than an inclusive one. This, Voase suggests, is often in contradiction to the very nature of a festival.

Such are the perceived economic, social and political benefits of hosting festivals and events, and the drives to utilise large events to stimulate tourism directly during an event, or indirectly at a later stage through imaging, that considerable effort and public investment goes into the process of bidding to host such occasions. This is a highly competitive process undertaken by countries and cities and as Steynburg and Saayman argue in chapter 6, it requires considerable attention. Drawing upon a review of work focusing mainly on sporting events, they provide a detailed discussion of the bidding process and its various phases in order to put forward a number of key success factors. Steynberg and Saayman's chapter considers factors in connection with the highly politicised issues that influence city authorities in their deciding whether or not to bid for the hosting of major events.

Away from the competition of bidding for events and focusing more upon the undertaking of more indigenous events, in chapter 7 Salem, Jones and Morgan focus upon the practicalities of managing festivals in a specific context. The context is that of Egypt which has long recognised the importance of cultural events as part of its tourism policy. Using three case studies of the Nile Bounty Festival, the Ismailia International Folklore Festival and the Aida Opera Concerts, this chapter proposes an organising framework or model of good practice to guide the study of decision making, planning, implementation and evaluation of cultural festivals and the feedbacks between these critical dimensions of festival management. They draw particular attention to the contexts and backgrounds of festivals that fail to achieve their objectives, their micro- and macro-political dimensions and the local specificities that were at work in the case of a major programme of festival development in Egypt.

Far removed from the festivals and events to emerge or be created out of social, cultural or economic need, Chapter 8 considers a highly specific natural event – that of the total eclipse of the sun – and the attempts to organise and manage this for tourists. Though total eclipses of the sun occur somewhere on the earth every eighteen months they last for only thirty seconds or so. Hartmann and Brown using participant observation methods, researched this occasion as it occurred in the Australian Outback, its build up, and the subsequent impact on the tourists who witnessed it. The chapter provides an interesting examination of the way this effectively uncontrollable occasion, was packaged for particular tourists types and the inherent difficulties of managing visitors – often in an amateur fashion – to a festival site. Also discussed is the relevance of the case for similar such events and the chapter suggests some useful methodological possibilities that participant observation techniques possesses for festivals researchers.

An essential aspect of contemporary festival organisation and management is that of regulation; an issue that can cause particular concerns for potential tourist audiences as one highlighted accident can have a major deterrent effect on future visitors. Consumer protection and the regulation of festival visitor behaviour and interactions with local communities draws attention to the law governing and affecting event organisers, audiences and participants. Here it soon becomes apparent that there are difficulties of legal definition and regulation in the complex and diverse field of festivals and events. It is also the case that owing to considerable variation in legal systems and legislation across the world, it is problematic to draw upon common guidelines. Storm, in chapter 9 discusses the complexity of regulatory issues in the context of rock festivals and highlights the case of the European Union's efforts to define and agree EU and national competence to legislate in this area. Pedersen (chapter 10) extends this discussion to the implications of a 'soft law' approach being developed at EU level alongside event organisers' attempts to self-regulate in the vital area of consumer health and safety in the area of cultural festivals and events.

The impacts of festivals and events have long been the subject of academic attention and increasingly are an important focus for festival organisers too. The economic outcome of festivals is arguably the most well covered type of impact and also the most contested in relation to measurement and assessment techniques. In chapter 11, Chhabra presents a case study based on two 'Scottish' highland games in the United States – the Grandfather Mountain Highland Games and the Flora Macdonald Highland Games – both derivative festivals from Scotland but with long histories nonetheless, and both attracting significant numbers of tourists. Chhabra not only points to the importance of tourist expenditure to the festivals studied in direct and indirect terms, but also to the importance of the regularity of such events. In doing so she also identifies a series of methodological issues that festival evaluators need to address.

Nurse (chapter 12) also directs attention to the economic impacts of festivals in his consideration of six festivals in the Caribbean, some well established and others not. Importantly, Nurse's work identifies the value of these festivals as a pull for tourists and specifically their ability to increase hotel occupancy. But while this chapter considers the economic value of festivals, it also evaluates the Caribbean festivals in a wider social and political context pointing to the benefits that accrue in terms of esteem, community development, spin offs to the entertainment sector and benefits generated by the export of the music festival model. Nurse's approach commends a political economy perspective on festivals that moves research on from the mere application of technical, positivist economic models.

Evaluating festivals in terms wider than just the economic is in line with the creative, cultural and social basis of festivals. It is necessary to locate festivals and tourism within on-going processes of development and change. In the case of the Dubai Shopping Festival, Gabr (chapter 13) draws out the significance and massive success of a festival recently created by a partnership between the government and the private sector. Gabr picks up on the neglected area of the relationships between festivals and the nature, development, aesthetics and 'fabric' of cities. The festival feeds off the importance of the shopping experience to tourists, both in the spaces of new shopping malls and traditional souks, and has stimulated a process of physical transformation and urban regeneration that marks out the city of Dubai as a tourist destination as well as a place for living .

The exploitation of large-scale cultural festivals and mega-events, such as the European Capital of Culture years as a focus for development and regeneration requires critical analysis. Exaggerated claims may be made about the economic benefits and international visitors that may be expected to flow from and to these events. Such events may also be accused of targeting downtown, city centre locations, primarily benefiting property and commercial developments, 'elite' art forms and middle class audiences. Policies and strategies for these large budget festivals need to go beyond an emphasis on economic considerations, with environmental, image, social/cultural and political issues needing to receive more prominence in festival studies. In chapter 14, Malta, Pinho and Escaleira illustrate these complexities in the context of the city of Porto in Portugal, where a combination of the 2001 European Capital of Culture, designation as a UNESCO World Heritage City and the hosting of part of the 2004 European football championships have contributed to the transformation of the city, although the question of international tourist arrivals failing to come up to expectations is noted. Their chapter also draws attention to the transnational nature of such cultural events, involving the European Union and United Nations agencies and raises questions about the balance between urban competitiveness and cooperation and city image formation and re-formulation in the context of globalisation. Their work connects well with Edwards and Moital's work (chapter 15) which discusses and evaluates the processes and outputs of the 1998 'World Fair' in the Portuguese capital.

In all, the chapters in this book address some critical issues in the examination of the marketing, management, development and politics of festivals and cultural events. It is hoped that these contributions will suggest new directions for researchers, policy makers and practitioners in this thriving and vibrant sector.

References

Allen, J., O'Toole, W., McDonnell, I. and Harris, R. (2002), *Festival and Special Event Management,* Sydney, John Wiley & Sons Australia.

Allen, K. and Shaw, P. (2001), *Festivals Mean Business: The shape of Arts Festivals in the UK,* London, British Arts Festival Association.

Atkinson, D., and Laurier, E. (1998), A Sanitised City? Social Exclusion at Bristol's 1996 International Festival of the Sea, *Geoforum,* Volume 29, Issue 2, May, Pages 199-206.

Boissevain, J. (Ed.) (1992), *Revitalizing European Rituals,* London, Routledge.

Boissevain, J. (Ed.) (1996), *Coping with Tourists: European Reactions to Mass Tourism,* Oxford, Bergahn Books.

Breen, H., Bull, A. and Walo, M. (2001), A comparison of survey methods to estimate visitor expenditure at a local event, *Tourism Management,* Volume 22, Issue 5, October, Pages 473-479.

Chacko, H. E. and Schaffer, J. D. (1993), The evolution of a festival: Creole Christmas in New Orleans, *Tourism Management,* Volume 14, Issue 6, December Pages 475-482.

Crompton, J. L., and McKay, S. L. (1997), Motives of visitors attending festival events, *Annals of Tourism Research,* Volume 24, Issue 2, Pages 425-439.

D'Angelo, M. and Vesperini, P. (1998), *Cultural Policies in Europe: a Comparative Approach,* Strasbourg, Council of Europe Publishing.

De Bres, K. and Davis, J. (2001) Celebrating group and place: a case study of a new regional festival, *Tourism Geographies,* Volume 3, Number 3, Pages 326-337

Falassi, A. (Ed.) (1987), *Time Out of Time: Essays on the Festival,* Albuquerque, University of New Mexico Press.

Faulkner, B. (1993), *Evaluating the Tourism Impact of Hallmark Events,* Occasional Paper No. 16. Australian Bureau of Tourism Research.

Formica, S. (1998), The development of festivals and special events studies. *Festival Management and Event Tourism,* 5 (3), 131-137.

Getz, D. (1991), *Festivals, Special Events and Tourism,* New York, Van Nostrand Reinhold.

Getz, D. (1997), *Event Management and Event Tourism,* New York, Cognizant Communications.

Goldblatt, J. (2002), *Special Events: Twenty-first century global event management,* New York, John Wiley.

Hall, C. M. (1997), *Hallmark Tourist Events: Impacts, Management and Planning,* Chichester, John Wiley.

Hinch, T. and Higham, J. (2003) *Sport Tourism Development*, Channel View Publications, Clevedon.

Hughes, H. (2000), *Arts, Entertainment and Tourism*, Oxford, Butterworth Heinemann.

Kates, S. M. and Belk, R.W. (2001), The Meanings of Lesbian and Gay Pride Day, *Journal of Contemporary Ethnography*, Vol.30, No.4, pp.392-429.

Larson, M. (2002), A political approach to relationship marketing: case study of the Storsjöyran festival, *International Journal of Tourism Research*, Volume: 4, Issue: 2, March/April, Pages, 119-143.

Long, P. E. (2000), After the Event – Perspectives on Organisational Partnerships in the Management of a Themed Festival Year, *Event Management*, Vol. 7 (1).

Manning, F. E. (1983), (Ed.) *The Celebration of Society: Perspectives on Contemporary Cultural Performances*, Bowling Green University Press.

Martorella, R. (1996), *Art and Business: An International Perspective on Sponsorship*, Westport, Conn., Praeger.

Mossberg, L. (Ed.) (2000), *Evaluation of Events: Scandinavian Experiences*, New York, Cognizant Communications.

O'Sullivan, D. and Jackson, M. (2002), Festival Tourism: A Contributor to Sustainable Local Economic Development? *Journal of Sustainable Tourism*, Vol 10 No 4.

Prentice, R. and Andersen, V. (2003), Festival as creative destination, *Annals of Tourism Research*, Volume 30, Issue 1, January 2003, Pages 7-30.

Quinn, B. (a) (2003), Symbols, practices and myth-making: cultural perspectives on the Wexford Festival Opera. *Tourism Geographies*, 5 (3), 329-349.

Quinn, B. (b) (2003), *Shaping Tourism Places: Agency and Interconnection in Festival Settings* in Cronin, M. and O'Connor, B. *Irish Tourism: Image, Culture and Identity*. Clevedon, Channel View Publications.

Ravenscroft and Matteucci, (2003), The Festival as Carnivalesque: social governance and control at Pamplona's San Firmin Fiesta, *Tourism, Culture and Communication*, Vol 4 pp. 1-15

Robinson, M., Evans, N., Long, P., Sharpley, R. and Swarbrooke, J. (2000) *Tourism and Heritage Relationships: Global, National and Local Perspectives*. Sunderland, Business Education Publishers

Roche, M. (2000) *Mega-events: Olympics and Expos in the Growth of Global Culture*, Routledge, London.

Saleh, F. and Ryan, C. (1993) Jazz and knitwear : Factors that attract tourists to festivals, *Tourism Management*, Volume 14, Issue 4, August Pages 289-297

Swarbrooke, J., Beard, C., Leckie, S., Pomfret, G. (2003) *Aventure Tourism: The New Frontier*, Butterworth Heinemann, London.

Van Koningsbruggen, P. (1997), *Trinidad Carnival: A Quest for National Identity*, Macmillan Education Ltd., London.

White, A. L. (1987), *Lost in Music: Culture, Style and the Musical Event*, London, Routledge & Kegan Paul.

Section 1

Marketing and Markets

Cultural Event Tourism: modelling performing arts tourism events and effective marketing strategies

Pandora Kay

Victoria University, Australia

Introduction

In Australia and many other Western cultures, there is a history of financial difficulty for locally-based performing arts companies and events. One current problem is how to increase attendances to performing arts, as those unable to attract new markets are faltering. Related problems are increasing competition and changing entertainment trends for some key markets. Direct competition for audiences is increasing due to an expanding number of performing arts events on offer, both locally and elsewhere to which highly mobile audiences are willing to travel. Indirect competition comes from other entertainment options including all other forms of art and cultural activities and an ever-expanding range of other entertainment options largely associated with new technology and changing entertainment preferences of some key markets such as the youth market. Even the live contemporary music scene laments declining audiences as the youth market increasingly prefers in-home entertainment options such as television and videos, burning their own CDs, internet-based entertainment; computer games and play stations.

Growing tourist markets represent new potential audiences for locally-based performing arts companies and events but the challenge is how to attract these tourists to attend performances. Effective marketing strategies are crucial to attracting markets, and this chapter presents a typology of performing arts tourist events and develops a procedural model for researching cultural event tourists and effective marketing strategies with a specific comparison between two forms of performing arts: arts festival events and locally-based performing arts. Although of particular relevance to Melbourne-based performing arts, this research is also of relevance to performing arts events located elsewhere in Australia or other Western cultures. It is also of relevance to cultural event tourism in general, particularly the marketing of locally-based cultural events to tourist markets.

Cultural life and the role of the performing arts within this, at the beginning of the 21st century continue to evolve in complex ways. Some similarities in the recent evolution of the performing arts can be noted across Western cultures. A recent major report on the performing arts in the United States over the past thirty years with recommendations for their future well-being (McCarthy *et al*, 1999), identifies some familiar current challenges for live performances in particular. Financial pressures, especially for medium-sized organisations, an increasingly competitive leisure market, and the impact of new technologies, especially recordings and broadcast performances via various media including the Internet and digital technology, are identified as particular challenges. While the number of organisations and performing arts infrastructure venues have increased during the 1980s and 90s, their real revenues have declined. Audience growth has occurred in the same period, but has largely resulted from population growth and increasing education levels, rather than an increase in the percentage of the population that engages in the arts and therefore future attendance levels may weaken. Mid-sized non-profit organisations are facing the greatest difficulty in attracting enough of the public to cover their costs and are most likely to disappear in the future. Hence the report's most important recommendation, is the need to stimulate demand for the arts in contrast with the concentration over the past half-century on building and strengthening the supply of artists, organisations and productions. Another finding of relevance to this chapter, is the acknowledgement of the increasing role of the marketplace, marketing and marketers in the delivery of the arts. Associated with this trend, future research needs identified in the report, are the examination of how individual tastes for the arts are formed and how the benefits of the arts can be identified and measured so that more diversified and innovative approaches to promoting the arts can be explored.

Some similar findings have been reported in relation to the performing arts in Australia, especially financial pressures, increased competition due to growth in the number of performing arts organisations, venues and productions, and the importance of audience development and marketing (ABS, 2000a; Nugent, 1999; Australia Council, 1999). Throughout the 1990s, the number and diversity of suppliers of high quality performing arts product increased. Some key areas of growth included self-entrepreneuring by subsidised venues; entrepreneuring of international productions (including spectaculars); increase in the number of, funding for, and attendances at major festivals; and touring activities by the major companies both within and outside their home State (Nugent, 1999). Growth in arts and cultural festivals is a very relevant issue for the performing arts industry and also for cultural event tourism. Most Australian States and Territories hold regular arts festivals, some on an annual basis (e.g. Melbourne Festival; Perth Festival, Sydney Festival), others every two years (e.g. Adelaide Festival; Brisbane Festival). The impact of festivals throughout the 1990s increased in terms of the number of festivals, audience attendances, government funding and private sector support (ABS, 2000a; Arts Victoria, 2000b, Nugent, 1999).

An enquiry into 31 major performing arts organisations (Nugent, 1999) found the vast majority are facing high and escalating fixed costs associated with lead times that determine how long in advance a company's cost structure becomes fixed. Primary cost drivers are labour costs, public expectations of production values, advertising rates, and venue hire charges. Production costs (including royalties) for a new work or a new production of an existing work in 1997 ranged from more than $700,000 for major dance and opera performances to an average of $200,000 for major theatre productions (Nugent, 1999). Competition also exists between art forms and has increased especially as the size of audiences who cross-over between the art forms increases. Established broadline theatre, opera and ballet have been most affected by alternative forms of entertainment that include new entrants such as festivals, and the rise of large scale commercial musicals, opera and dance spectaculars, as well as film and CDs (Nugent, 1999).

In comparison with their international peers in the US and the UK, some Australian major performing arts companies earn more box office, including The Australian Ballet, Opera Australia, Melbourne Theatre Company (MTC) and Sydney Theatre Company (STC). Consequently, in terms of revenue generation, these companies are classified as a box office led model in contrast with the prevailing models in the US and the UK which are more private sector for the former, and government led for the latter (Nugent, 1999). Therefore audience development and the role of marketing in attracting audiences are even more crucial for major performing arts companies in Australia.

Arts marketing and audience development are also priorities in Australia acknowledged by the lead arts body, the Australia Council as, "developing new audiences, diversifying audiences and increasing attendances enhances the sustainability and success of the performing arts sector"

(Australia Council, 1999). In relation to arts marketing and audience development, the Australia Council (1999) further acknowledges, "an important first step is to understand the composition and needs of particular audiences so that marketers can strategically target promotion of specific performances".

These research findings emphasising a need for increased performing arts attendances, audience development and audience diversification, highlight the potential of growing tourist markets as new audiences for the performing arts and the important role of marketing in attracting any market as an audience including tourists. Knowledge of how to attract tourist markets to locally-based cultural events is important for the performing arts as well as from a tourism perspective. For the performing arts, attracting tourist markets will contribute to maintaining a diverse range of locally-based performing arts in Western cultures at a time when funding is declining and new markets are needed. If inbound tourists are attracted to locally-based performing arts events, this further develops the arts as an export industry. From a tourism perspective, attracting tourists to locally-based performing arts events increases tourist's cultural experiences and expenditure and may result in new tourists being attracted to a destination. If inbound tourists are attracted, this in turn increases the destination's foreign exchange earnings. While this research focuses on performing arts events, it is also of relevance to marketing other forms of cultural events to tourist markets generally. Similarly, while it largely focuses on event tourism at performing arts events in Melbourne, Australia, it is of relevance to cultural event tourism located elsewhere in Australia or other developed countries.

A brief literature review is firstly undertaken to identify and develop an overview of relevant theories on the marketing of cultural event tourism. Existing data of relevance to cultural tourism in Australia and Melbourne is then analysed to determine the significance of cultural event tourism in these geographic areas to date, to identify further variables of relevance to the marketing of cultural event tourism, and to determine the role of marketing in cultural event tourism. Any gaps in the existing data will also be identified. From the initial literature review and analysis of existing data, conceptual frameworks and models of relevance to effective marketing of performing arts events to tourists will then be developed. The conceptualisation and development of these frameworks and models will include further in-depth consideration of the supporting literature for each of the key concepts.

Arts events tourism

Cultural event tourism and tourists take several forms. In this chapter cultural event tourists (Figure 1) are categorised firstly by type of tourist (i.e. international, national – interstate and intrastate – and day visitors), then by primary purpose of visit (i.e. visiting friends and relatives, holiday/leisure, or business) and then by type of cultural event activity attended (i.e. locally-based major performing arts). This typology of performing arts event tourists, considers these forms of cultural event tourism as a sub-group of cultural tourism based on type of activity attended, and actual tourist behaviour. This definition, in turn, is based on an operational/behavioural definition of tourism as the 'activities of persons' (UN & WTO, 1994; WTO, 1985; Alzua *et al*, 1998).

The definition is made operational through existing or additional data that can be readily collected, and it relates closely to existing relevant data such as the Bureau of Tourism Research annual *International Visitor Survey* (e.g. BTR, 2000a), annual *National Visitor Survey* (e.g. BTR, 2001), and existing studies of cultural tourism in Australia by inbound visitors (Foo & Rossetto, 1998) and by domestic tourists (CMCSWG, 1997).

The above definition also requires 'major performing arts events' to be defined as the type of cultural activity attended that is of interest in this chapter. Typologies of performing arts events vary depending on whether they have been developed from an arts industry perspective (e.g. Australia Council, 1999; ABS, 1999, 2000a; Arts Victoria, 1997a, 1997b) or as part of cultural activities identified within tourism research (e.g. Foo & Rossetto, 1998; CMCSWG, 1997; BTR 2000a, 2001).

Figure 1 *Performing arts event tourist typology*

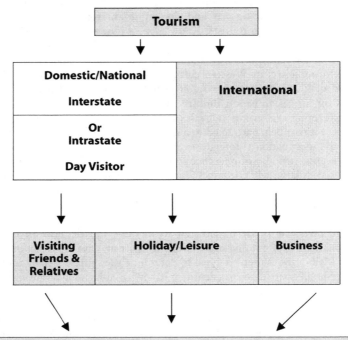

Source: based on WTO, 1985; UN & WTO, 1994; Arts Victoria, 1997a,b; CMCSWG, 1997; Australia Council, 1999; ABS, 1999, 2000a; Foo & Rossetto, 1998; Australia Council, 1999; BTR, IVS, NVS.

In this typology, performing arts event tourists are a sub-group of cultural event tourists based on the overall cultural activity category 'performing arts' as categorised in Figure 1, and the definition of 'major, locally-based live performing arts' as defined below. The six performing arts sub-categories include two of the six sub-categories of the cultural activity typology used in research on inbound cultural tourists to Australia (Foo & Rossetto, 1998), namely, festivals or fairs (music, dance, comedy, and multi-arts but excluding the forms of visual arts, and heritage *per se*); and performing arts or concerts (theatre, opera, ballet, classical and contemporary music). The performing arts sub-category of 'musical theatre' is additional to the six sub-categories used by Foo and Rossetto (1998) and is included here as a separate sub-category in acknowledgement of its major contribution to paid performances in Australia as identified by research on the performing arts sector (ABS, 2000a).

Major, Locally-based, Live Performing Arts Events are distinct from recorded or broadcast events and are held regularly (i.e. either for a season annually, or for several seasons per year), by number of paid performances (i.e. a total of more than 100 performances per year, season or festival); by number of employees (i.e. more than 100 employees per organisation), held in a large capital site (e.g. local performing arts venues with capacity of more than 500), with a large investment in production for a new work or a new production of an existing work (more than $200,000), and those performances that are locally-based (i.e. held in their resident city rather than on tour) (ABS, 2000a; Nugent, 1999; McCarthy *et al*, 1999).

Associated definitions

- *International:* any trip by a temporary visitor from another country who spends at least one night but not more than one year for the purposes of business or leisure and who attends at least one performing arts event tourist activities during their stay (based on IVS in BTR, 2000a, 2000b).

- *Domestic:* any trip within in this case Australia by a person residing in Australia, irrespective of nationality, travelling over 40 kms from their usual residence, involving a stay of at least one night away from home, who attends at least one of the above mentioned performing arts event tourist activities during their stay (based on WTO and UN definitions cited in CMCSWG, 1997; Foo & Rossetto, 1998).

- *Interstate:* residents from outside the state of in this case Victoria, visiting the state for at least one night (based on NVS in BTR, 2001; CMCSWG, 1997).

- *Intrastate:* in this case residents of the state of Victoria travelling over 40kms within their own state's boundaries to visit Melbourne for at least one night (based on NVS in BTR, 2001; CMCSWG, 1997).

- *Day Visitors:* Those who travel for a round trip distance of at least 50 kilometres, are away from home for at least 4 hours, and who do not spend a night away from home as part of their travel (excludes same day travel as part of overnight travel, and routine travel, such as commuting between work/school and home (based on NVS in BTR, 2001).

The above operational/behavioural definition of cultural event tourism does not define and categorise cultural event tourists by attitudinal and motivational factors as well as behavioural dimensions consistent with a multi-dimensional typology and segmentation approach advocated by some authors (e.g. Alzua *et al*, 1998; Lang & O'Leary, 1997). Alzua *et al* (1998) argue that a shortcoming of market segmentation research in tourism marketing has been to typically derive groups by clustering respondents on the basis of only one dimension e.g. behaviours or attitudes. They emphasise the importance and advantages of integrating attitudinal and behavioural characteristics in multi-dimensional segmentation as the former may trigger or drive the behaviour as exemplified by attitudes such as benefits sought at a destination by travellers which may influence travellers to choose within a preferred set of alternative activities, or to participate more often or widely. Examples of attitudinal characteristics of relevance to typologies and segmentation of tourists include motivations, benefits pursued, attitudes, philosophies, expectations, barriers or fears preventing attendance, preferences regarding travel, destination or marketing. An aim of this chapter is to develop a conceptual framework and model that includes cultural event tourists being defined and categorised by psychological attitudinal and motivational factors as well as by behavioural factors.

From a review of relevant literature, especially studies involving both empirical and conceptual research but focusing largely on the allied areas of tourism, leisure and recreation (e.g. Morrison *et al*, 1994; Lang & O'Leary, 1997; Alzua *et al*, 1998; Nicholson & Pearce, 2000, 2001; Sung, *et al*, 2000; Frochot & Morrison, 2000), relevant concepts to developing effective marketing strategies for performing arts events to attract tourist markets are an understanding of who is being attracted, together with why and how they are attracted, for this in turn determines their ultimate behaviour. If the tourism market for performing arts events can be subdivided by distinguishable characteristics into differentiated groups in accordance with the accepted theoretical principle of market segmentation in general (e.g. Kotler, 1991) and for tourism markets specifically (e.g. Middleton, 1994; Morrison, 2001, Smith, 1989), then this marketing theory advocates developing unique marketing strategies for each of these groups. While the strategic importance of market segmentation among academics and practitioners is widespread, Morrison *et al* (1994) acknowledge a lack of consensus on how to divide travel markets into their component segments, that is, how many and which variables to use to divide the market and the exact procedure to follow in segmentation. Travel and tourism benefit segmentation research have tended to use a two-step method combining factor and cluster analysis: using factor analysis firstly to reduce the original list of benefits to a smaller number of underlying dimensions and then cluster analysis to group these dimensions into a number of clusters (Frochot & Morrison, 2000). Another criticism of segmentation work to date identified by Smith (1989) and Morrison *et al* (1994) is its main use to merely describe groups of people, *a priori* methods, rather than to predict or explain behaviour, *a posteriori* methods. One example of an *a posteriori* market segmentation technique, is benefit segmentation as the composition of segments is unknown in advance of analysis (Frochot & Morrison, 2000).

Therefore a modified version of the three-step model originally developed by Morrison *et al* (1994) for segmenting travel markets and adapted by Alzua *et al* (1998) for segmenting cultural and heritage tourism for UK outbound international travellers, is of relevance to developing effective marketing strategies to attract tourists to performing arts events. This model uses individual segmentation bases or criteria in three sequential roles to divide the travel market into its principal subdivisions, to differentiate travellers, and then to describe travellers within segments. One modification to be incorporated in this proposed conceptual framework is the integration of both attitudinal and behavioural characteristics as part of the segmentation methodology recommended by Alzua *et al* (1998).

In terms of the segmentation process used by Alzua *et al* (1998) in their benefit segmentation research, firstly the outbound UK cultural and heritage tourism market were divided by activity, then a two-stage cluster analysis using both behavioural and attitudinal dimensions to differentiate the market into five distinct groupings among these cultural tourists was undertaken, then the differences between these five clusters were described on the relevant variables. The two-stage cluster analysis incorporated an hierarchical cluster method (e.g. Ward's Method: minimum variance method) to produce a range of cluster solutions from which the researcher must select a solution, represented by a specific number of clusters from this range (Frochot & Morrison, 2000), and, in the second stage, the former results were used as starting points for subsequent non-hierarchical (K-means) clustering (Alzua *et al*, 1998).

When profiling benefit segments, Frochot and Morrison (2000) argue against using only statistical tests (e.g. chi-square analysis, ANOVA, and discriminant analysis) to determine the number of benefit segments through cluster analysis. They claim it is insufficient and recommend studies should at least evaluate the average visitor spend per segment (or profitability) and ideally should also include an evaluation of accessibility and reachability as portrayed in the Loker and Perdue study (1992).

Benefit segmentation has been popular in travel and tourism research and Frochot and Morrison (2000) attribute this to the belief that benefits are related to travellers' motivations. However, they also acknowledge that there is no universally accepted set of tourist motivations and the exact link between benefits sought and motivation is still to be tested and proven. Alzua *et al* (1998) combined past and future experiences, collecting information on socio-economic and demographic variables, travel characteristics, destinations visited and destinations most likely to visit, activities engaged in when on the most recent trips, travel philosophy, benefits sought, product segments and media habits.

Existing research and data gaps

From the performing arts perspective in Australia, some research has been undertaken of performing arts audiences and the marketing of performing arts (Australia Council, 1999; Arts Victoria, 1997a, 1997b), but none of this research includes tourist audiences or markets.

From the cultural tourism perspective, empirical research to date in Australia has focused on either international tourists (Foo & Rossetto, 1998) or domestic cultural tourists (CMCSWG, 1997). Different methodologies were used, namely, the former as a supplementary survey in 1995 to the International Visitor Survey (IVS) and the latter as a supplementary survey to the ABS survey of attendances at selected cultural venues in Australia (ABS, 1991, 1995, 1999). Neither of these studies develops any further marketing strategies apart from the segmentation of the cultural tourist market for international and domestic tourists in Australia, with each study focusing on either international or domestic cultural tourists respectively. Other research relevant to cultural event tourism in Australia is in the annual surveys of international and national visitors (BTR, annually and quarterly). While the definition of cultural activities used in each of these studies differs, they do provide characteristics for all tourists, segmentation on several bases such as by broad purpose of visit (i.e. holiday/leisure; business, visiting friends and relatives), and most importantly in terms of this chapter's research focus, further information about cultural activity participation, but no details on the characteristics of these cultural tourists *per se*.

Significance of performing arts cultural event tourism in Melbourne, Victoria

The Melbourne geographic area located within the state of Victoria is a focus of this chapter as the number of tourists to Victoria per annum based on the latest published data, total just over 19 million which is a very substantial market for any Melbourne-based attraction, and especially when compared with Melbourne's resident population of almost 3.5 million, 2.5 million of whom are 15 years of age or older (ABS, 1996, 2000b). The 19 million tourist visitors are comprised of just over one million international tourists (BTR, 2000b), 18 million domestic overnight visitors consisting of more than 4.7 million interstate visitors and 13.3 million intrastate visitors (BTR, 2001). The one million international visitors is the second highest number of international visitors to a selected destination in Australia, ranking after Sydney (2.4 million) (BTR, 2000b). Of these inbound international visitors to Melbourne, the significant market sources in ranking order are

UK (144,700, 14%), New Zealand (139,300, 14%), USA (121,700, 12%), Japan (73,000, 7%), Singapore (61,800, 6%) and Germany (47,500, 5%) (BTR, 2000b). This differs slightly from the profile of total international visitors to Australia which totalled nearly 4.5 million for the year ending June 2000, where the top six significant market sources in ranking order are New Zealand (16%), Japan (15%), UK (12%), US (10%), Singapore (6%) and Germany (3%). If day visitors are taken into consideration, an additional 44.5 million day visitors visited the state of Victoria in 1999, consisting of 1.2 million interstate visitors and 43.3 million intrastate visitors (BTR, 2001).

On the performing arts event supply side, Melbourne hosts an annual major arts festival and fringe arts festival in September/October, a comedy festival midyear, and is home to several major performing arts companies including the Melbourne Symphony Orchestra, Orchestra Victoria, and one of Australia's oldest and largest theatre companies, the Melbourne Theatre Company (MTC) established in 1953 and employing more than 116 permanent, full-time staff (Nugent, 1999). Melbourne also has an impressive range and number of major performing arts venues including the Victorian Arts Centre Concert Hall (capacity 2,700), State Theatre (2,000), Playhouse (900); Regent (2,200), Myer Music Bowl (2,000), Her Majesty's (1600), Princess (1,400); Comedy (1,000), Athenaeum (950), and Forum (800) (Nugent, 1999).

If for example, Melbourne Theatre Company attracted one per cent of the 19 million combined tourist visitors, this would be 190,000 visitors that would result in $5.7 million additional annual earned revenue at the average ticket price of $30.

A snapshot picture of cultural event tourism in the Melbourne geographic area and Australia as a whole is difficult to determine from existing research which has used different methodologies (e.g. surveying a sample of all international tourists versus surveying a sample of visitors to selected cultural venues), different tourist populations (e.g. international or national visitors) and often does not provide detailed analysis of tourist participation in cultural events as distinct from participation in cultural tourism in general. There is also a lack of detailed analysis for cultural event tourism in specific geographic areas such as Melbourne. Furthermore, most of the cultural tourism data is now quite dated.

Significance of cultural event tourism for international visitors in Australia

Details of international visitor attendance at cultural events and their characteristics and motivations is only available for Australia as a whole and is part of a broader study of cultural tourism in Australia undertaken in 1995 (Foo & Rossetto, 1998). For cultural tourism overall in Australia, approximately 62 percent or 2.1 million of all international visitors to Australia in 1995 (3.427 million) participated in at least one cultural activity. The market source of these cultural tourists by country of residence – Asia (45%), Europe including the UK (28%), New Zealand (15%) and North America (10%) – was found to be rather consistent with the distribution of all inbound visitors for the period except for a higher proportion of visitors from Europe and North America being likely to visit cultural attractions in Australia than other groups of visitors. By type of cultural activity, of the six cultural activity categories included in the research, cultural events ranked third and sixth respectively for visits to performing arts or concerts (15% of visits) and visits to festivals or fairs (4% of visits). The respective rankings of the other cultural activity categories were visiting museums or art galleries (31%), historic or heritage buildings, sites, monuments (27%), Aboriginal sites and cultural displays (15%) and visiting art or craft workshops or studios (9%). These attendances suggest the untapped potential that inbound tourists present to cultural events and in particular to organisers of festivals and fairs.

Limitations of this research are that it does not give a breakdown of the extent of cultural tourism in each State/Territory cross-tabulated by type of cultural activity. Nor is there published analysis of sources of information used by inbound cultural visitor by type of cultural activity cross-tabulated with demographic characteristics such as age, gender, country-of-residence, occupation, main purpose of visit, duration of stay, or preferred language.

Significance of cultural event tourism for domestic tourists

Similar research of cultural event tourist motivations and other influencing factors does not exist for national tourists and day visitors in Australia. Research of national or domestic tourist interest in cultural events in Australia to date has largely been based on analysis of the NVS (BTR, annual reports) and a detailed supplementary survey of attendances at selected cultural venues by Australian residents while staying away from home undertaken in 1994 (CMCSWG, 1997). Only a limited picture of cultural event tourism for domestic tourists can be gleaned from the latter research where different performing arts activity categories were included, for example, 'opera or musical theatre' and 'popular music', and festivals or fairs were not included as a separate category in this research. For day visitors, it is not possible to determine the significance of either performing arts or festival activities as they are part of a broad arts heritage activity category (e.g. BTR, 2001). The significance of cultural event tourism for all domestic tourists in Australia (interstate and intrastate) from the most recent published information (BTR, 2001), is only two percent for performing arts activities (theatre, concerts or other performing arts), and two percent for festivals/fairs or cultural events, but in numbers each of these represents just over 1.4 million of almost 73 million overnight visitors in 1999. Analysis of activities by State/Territory visited, shows Victoria and Queensland were the States with the highest percent of visitors attending performing arts activities (3% each) of a similar number of overnight visitors (approximately 16.5 million each). An additional 3% of Victoria's overnight visitors attended festivals/fairs or cultural events.

What can be seen from the research of domestic cultural tourism (CMCSWG, 1997) is how the distribution of tourist attendances at various forms of performing arts differs, and a potential to increase tourist attendances for all forms. The performing arts component of this cultural tourism by domestic tourists firstly for Australia as a whole and then for the state of Victoria, with some comparisons to other cultural activities, follows with some comparisons to other selected types of cultural activities. Festivals or fairs were not included as a category in this research.

Australian domestic tourist attendances at selected cultural venues as a percentage of total attendances were highest for museums (40%), followed by art galleries (36%), with a lower percentage for all forms of performing arts combined (15.3%). By performing art categories, the percentage of domestic tourist attendances in order of ranking importance were opera or musical theatre (19.7%), popular music (17.5%), dance (15%), theatre (13.8%), classical music (13.2%) and other performing arts (10.2%). On a state basis, Victoria received 563,000 interstate visitors at cultural venues, whose attendance at all forms of performing arts combined (33.7%) was greater than for museums (28%) or art galleries (25%), and by type of performing art activity comprised opera or musical theatre (10.1%), popular music (9.7%), theatre (5.6%), classical music (2.4%), dance (2.1%), and other performing arts (3.8%). In the same period, Victoria received 692,000 intrastate visitors at cultural venues, whose attendance at all forms of performing arts combined (37.6%) was far greater than for museums (22.3%) or art galleries (18%), and by type of performing art activity comprised popular music (15.0%), opera or musical theatre (8.4%), theatre (5.3%), classical music (2.4%), dance (2.0%), and other performing arts (4.5%).

In terms of the characteristics of interstate cultural event visitors, the main geographic sources were New South Wales (42%), South Australia (18.3%), and Queensland (15.3%). There were more females than male visitors (54.5% c.f. 45.5%), the main family status group were couples without children (35.6%) and there was a fairly even spread across all five age groups (22.4% 25-34 years; 21.2% 35-44 years; 20.3% 15-24 years; 18.3% 45-54 years; and 17.7% 55 years or more). (Arts

Victoria, 2000a, 2000b). Within the performing arts, attending the opera or musical theatre was more popular amongst females (12%) than males (7.8%), while a higher proportion of males attended popular music performances (11.8% c.f. 8%) (CMCSWG, 1997).

Characteristics of cultural event tourists in Australia

Distinguishing characteristics of international cultural event tourists cannot be determined from existing research except for a breakdown of country-of-residence for international visitors to Melbourne by one broad cultural event activity, i.e. Melbourne festivals/events/theatre (BTR unpublished data 1996 cited in Arts Victoria, 2000b). From this research, 11.7 percent of all international visitors to Melbourne in 1996 attended Melbourne festivals/events/theatre. Of these international visitors, the ranking of visitors by country-of-residence, 33 percent were from Asian markets within which 6.3 percent were from Japan, with other major markets being North America (16.4%), New Zealand (14.8%), UK (11.6%) and all other countries (23.5%). While the distribution of these cultural event tourists is similar to the distribution of international visitors to Australia by country-of-residence and hence the largest number of visitors are from the Asian continent in both instances, a higher proportion of visitors from North America, NZ and UK sought cultural event experiences while in Australia. These findings are similar to those for cultural tourists in general by international visitors to Australia (Foo and Rossetto, 1998). This detailed research however, does not provide analysis of tourist characteristics by type of cultural activity from which the characteristics of cultural event tourists could be analysed specifically.

Research variables of relevance to cultural event tourists

Research of cultural tourism in Australia by international visitors (Foo & Rossetto, 1998) includes cultural visitor demographic characteristics and motivations, whether any planning was involved, and sources of information used. This research also segments international cultural tourists as 'specific' or 'general' – a cultural tourist segmentation also used by Richards (1996) in relation to European tourism and cultural attractions. The research further analyses motivations, planning and information at specific types of cultural sites including performing arts or concerts and festivals or fairs. Foo and Rossetto (1998) acknowledged that future research exploring when visitors plan their visits rather than just whether any planning is involved is important as such data, combined with data collected on information sources, is valuable in the distribution of promotion and marketing materials.

From the research of motivating factors at cultural sites (Foo & Rossetto, 1998), different types of cultural events – performing arts or festivals and fairs – demonstrate some differences in motivating factors. While most visitors to cultural events were influenced by the social aspect of the experience (13%, 12% respectively), visitors to performing arts also had to be interested in the performance (52%) whereas visitors to festivals and fairs were less likely than most cultural international tourists to have a specific desire to visit this type of event (17%). Other motivating factors for performing arts attendances were as part of their package tour (15%), rest and relaxation (11%), to experience something Australian (11%). For festival or fair attendances, key motivating factors were a break from their normal schedule (26%), and the opportunity to experience something Australian (27%). Very few visitors to festivals or fairs attended as part of a package tour (1%). Motivational factors other than those included in the survey were identified by cultural tourists in general, namely, recommendations (8%), promotional material (7%), and previous visits (6%).

The research of planning and information sources used by cultural tourists at cultural sites (Foo & Rossetto, 1998) shows sources used by cultural event tourists differ for performing arts or festivals and fairs as well as with other cultural activities. The majority of performing arts attendances were pre-planned prior to the visit (54%) whereas festival or fair attendances tended to be made on impulse with only 25% planning to do so. Up-to-date sources of information were favoured by performing arts cultural tourists: word of mouth (46%), advertising (43%), travel agents and travel brochures (30%), in preference to guidebooks (6%) or books and other forms of literature (1%). Those festival or fair visitors who planned their visit used similar sources of information: word of mouth (46%), advertising (40%), travel agents and travel brochures (30%), and also guidebooks and travel magazines (30%).

Broad trends in overseas visitor satisfaction at Australia's cultural sites were measured to identify development opportunities available to the cultural industry. In this research (Foo & Rossetto, 1998), satisfaction was assumed when an individual's level of interest in a particular activity increased as a result of experiencing the activity and postulated by their intentions if an individual chose to seek an experience again. Festivals or fairs offer the largest untapped potential for inbound cultural tourists as the cultural activity with the smallest number of attendances by inbound cultural tourists (4%), the least pre-planning of attendance (25%), low levels of interest prior to their visit (38% very interested, 39% fairly interested), but those who did attend were highly satisfied and desired more of the same in future visits. In contrast the performing arts events had the highest levels of interest prior to their visit (72% very interested, 18% fairly interested), with these interest levels being maintained (40%) if not increased (60%) as a result of attending the event. More than 50 percent of attendees indicated they would attend the same event in future visits to Australia.

There is other research of marketing the performing arts to local audiences in Australia which does not include tourist visitors but is relevant as it identifies factors of importance in the audience decision-making process, the sources of information used, and preferred timing of ticket purchase (Australia Council 1999). Some categories for each of these items in this research differ to those of the inbound cultural tourism research (Foo & Rossetto, 1998) and the findings for each item were further analysed by different attitudinal clusters and frequency of attendance over the past 2 years with some significant differences emerging. Other research of performing arts audiences in Victoria, includes attendance motivations, barriers to increased attendance, and influences on the decision to attend (Arts Victoria, 1997a,1997b).

Conceptual frameworks and models

In terms of researching and modelling cultural event tourism and effective marketing to attract tourists to cultural events, an understanding of who, why and how is needed. Knowledge and understanding about why and how tourists are influenced and decide to attend cultural events is needed and this involves an understanding of the complex determinants and influencing factors of cultural event tourism motivation as this is what triggers and drives actual behaviour. The other important set of information concerns the sociodemographic characteristic profile of cultural event tourists, or in other words, descriptive analysis of who goes (and does not go) to cultural events. If there are distinguishable sub-groups within any of these variables, marketing theory recommends market segmentation be undertaken so that unique marketing strategies can then be developed for each target market segment. Determining the target markets is an additional step in the process, once the segmentation has been performed. Then marketing strategies can be developed for each of the identified and selected target markets. A procedural model outlining this conceptual framework has been developed (Figure 2).

Figure 2   *Procedural model for researching performing arts event tourists and effective marketing strategies*

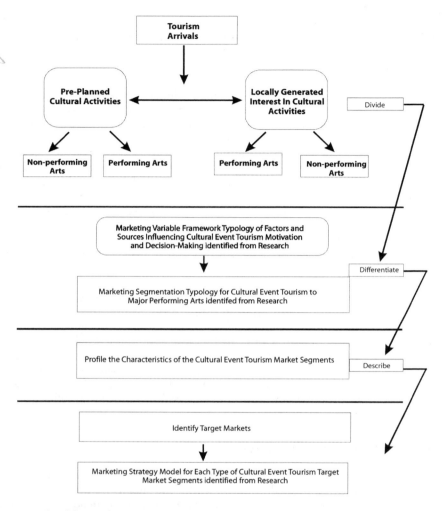

Source: *Developed from Literature Review and based on Morrison et al,1994; Alzua et al, 1998.*

Implications for performing arts and cultural event tourism research

In implementing the proposed model for researching, measuring, classifying and marketing to cultural event tourists, the following two typologies and one associated model will need to be developed:

(a)   A typology of determinants of cultural event tourist motivation and behaviour.

(b)   A typology of cultural event tourism market segmentation and appropriate segmentation variables of tourist markets for the performing arts.

(c) A model of the decision-making processes for performing arts event tourists that determine what events they attend including identification of key influences, sources of information and planning undertaken.

Furthermore, in implementing the proposed conceptual framework and model for researching performing arts event tourists and developing the associated required typologies and models, the following ongoing debates identified in the literature as being of particular concern will need to be addressed:

- What variables should be used to measure, classify, profile, explain and possibly predict, or influence cultural event tourist behaviour rather than merely describe groups of people? (e.g. Smith, 1989; Morrison *et al*, 1994).

- What are the descriptive factors and what are the causal factors? (e.g. Hayley, 1968 research of benefit segmentation application to the toothpaste market).

- What are the dependent variables and the independent variables? (e.g. Smith, 1989; Morrison *et al*, 1994).

- Should the variables be selected a priori (deductive or experience-based) or a posteriori (inductive or fact-based)? (e.g. Morrison *et al*, 1994).

- The need to use multi-dimensions rather than just one dimension in market segmentation i.e. activities undertaken and other manifested behaviour, attitudes, sociodemographic characteristics, as well as benefits sought, expectations, motivations, philosophies, preferences, and future intentions (e.g. Alzua *et al*, 1998 research of attitudinal and behavioural characteristic benefit segmentation of the outbound UK cultural and heritage tourism market; Lang & O'Leary, 1997 study using motivation, participation and preference for segmenting the outbound Australian nature travel market).

- How many and which dimensions should be used to divide, segment, differentiate and describe a market and in which sequence or order should they be applied? (e.g. Morrison *et al*, 1994; Alzua *et al*, 1998).

- What characteristics, variables or bases are relevant to segmenting and profiling cultural event tourists e.g., geographic, demographic, psychographic, behavioural, usage, purpose of travel, benefit, price, channel of distribution, or product-related? (based on Kotler, Lewis & Chambers, Middleton, Morrison and Smith, cited in Morrison *et al*, 1994).

- What is the optimum size, composition, sequencing and number of segmentation variable set? (e.g. Morrison *et al*, 1994).

- What motivations and influencing factors to include as relevant to understanding cultural event tourist behaviour, preferences and responses to marketing strategies?

- The relationship between benefits sought and motivations, with a widespread belief in tourism research that benefits are related to traveller's motivations (see Frochot & Morrison, 2000) and that traveller's motivations have always been portrayed as a critical variable in the decision-making process (e.g. Crompton, 1979; Lundberg,

1971), hence the greatest interest and application of benefit segmentation has been in travel, tourism, leisure, and recreation fields (Frochet & Morrison, 2000).

- The need to include specific characteristics of a given location, facility or event (e.g. Bonn, 1984 in relation to downhill skiers in North Carolina; and Nicholson & Pearce, 2001 identification of event-specific factors in relation to visitor motivations and attendance at four different types of events in NZ including two music festivals; see Frochet & Morrison, 2000).

- The need for further studies to better profile travellers including questions about:

  ➤ how the tourists can be reached and what information sources do they need? (Lang & O'Leary, 1997);

  ➤ do travellers among clusters have different trip-planning horizons? (Lang & O'Leary, 1997; Foo & Rossetto, 1998);

  ➤ do travellers from different countries have similar travel and activity patterns? (Lang & O'Leary, 1997).

- Consideration also needs to be given to internal and external factors that can affect the configuration of segments e.g. fashion trends, economic trends, and competition (Hayley, 1985).

- When to undertake research of visitor benefits and motivations, e.g. surveying tourists prior to departure, following their trips or activities, about their recent past behaviour, about future intended experiences; during and after the cultural event experience (e.g. for discussion see Frochet & Morrison, 2000).

- Where to undertake research of cultural event tourists e.g. at a single cultural event in one venue; at a single cultural event held across several venues (e.g. Formica & Uysal, 1998 research of visitors to Spoleto Festival in Italy); across several cultural events; at selected cultural venues (e.g. CMCSWG, 1997; ABS; 1991; 1995; 1999); across several different types of events including cultural events (e.g. Nicholson & Pearce, 2000, 2001); by sampling tourists (cultural event attenders and non-attenders) in non-event public spaces; sampling tourists at departure points such as airports (e.g. Foo & Rossetto, 1998); sampling tourists when they have returned home.

- What statistical methods should be used to undertake market segmentation, i.e. cluster analysis, factor analysis, combinations of both, the role of discriminant analysis or analysis of variance (e.g. ANOVA) to test for significance among clusters (for discussion see Frochot & Morrison 2000).

- In determining whether the number of segments is sufficient, selecting target markets and identifying segments that deserve separate marketing treatment, consideration should also be given to general marketing principles such as profitability, accessibility and reach in addition to using statistical tests (e.g. Loker & Perdue, 1992, Frochot & Morrison, 2000).

Conclusion

Understanding and modelling cultural event tourism characteristics, motivation and behaviour in order to develop effective marketing strategies is a complex area of tourism research with many ongoing debates and gaps in empirical data and conceptual knowledge. While there is a large amount of literature on travel and tourism motivation and benefit market segmentation (e.g. Crompton, 1979; Hayley, 1985) and a growing body of literature on festival event tourist motivation and characteristics (e.g. Nicholson & Pearce, 2000; 2001), very little empirical and conceptual research of relevance to performing arts and cultural event tourism has been undertaken. Existing statistical data of the performing arts in Australia and other developed countries indicates an existent need and untapped potential to increase tourist markets to attend these events. Researching and developing effective marketing strategies will be crucial in this process.

References

ABS (1991), *Attendance at Selected Cultural Venues, Australia, 1991*, Cat. No.4114.0, Australian Bureau of Statistics, Canberra.

ABS (1995), *Attendance at Selected Cultural Venues, Australia, 1995*, Cat. No.4114.0, Australian Bureau of Statistics, Canberra.

ABS (1996), *1996 Census Melbourne Statistical Division*. Australian Bureau of Statistics, Canberra.

ABS (1999), *Attendance at Selected Cultural Venues, Australia, April 1999*, Cat. No.4114.0, Australian Bureau of Statistics, Canberra.

ABS (2000a), *Performing Arts Industries, Australia, 1999-2000*, Cat. No. 8697.0, Australian Bureau of Statistics, Canberra.

ABS (2000b), *Year Book 1999*, No. 83, Cat. No. 1301.0, Australian Bureau of Statistics, Canberra.

Alzua, A., O'Leary, J. T. & Morrison, A. M. (1998), "Cultural and Heritage Tourism: Identifying Niches for International Travellers", *The Journal of Tourism Studies*, 9 (2), 2-13.

Arts Victoria (1997a), *Dance Audiences in Victoria, Factsheet 2*, Arts Marketing Taskforce, Arts Victoria, Melbourne.

Arts Victoria (1997b), *Theatre Audiences in Victoria, Factsheet 3*, Arts Marketing Taskforce, Arts Victoria, Melbourne.

Arts Victoria (2000a), *Arts Count*, Arts Victoria: Melbourne.

Arts Victoria (2000b), *The Arts Industry in Victoria: A Statistical Overview*, Arts Victoria, Melbourne.

Australia Council (1999), *Selling the Performing Arts*, Australia Council for the Arts, Sydney.

Bonn, M. A. (1984), "Understanding Skier Behaviour: An Application of Benefit Segmentation Market Analysis to Commercial Recreation", *Society and Leisure*, 7 (2), 397-406.

BTR (2000a), *Annual Results of the International Visitor Survey International Visitors in Australia 1999*, Bureau of Tourism Research, Canberra.

BTR (2000b), *Quarterly Results of the International Visitor Survey: International Visitors in Australia June 2000*, Bureau of Tourism Research, Canberra.

BTR (2001), *Annual Results of the National Visitor Survey Travel by Australians 1999*, Bureau of Tourism Research, Canberra.

CMCSWG (1997), *Domestic Cultural Tourism in Australia 1994-95*, Cultural Ministers Council Statistics Working Group, Canberra, Australia.

Crompton, J. L. (1979), "Motivations for Pleasure Vacation", *Annals of Tourism Research*, 6 (4), 408-424.

Foo, L. M. & Rossetto, A. (1998), *Cultural Tourism in Australia: Characteristics and Motivations*, BTR Occasional Paper No.27, Bureau of Tourism Research, Canberra.

Formica, S. & Uysal, M. (1998), "Market Segmentation of an International Cultural-Historical Event in Italy", *Journal of Travel Research*, 36 (4), 16-24.

Frochot, I. & Morrison, A. M. (2000), "Benefit Segmentation: A Review of its Applications to Travel and Tourism Research", *Journal of Travel and Tourism Marketing*, 9 (4), 21-45.

Hayley, R. (1968), "Benefit Segmentation: A Decision-oriented Research Tool", *Journal of Marketing*, 32, July, 30-35.

Hayley, R. (1985), *Developing Effective Communication Strategies – A Benefit Segmentation Approach*, Wiley, New York.

Kotler, P. (1991), *Marketing Management: Analysis, Planning, Implementation, and Control*, 7th Edition, Prentice-Hall, New Jersey.

Lang, C-T. & O'Leary, J. T. (1997), "Motivation, Participation, and Preference: A Multi-segmentation Approach of the Australian Nature Travel Market", *Journal of Travel & Tourism Marketing*, 6 (3/4), 159-180.

Loker, L. E. & Perdue, R. R. (1992), "A Benefit-based Segmentation of a Nonresident Summer Travel Market", *Journal of Travel Research*, 31 (1), (1992), 30-35.

Lundberg, D. E. (1971), "Why Tourists Travel", *The Cornell H.R.A. Quarterly*, 26:February 75-81.

McCarthy, K. F., Brooks, A., Lowell, J. & Zakaras, L. (1999), *The Performing Arts in a New Era*, RAND/The Pew Charitable Trusts, United States.

Middleton, V. T. C. (1994), *Marketing in Travel and Tourism*, 2nd Edition, Butterworth-Heinemann: Oxford.

Morrison, A. M. (2001), *Hospitality and Travel Marketing*, 3rd Edition, Delmar Thomson Learning, Albany.

Morrison, A. M., Hsiech, S., & O'Leary, J. T. (1994), "Segmenting the Australian Domestic Travel Market by Holiday Activity Participation", *The Journal of Tourism Studies*, 5 (1), 39-56.

Nicholson, R. & Pearce, D. G. (2000), "Who Goes to Events: A Comparative Analysis of the Profile Characteristics of Visitors to Four South Island Events in New Zealand", *Journal of Vacation Marketing*, 6 (3), .236-253.

Nicholson, R. & Pearce, D. G. (2001), 'Why Do People Attend Events: A Comparative Analysis of Visitor Motivations at Four South Island Events", *Journal of Travel Research*, 39: May 449-460.

Nugent, H. (1999), *Securing the Future: Major Performing Arts Inquiry Final Report*, Department of Communications, Information Technology and the Arts, Canberra.

Richards, G. (1996), "Production and Consumption of European Cultural Tourism", *Annals of Tourism Research*, 23 (2), 261-283.

Smith, S. L. J. (1989), *Tourism Analysis*, Longman Scientific & Technical, Essex.

Sung, H. Y., Morrison, A. M. & O'Leary, J. T. (2000), "Segmenting the Adventure Travel Market by Activities: From the North American Industry Providers' Perspective", *Journal of Travel and Tourism*, 9 (4), 1-20.

UN & WTO (1994), *Recommendations on Tourism Statistics,* United Nations, New York.

Woodside, A. G. & Jacobs, L. W. (1985), "Step Two in Benefit Segmentation: Learning the Benefits Realised by Major Travel Markets", *Journal of Travel Research*, 24 (1), 7-13.

WTO, (1985), The State's Role in Protecting and Promoting Culture as a Factor of Tourism Development and the Proper Use and Exploitation of the National Cultural Heritage of Sites and Monuments for Tourism. Report to the Secretary-General on the General Programme of Work for the Period 1984-85, World Tourism Organisation: Madrid.

Motivations for Attendance at the 2001 Sidmouth International Festival: fun, family, friends, fulfilment or folk?

Peter Mason and John Beaumont-Kerridge

University of Luton, UK

Introduction

Historically, many festivals in Britain and other parts of Europe, have been linked to a religious calendar (Bowdin *et al*, 2001), and were often mainly of local importance. However, by the twentieth century, in developed countries such as Britain, governments had realised the importance of, for example, agricultural and industrial events/exhibitions, to generate a feeling of pride in the nation. During the 1950s and 1960s, a number of arts and popular music festivals developed in Britain. By the last quarter of the twentieth century many events were becoming 'professionalised' in terms of their organisation, promotion and management. Special events celebrating authentic folk culture had become increasingly popular during the 1970s in developed countries (Getz and Frisby, 1988; Janiskee, 1994; Raybould *et al*, 1999). Such events, which often began as small scale, locally oriented and organised were becoming professionally run and targeted at a national audience during this period.

According to its organisers, the Sidmouth International Festival (SIF) is the largest folk festival of its kind in Europe (S.Heap, pers comm., 2001). The Festival takes place during the second week of August, and in excess of 60,000 visitors come to the small coastal resort in Devon, in South West England, that has a resident population of only 12,000 (S Heap, pers. comm., 2001). The Festival has been held annually since 1955, but in its early days was small scale and locally-oriented in terms of performers and audience. However, by the late 1960s it was a major folk festival in the UK and, for at least the last quarter century, has provided visitors with an opportunity to watch internationally renowned folk singers and musicians. Traditional dance troupes from the UK, but also from Europe, Africa, Asia and the Pacific Region, have helped give the Festival its international dimension. Unlike many similar events, the Festival is dispersed around the town itself, in a wide variety of venues, including cinemas, theatres, clubs, public houses and church halls as well as in specially erected marquees. Originally organised by the English Folk Dance and Song Society, by the 1990s it was run by an organisation that specialises in music events called Mrs Casey's Music. Although the Festival has been in existence for almost half a century, no research relating to tourism associated with the event has been published.

Motivations for festival attendance

Understanding the behaviour of tourists is an important area of tourism research (Ryan, 1997). Behaviour is usually linked to motivation. Not only is information on motivation and behaviour useful in its own right for academic researchers, but also it can aid operators of festivals and events with marketing and management (Raybould *et al*, 1999). Behaviour can be influenced by a number of factors including cultural conditioning, social influences, perception and education, but as Crompton and McKay (1997) indicated motives are the starting point of the decision making process that leads to particular types of behaviour. It is in the related fields of psychology and sociology that researchers have developed a number of significant theories on motivation.

In the field of cognitive psychology, motives are seen as largely a function of the expected consequences of future human behaviour (Dunn-Ross and Iso-Aloha, 1991). In this sense, motives can be considered as internal factors that have initially aroused a person and then direct his or her behaviour (Iso-Aloha, 1980). The main components of a general psychological model of motivation are needs and motives, behaviour or activity, goals or satisfactions and feedback (Harrill and Potts, 2002).

Mannell and Kleber (1997:190) provide an example to indicate the links between the main concepts in this psychological model:

> "People who have a strong need or desire to be with others (*motive*) may attempt to engage in leisure activities, such as going to bars and drinking that allow them to increase their interactions with other people (*behaviour*) in hopes of developing more friendships (*goal and satisfaction*)."

This is an iterative model in that the feedback component leads back into the initial needs and motivations (Harrill and Potts, 2002). In other words, during an activity an individual interacts with the environment in which the activity takes place and possibly with others involved in the activity and this results in more, or perhaps, different motivation.

One of the important psychological models of motivation in relation to tourism that has emerged is Iso-Aloha's (1980) two-dimensional model. The two dimensions in the model can be summarised as 'seeking' motives and 'escaping' motives (Pearce, 1993). In Iso-Aloha's model, individuals seek personal and interpersonal rewards and at the same time wish to escape personal and interpersonal environments. The main criticism of Iso-Aloha's model is that, with only two dimensions, it is limited by its level of aggregation (Raybould *et al*, 1999).

A number of sociological theories have been put forward for motivation in the tourist literature. One of the earliest was that of Cohen (1972) who subdivided tourists into four types, based on motivation. Cohen asserted that the main variables forming the basis of his theory and hence leading to the fourfold classification were 'strangeness' versus 'familiarity'. Hence at one end of his continuum was the 'organised mass tourist' seeking familiarity in holiday surroundings, while at the other end, the 'drifter' is willing to accept far more 'strangeness'.

Cohen developed his theory to investigate how various types of tourist might interact with host communities. This approach also influenced Plog (1972) who developed a continuum, using two concepts allo-centric and psycho-centric. Plog suggested that psycho-centric individuals are concerned primarily with the self, are inhibited and relatively non-adventurous. In terms of tourist behaviour, psycho-centrics want the familiar and are unlikely to travel great distances to explore new tourism destinations. Conversely Plog asserted allo-centrics are confident, naturally inquisitive and seek out the unfamiliar when travelling. Both Cohen's (1972) and Plog's (1972) models have been tested, but with varied success and have not met with universal acceptance. Nevertheless, they remain as key theories in tourism motivation, although both are largely descriptive rather than explanatory, which means they lack predictive validity (Harrill and Potts, 2002). Dann's (1977) theory is in a similar vein to Cohen's (1972). Dann argued that tourist motivation can be best understood as the relationship between 'push' and 'pull' factors, although he actually used the concept of anomie (the desire to escape from societal norms) and ego-enhancement (the pull factor). Similar ideas were put forward by Manfredo *et al* (1996) when they indicated that those seeking leisure and tourism experiences do so because of a perceived inequity between their existing state and their desired state. Although the models of Dann (1977) and Manfredo *et al* (1996) are largely sociological, they show great similarities with Iso-Aloha's (1980) two-dimension psychological model.

A number of these sociological and psychological theories tend to imply that motivation is a fairly static concept. However, Pearce (1988) using the concept of a 'travel ladder' when investigating motivation for tourism, suggested that motivations are multivariate and dynamic, changing particularly as a result of ageing and life-cycle stage, as well as being influenced by other people. Pearce acknowledged that he was influenced by the work of the psychologist Maslow (1954), who created a hierarchical range of needs, from low level, primarily physical needs to high level intellectual needs. Maslow termed these needs, in ascending sequence, 'physiological', 'safety', 'social', 'self esteem' and 'self development'. Pearce, using Maslow's (1954) ideas, proposed the following tourism motivation categories: 'relaxation', 'excitement and thrills', 'social interaction', 'self esteem and development' and 'fulfilment'.

Despite a number of theoretical perspectives on tourism motivation, Fodness (1994) pointed out that there was little empirical research on the reasons that people travel for tourist experiences. A number of reasons were given for this, including the general lack of motivation research in tourism, as well as confusion over the application of social and psychological theories to tourism. Ryan and Glendon (1998) appear to contradict Fodness when claiming there are a large number of motivation studies in tourism. However, they provide support for Fodness, when indicating a major problem in tourism motivational research, is that comparison is difficult, as researchers have used different models and different research instruments.

In terms of festivals, as recently as the late 1990s, Crompton and McKay (1997) indicated there was very little research into motives for festival and event attendance. As Raybould *et al* (1999) suggested, when agreeing with this view, this indicates that those marketing festivals have been slow to support this type of research. Nevertheless, Getz (1991) has used the ideas of Maslow (1954) to specifically investigate the motives for festival attendance and he created a three 'generic needs' model. These generic needs are as follows: 'physical needs' (including eating, drinking, taking exercise, relaxing and finding sexual gratification); 'social needs', (including seeking friendship, socialising with friends and family, seeking romance and seeking cultural roots); and 'personal needs', (including searching for knowledge, seeking new experiences, being creative and fulfilling ambitions).

A number of researchers have used factor analysis in empirical research about motivation in the field of tourism and leisure. Although different labels have been attached to the dimensions identified by various researchers, common themes have emerged and, according to Raybould *et al* (1999), by the 1990s a generally accepted terminology was in use and this tends to confirm a wider range than Iso-Aloha's (1980) two dimensions model. For example, a relatively early study (Crompton 1979), involving the use of semi-structured interviews to investigate reasons for taking leisure vacations, identified nine motivational dimensions, while the work of Fodness (1994) who investigated motivations for taking holidays led to identification of five 'vacation themes'.

There are few empirical motivational studies specifically focusing on festivals and events (Raybould *et al*, 1999). However Uysal *et al* (1993) made use of Iso-Aloha's two-dimensional model when studying a festival in South Carolina, USA. Their research suggested five important motivational factors: escape, event novelty, excitement, socialisation and family togetherness. Uysal *et al*'s research indicated that these factors were important to all visitor groups to this festival. Very similar findings were also produced by Mohr *et al* (1993) when investigating a hot air balloon festival, also in South Carolina, although here family togetherness and socialisation were regarded as more important by visitors. In a study of three different festivals, Scott (1996) reported that the theme of each of the festivals had a strong bearing on the motivations indicated by visitors.

The most relevant piece of empirical research for this study is that conducted by Raybould *et al* (1999). Their research focused on the Woodford Folk Festival in Australia. According to Rickards (1998), the Woodford Folk Festival is the biggest in the southern hemisphere. In addition to the focus on folk music and dance, there are a number of other similarities between the Woodford Folk Festival and the SIF. Both stress the importance of culture, there is an international dimension at each, there is a strong element of participation, each has a separate Children's festival and both have a strong feeling of camaraderie built up by groups of 'regulars' who attend each festival year after year. Like the SIF, the Woodford Folk Festival is an annual festival. However, it has not been running as long as the SIF, having been established in 1987 and also is based at a special site rather than being in a town. By 1997/8 the Woodford Festival featured over 2000 performers in 20 venues and there were over 28,500 ticket holders (Perrett and Raybould, 1998).

Methodology

As Raybould *et al* (1999) indicated a key problem with research into short-term events such as festivals, is that of the inability to conduct a pilot study. Hence, given the similarity of the SIF to the Woodford Folk Festival, it was decided to use the general approach and a number of the specific questions used by Raybould *et al* (1999). Part of the rationale for the use of Raybould *et al*'s approach was that, in the creation of their motivation factor questions, they acknowledged the contribution of other significant festival researchers, including Crompton, (1979), Beard and Ragheb, (1983) and Uysal *et al* (1993). This approach also had the advantage of allowing direct comparisons to be made between the results from the SIF and the Woodford Folk Festival. However, an important difference between the SIF study and the Woodford Folk Festival research was that the SIF research was part of a bigger study also investigating tourism impacts and satisfaction levels at the Festival.

Using the approach of Raybould *et al* (1999) the research instrument was a questionnaire. Following on from a number of demographic questions and those concerned with trip characteristics, respondents were asked to indicate the extent to which they agreed or disagreed with each of twenty statements on a five point Likert-scale, where '5' was 'strongly agree' and '1' 'strongly disagree'. Each statement began with "I attended the Sidmouth International Festival ...." and ended with a motive for attendance (e.g. 'to develop my skills' or 'to interact with others'). Such attitudinal surveys are now commonly used in tourism motivational research (see Ryan, 1995, Mason and Cheyne, 2000) and are seen as appropriate way to gain information where other techniques cannot be effectively deployed. The design of the statements used in the Likert-scale question was informed largely by the research conducted by Raybould *et al*, (1999). However, Raybould *et al* used twenty-four statements and some of these were considered inappropriate for the SIF research. In total seventeen of the twenty questions used in the SIF research were taken directly from Raybould *et al*'s research.

The three other SIF research questions focused on aspects believed significant at the SIF. Two questions were concerned with the degree of involvement in musical activities (see Figure 1, statements i and q) and the other about the international nature of the SIF (see statement f in Figure 1).

Approximately 500 (490) copies of the questionnaire survey were distributed during the Festival week August 3rd –10th 2001. Using a team of four researchers, these were distributed at nine sites, over six days of the Festival (Saturday 3rd to Thursday 8th August). Two of the research team had visited the Festival on a number of occasions previously and used this experience to select appropriate sites. Following the technique used by Raybould *et al* (1999), every third person passing a particular point at each of the nine sites was selected and given a copy of the questionnaire to be completed on the spot. Although no precise record was kept of those refusing to complete the questionnaire, this was believed by the team of researchers to be less than ten visitors. Research took place at selected times between midday and 9pm and researchers spent approximately one hour at each of the nine sites. A total of 420 completed questionnaires were returned, of which 411 were usable, as 9 failed to specify the gender of respondents.

Results

Demographic data

The demographic data from the questionnaire survey indicated that just over half (54%) of those questioned in the questionnaire survey were female and just under half (46%) were male. In terms of age, over 70% of Festival visitors were over 40 years old (including 18% over 60 years old). Only 16% were under 30 years old. Festival visitors were generally well educated, with just over half the respondents (52%) having at least an undergraduate degree, including over a fifth (22%) with a post-graduate qualification.

Different types of visitor groups attended the Festival. Approximately a third were 'traditional couples', another third were couples without children and approximately a quarter were 'solo' without children. Approximately 10% were single parents. The majority of visitors were relatively well off. The household income of 44% of respondents was in excess of £30,000 per annum. (The average annual income in late 2001 was £23,600). In relation to place of residence, just under a quarter of visitors (24%) were from Devon including 14% from the East Devon and Exeter region and approximately one fifth (18%) were from elsewhere in the South West. However, at least two in every five (41%) came from a region encompassing the Midlands, South-East England and East Anglia. This indicates that at least in terms of visitors, the Festival is of national importance. A small proportion of the sample (3%) came from continental EU countries and another 3% from other overseas countries.

Three quarters of respondents had visited the Festival before (with a third visiting more than five times before). However just under a quarter (23%) were making their first visit to the Festival. The Festival is important in terms of the tourism sector 'Visiting Friends and Relatives'. Over half of respondents (54%) attended with family members and/or friends. However, another visitor niche (approximately a third of respondents) was made up of couples. Approximately half the visitors (53%) had season tickets and just under half (47%) were day visitors. In terms of transport to the Festival, over 90% of respondents used a car. In addition, as approximately 4% of visitors indicated that they used a camper-van, almost nineteen out of twenty Festival visitors arrived in a private motor vehicle. Most of the small number, who travelled by train, were overseas visitors.

Festival visitors used a wide range of accommodation. One fifth of respondents were camping at a Festival site, another 14% were camping elsewhere and 7% stayed in caravans. Approximately 11% stayed in bed and breakfast accommodation, 9% were in self-catering accommodation and 8% in hotels. Approximately 12% stayed with friends and relatives. However approximately one fifth (19%) were visiting the Festival from home.

Motivation

The major instrument for investigating motivation was a Likert scale questionnaire involving twenty statements. These statements are shown in Figure 1, and this also indicates the mean score for each statement, which began with 'I attended the Sidmouth International Festival':

Figure 1 *Motivation statements with mean scores*

(a)	To escape	2.9
(b)	To be with friends	3.5
(c)	As I enjoy the Festival crowd	3.9
(d)	To be entertained	4.6
(e)	To be creative	3.0
(f)	To experience an international festival	3.7
(g)	To be with my partner/family	3.5
(h)	To expand my knowledge	3.4
(i)	To watch musical events	4.5
(j)	As this Festival is unique	3.8
(k)	As a break from my normal routine	3.9
(l)	To meet new people	3.3
(m)	To be involved and participate	3.3
(n)	To develop my skills	2.8
(o)	It sounded like fun	3.9
(p)	To challenge myself	2.6
(q)	To take part in musical activities	3.0
(r)	As I thought my family would enjoy it	2.7
(s)	To interact with others	3.4
(t)	To do things with my family	2.9

As Figure 1 indicates, statements relating to 'seeking entertainment' ('To be entertained', 4.6, and 'Sounded like fun' 3.9) achieved particularly high means. The nature of the Festival itself ('To watch musical events' 4.5, 'As this Festival is unique', 3.8, 'As I enjoy the Festival crowd', 3.9 'To experience an International festival, 3.7) was also viewed as important. The statement relating to escaping mundane environments ('As a break from normal routine, 3.9) scored highly, although the more generic ('To escape', 2.9) which was the first of the statements in the question, did not achieve a particularly high mean.

Overall, statements relating to family activities, social interaction and learning were ranked less highly. However, these means ignore variability within the visitor sample. One of the key aims of this research was to discern variables, that influence visitor motivations and any relationships between motivations, and to this end the data was analysed, using factor analysis and analysis of variance (ANOVA).

Prior to conducting factor analysis, two tests, the Kaiser-Meyer-Olkin (KMO) Measure and Bartlett's Test of Sphericity (BTS) were conducted. The results, showing a relatively high KMO measure of 0.823 (normally acceptable above 0.5) and a BTS result of Chi squared = 2462.57, confirmed that the data was suitable for factor analysis. Exploratory factor analysis produced five factor groupings, but only three of these were fully acceptable in relation to the Cronbach Alpha test (normally at 0.7 and above). These factors are shown in Figure 2.

Figure 2 *Factor analysis results*

Factor 1 (Cronbach Alpha 0.88) (**Learning**)

To be creative

To be involved and participate

To develop my skills

To challenge myself

To take part in musical activities

To interact with others

Factor 2 (Cronbach Alpha 0.80) (**Family**)

To be with my partner/family

As I thought my family would enjoy it

To do things with my family

Factor 3 (Cronbach Alpha 0.69) (**Passive Entertainment**)

To be entertained

To experience an international festival

To watch musical events

Factor 4 (Cronbach Alpha 0.52) (**Escape**)

To escape

As a break from my normal routine

It sounded like fun

Factor 5 (Cronbach Alpa 0.54) (**Social Stimulation**)

To be with friends

As I enjoy the Festival crowd

In the factor analysis the following statements did not correlate: 'To expand my knowledge', 'The Festival is unique' and 'To meet new people'.

Each of the five factors in Figure 2 has been given a label. These five factors have been labelled based upon the individual items contained in each group and consistent with the literature, and in particular influenced by the work of Raybould *et al* (1999). These five factors identified in the SIF study were as follows: (1) Learning, (2) Family, (3) Passive Entertainment, (4) Escape and (5) Social Stimulation.

ANOVA was conducted in relation to the twenty motivation statements in the Likert scale and the demographic and visitor trip variables. Statistically significant differences (at the 0.05% level) were found in terms of the motivation statements in relation to the following variables: gender, education level, the marital/family status of respondents, the nature of the ticket purchased, with whom respondents attended the Festival and whether respondents had attended the Festival before.

In terms of gender, females provided statistically significantly higher means than males for eight of the twenty statements. These statements are shown in Figure 3.

Figure 3 *Motivation statement responses provided by females achieving a statistically higher mean than those provided by males*

As I enjoy the Festival crowd

To experience an international festival

This Festival is unique

As a break from my normal routine

To meet new people

It sounded like fun

To challenge myself

As I thought my family would enjoy it

The education level of visitors affected responses to the motivation statements. In summary, a number of statements achieved a statistically significant higher mean score from visitors with at least an undergraduate degree and/or a post graduate degree, compared with responses from those with an education up to only 'secondary' or 'A' level. These statements were as follows: 'To be creative', 'To expand my knowledge', 'To challenge myself', and 'To be involved and participate'.

A number of statistically significant differences were found in terms of the responses to the motivation statements in relation to 'family status' (or what was termed on the questionnaire 'current situation'). Hence, perhaps not surprisingly, those respondents who indicated their current situation was 'Family' provided the highest means for 'To do things with my family' and 'As I thought my family would enjoy it'. Nevertheless, these responses may be said to provide evidence of the 'reality' of the data. Both the groups 'Solo' and 'Solo with children', provided responses with statistically significantly higher means than for the 'Family' and 'Couple/no children' in response to a number of the statements. These statements are shown in Figure 4.

Figure 4 *Responses from 'Solo' and 'Solo, no children' visitors achieving statistically higher means than responses from 'family' and 'couple, no children'*

To be creative

To meet new people

To develop my skills

To challenge myself

To take part in musical activities

To interact with others

Ticket type was revealed as influencing motivation. Day ticket holders provided responses with statistically higher means in terms of all the 'family' related motivation statements. However, season ticket holders gave responses with statistically higher means in relation to eight of the statements. These are shown in Figure 5

Figure 5 *Season ticket holder motivation responses with statistically significant higher means than those provided by day ticket holders*

To be with friends
To be creative
To expand my knowledge
To meet new people
To be involved and participate
To develop my skills
To take part in musical activities
To interact with others.

In general terms, those who attended the Festival with friends and/or family gave responses with higher means, in terms of the 'family motivations' and the statements 'To be with friends' and 'To interact with others', than other groups. Those who attended 'Alone' gave responses with higher means for the following statements: 'To meet new people', 'To interact with others' 'To develop my skills' and 'To challenge myself'.

Those who had attended the Festival before, in general, gave responses with higher means to a majority of the statements, than those who had not attended before. Figure 6 shows these statements.

Figure 6 *Responses of those who had attended the Festival 'at least once before' with statistically higher means than responses from those who had not attended the Festival before*

To be with friends
To enjoy the Festival crowd
To be entertained
To expand my knowledge
The Festival is unique
To develop my skills
To take part in musical activities
To interact with others

Discussion

In general terms, it is possible to view the motivations for attendance at the SIF as fitting into two broad categories, that of 'push and 'pull' (Dann, 1977; Iso-Aloha, 1980; Manfredo *et al*, 1996; Pearce, 1993). The motivations for SIF attendance also conform largely to Getz (1991) 'three generic needs' model of festival attendance and in particular his 'social needs' and 'personal needs' appear as key motivations.

In terms of the details of the research questions, the specific motivation achieving the highest mean in the SIF research, 'to be entertained', also achieved the highest mean in the research conducted by Raybould *et al* (1999) at the Woodford Folk Festival. Results from the SIF also confirm the findings of Raybould *et al*, in that the nature of each of the festivals, in terms of their focus on folk music, appeared to be very important motivations for attendance. This finding also supports that of Scott (1996) where the theme of a particular festival was revealed as a major motivational factor for attendance.

Raybould *et al*'s (1999) findings suggested that 'escaping mundane environments' was an important motivation for festival attendance. Those attending the SIF also indicated that this motivation was significant, but it appears that this motivation was not as strong as for attendance at the Woodford Folk Festival. The SIF research, revealed that family activities, social interaction and learning were less important motivations than 'seeking entertainment' and 'the nature of the festival'. These are identical results to those revealed by Raybould *et al* at the Woodford Folk Festival.

However, factor analysis of the SIF results produced similarities with, but not identical findings to, those of Raybould *et al*. Raybould *et al* identified five groupings after factor analysis: 1) Learning, 2) Family 3) Social Stimulation, 4) Authenticity and Uniqueness and 5) Escape. The SIF also produced five groupings, although groupings 4 and 5 did not achieve Cronbach alpha scores quite large enough to indicate a sufficiently high degree of reliability. Four of the SIF groupings had identical labels to those of Raybould *et al* ('Learning', 'Family', 'Social Stimulation' and 'Escape'). However, the individual items in each were not identical. One of the important differences was that the item 'To interact with others' was in the factor 'Social Stimulation' in Raybould *et al*'s study, but in the 'Learners' factor in the SIF research. The SIF research also produced a category labelled 'Passive Entertainment' which was not found as a factor at all in the Raybould *et al* study. However this category 'passive entertainment' could be equated with Pearce's (1988) 'relaxation' category. The concept of 'authenticity', per se, was not included in the SIF research and hence no factor with this label was produced.

The results from the ANOVA indicated some important demographic and trip variables influencing motivations at the SIF. Almost half (eight) of the motivation statements achieved statistically higher means in answers from the female respondents. Only a limited amount of research has focused on gender variations in attitudes to tourism (see Mason and Cheyne, 2000), hence these results are particularly interesting. These motivation statements of female visitors were, in general, concerned with 'escape' and 'participation', hence both the 'push' and 'pull' factors (Dann, 1977; Iso-Aloha, 1980; Manfredo *et al*, 1996; Pearce, 1993) appeared important. The female respondents also provided a statistically higher mean for the statement 'As I thought my family would enjoy it'. Mason and Cheyne (2000) recorded greater concern with family issues in relation to tourism by female respondents. Results from the SIF study may provide an indication that female visitors have a somewhat different 'world view' (see Pearce *et al*, 1996) to the male visitors. However, more detailed research at the SIF would be needed to confirm this.

The results relating to 'current situation' (e.g. 'solo', 'couple/no children' etc.) from the SIF study mirror very closely those achieved by Raybould *et al* (1999) as do those for the nature of festival attendance (e.g. 'with friends', 'with family' etc.) and motivations. Of particular importance here was that those without children and/or attending alone were more likely to provide higher mean scores for 'learning' motivations, such as 'To develop my skills' and 'To challenge myself'.

The SIF study indicated that those with higher education qualifications were more likely to want to attend the Festival to be involved in 'Learning'; situations, than those with lower qualifications. This result was not achieved by Raybould *et al* at the Woodford Festival, as here educational level was not found to have any effect on the five factors.

Ticket type and previous attendance were variables that influenced the mean scores of motivation statements at the SIF. Day ticket holders were motivated to a greater extent than season ticket holders by 'Family' factors. By contrast, season ticket holders provided responses with higher means to responses than from day ticket holders for eight of the motivation statements. These motivation statements were largely within the 'Learning' and 'Social Stimulation' groupings. Very similar results to these were found by Raybould *et al* at the Woodford Folk Festival. Raybould *et al* also found important differences between the motivations of those who had attended the Festival before and those who had not. More frequent visitor to the Woodford Folk Festival indicated that 'Escape', and 'Authenticity' issues were particular important. For SIF visitors who had attended the Festival at least once before, eight motivations achieved a statistically higher mean compared to the responses from those who had not attended before. These motivation statements covered four of the five major factors: 'Learning', 'Social Stimulation' 'Family' and 'Passive Entertainment'. Hence, it can be suggested that those who had attended the SIF before, and particularly those who had visited more than five times, probably have a better understanding of the benefits the Festival has on these factors. In this way, it is possible to argue that for those who have attended before, these are very much 'pull' factors (Crompton 1979, Iso-Aloha, 1980) encouraging and bringing them back to the SIF year after year.

It might be assumed that age would be an important variable in relation to motivation for Festival attendance. Raybould *et al*, in fact, found that age was important in their study. However in relation to the SIF, although there was some indication of different motivations for attendance, with younger visitors indicating that 'Learning' was more important, while older visitors that 'Family' was more important, these differences were not statistically significant.

Raybould *et al* argued that very little motivational research has been conducted at festivals with the intention of improving marketing or management. However, when taken together, the findings from the factor analysis and ANOVA at the SIF have some important implications for both marketing and management. In particular, it would appear that those who comprise regular visitors are looking for a different type of Festival experience compared with first time visitors. Hence, marketing material needs to be more specifically targeted at these different types of visitors. Also, the relatively old age of many visitors, needs to be noted by those involved in marketing and managing the SIF. There was some anecdotal evidence, gained during the research process, that up to three generations of the same families now regularly attend the Festival. Nevertheless, older visitors will need to be replaced by younger ones, if the long-term sustainability of the SIF is to be ensured.

Conclusions

Research results at the SIF were similar, in several ways to those found by Raybould *et al* (1999) at the Woodford Folk Festival, but also provided evidence of important differences. Motivations relating to 'seeking entertainment' as well as those concerned with the nature of each of the festivals were particularly important for attendance at both festivals. Another similarity was that family activities, social interaction and learning were less important motivations at both festivals. However, the factor analysis and ANOVA at the SIF provide details of some differences in motivation between the two festivals, as well as indicating links between demographic and trip variables in relation to motivations. Hence, the SIF respondents with higher qualifications were more likely to be involved in 'Learning', season ticket holders were also more likely to be 'learners', rather than passive participants, those who had attended the Festival more than five times previously were more likely to be 'learners', those who attended with friends and family wanted family entertainment, more than couples and single parents, and women generally had more positive views on the Festival than men.

When combining the results from the factor analysis and ANOVA, it was possible to indicate the following groups by motivation:

(a)   Those who had attended the Festival several times before and were motivated by the desire to challenge themselves by taking part in learning situations. Social stimulation involving meeting up with friends and relatives was also important to this group.

(b)   Those who were more passive in their response to the Festival, enjoying watching, 'being entertained', more than taking part in events.

(c)   Those who were mainly family orientated in their motivation, comprising both long-term visitors and those who had attended only once before.

(d)   Those who were attending the Festival for the first time and were mainly motivated by social factors and family activities.

(e)   Those who were escaping routine, comprising more women than men.

All the components listed in the sub-title of this chapter were major motivations for attendance at the SIF. However, if seeking 'fun' (entertainment) and 'folk' (the nature of the festival itself) were the key motivations, 'friends' and 'family' were also very important and fulfilment, which could be achieved through 'learning' opportunities at the Festival, was also shown to be particularly significant.

References

Beard, J. and Ragheb, M. (1983), Measuring leisure motivation, *Journal of Leisure Research*, 15 (3,) 219-228.

Bowdin, G. McDonnell, I. Allen, J. and O'Toole, W. (2001), *Events Management*, Oxford, Butterworth Heinemann.

Cohen, E. (1972), Towards of sociology of international tourism, *Social Research*, 39 (1), 164-182.

Crompton, J. (1979), Motivations for pleasure vacations, *Annals of Tourism Research*, 6 (1), 408-424.

Crompton, J. and McKay, S. (1997), Motives of visitors attending festival events, *Annals of Tourism Research*, 24 (2), 425-439.

Dann, G. (1977), Anomie, ego-enhancement and tourism, *Annals of Tourism Research*, 4 (4), 187-219.

Dunn-Ross, E. and Iso-Aloha, S. (1991), Sightseeing tourists' motivation and satisfaction, *Annals of Tourism Research*, 12, 256-262.

Fodness, D. (1994), Measuring tourist motivation, *Annals of Tourism Research*, 21 (3), 555-581.

Getz, D. (1997), *Event Management and Event Tourism*, New York, Cognizant Communications Corporation.

Getz, D. and Frisby, W. (1988), Evaluating management effectiveness in community run festivals, *Journal of Travel Research*, 27 (3), 22-27.

Harrill, R. and Potts, T. (2002), Social Psychological Theories of Tourist Motivation: Exploration, Debate and Transition, *Tourism Analysis*, 7, 105-114.

Iso-Aloha, S. (1980), The Social-psychology of Leisure and Recreation, Iowa, Brown.

Iso-Aloha, S. (1982), Towards a social psychological theory of tourism motivation: a rejoinder, *Annals of Tourism Research*, 9 (2), 256-262.

Janiskee, R. (1994), Some macro-scale growth trends in America's community festival industry, *Festival Management and Event Tourism*, 2, 10-14.

Manfredo, M. Driver, B. and Tarrant, M. (1996), Measuring leisure motivation, a meta-analysis of the recreation experience preference scales, *Journal of Leisure Research*, 28 (3), 188-213.

Mannell, R. and Kleber, D. (1997), *A Social Psychology of Leisure*, State College Pennsylvania, Venture Publishing.

Maslow, A. (1954), *Motivation and Personality*, Harper, New York.

Mason, P. and Cheyne, J. (2000), Resident Attitudes to a Tourism Development, *Annals of Tourism Research*, 27 (2), 391-411.

Mohr, K. Backman, K. Gahan, L. and Backman, S. (1993), An investigation of festival motivations and event satisfaction by visitor type, *Festival Management and Event Tourism*, 1 (3), 89-97.

Pearce, P. (1988), The Ulysses Factor: Identifying Visitors in Tourists Settings, Springer-Verlag, New York.

Pearce, P. (1993), Fundamentals of Tourist Motivation: in Pearce, D and Butler, R, (Eds) *Tourism Research: Critiques and Challenges*, London, Routledge 113-134.

Pearce, P. Moscardo, G. and Ross, G. (1996), *Tourism Community Relationships*, London, Pergamon.

Perret, A. and Raybould, M. (1998), *A report on the visitor survey conducted at the 1997/8 Woodford Folk Festival*. Unpublished report to the Queensland Folk Federation. Centre for Tourism and Hotel Management, Griffith University.

Plog, S. (1972), *Why destination areas rise and fall in popularity*. Paper presented to the Southern California Chapter of the Travel Research Association, San Diego.

Raybould, M. Digance, J. and McCullough, C, (1999), Fire and Festival: Authenticity and Visitor Motivation at an Australian Folk Festival, *Pacific Tourism Review*, (3), 201-212.

Rickards, B. (1998), 'The Wonder of Woodford', Gold Coast Weekender (December 12-13th) The Gold Coast Bulletin p.26.

Ryan, C. (1995), *Researching Tourist Satisfaction*, London, Routledge.

Ryan, C. and Glendon, I. (1998), Application of a leisure motivation scale to tourism, *Annals of Tourism Research*, 25 (1), 169-184.

Scott, D. (1996), A comparison of visitors motivations to attend three urban festivals, *Festival Management and Event Tourism*, 3, 121-128.

Uysal, M. Gahan, L. and Martin, R. (1993), An investigations of event motivations: a case study, *Festival Management and Event Tourism*, 1 (1), 5-10.

Festival Planning:
the case of the 2000 Daejeon Science Festival, Korea

Hoon Lee
Hanyang University, Korea

Gang Hoan Jeong and Ralph Cousins
Paichai University, Korea

Introduction

Festivals and special events are one of the fastest growing forms of leisure and tourism related phenomena (Getz, 1997; Burr, 1977). Events can be described as tourist attractions, development catalysts, and image builders for attractions and destination areas (Getz, 1997). These events are often seen as an expression of the social norms and values of the community. Festivals and special events are a cultural demonstration of community life, tradition, and values, and have several impacts such as creating or enhancing a positive image and bringing money to the community economy (Uysal & Gitelson, 1994). Therefore, the development of new festivals in a region is one strategy for celebrating their assets or recognizing their identification, and for marking the attractions of that tourism destination.

Despite the importance of festivals and events, comparatively few studies have been conducted, until recently, on their planning model (Hall, 1992). Chacko & Schaffer (1993) also mentioned that there is a lack of information relative to the planning process and the planning model of a festival; from the birth of an idea, to the process of the planning and the effects of the festival.

Getz (1997, p.72) mentions that "planning is always future oriented, focusing on the formulation of goals and the means to achieve them." McDonnell, Allen, & O'Toole (1999) further state that the planning process is usually broken down into the two key processes of strategic and operational planning. Strategic plans are long-term, directional, and usually single-use plans while operational plans are short-term, specific, and standing, thus able to be reused in future events.

Several researchers have suggested a planning process for tourism developments and tourism products. Getz (1997) proposed a seven-stage strategic planning process for events and event tourism; (a) mandate, purpose, or mission, (b) visioning and goal setting, (c) situation analysis, (d) market research, (e) issues identification, (f) strategy formulation, and (g) implementation. "Its logic is straightforward, although developing the process can be quite complex. It does not have to be linear, but can combine and repeat elements of the various stages." (Getz, 1997, p. 93). The WTO (1998) suggest that tourism planning should be accomplished according to a systematic process.

Therefore the WTO (1998) recommends a general seven-stage planning process; study preparation, determination of development objectives, surveys and evaluations, analysis and synthesis, policy and plan formulation, recommendations, and implementation and management.

Similarly, Handfield, Ragatz, Petersen, and Monczka (1999, p.64) developed a conceptual model of the product development process "after reviewing a number of companies' supplier integration processes and compiling their best practices into a generic process model." The five stages include idea generation, business/technical assessment, product/process/service concept development, product/process/service design and development, and prototype build, test and pilot/ramp-up for operations. In terms of the components model or total level, Gunn (1994) suggested that the tourism planning process should predict a better future, incorporate all three sectors – attractions, infrastructure, and transportation, become more interactive, and include social goals as well as economic benefits. Smith (1994) tried to consider tourism as an industry that is characterised by a generic product and production process. Thus in doing so, he suggested that the tourism production process consists of primary inputs (resources), intermediate inputs (facilities or attractions), intermediate outputs (services), and final outputs (tourists experience).

Ideally, festival developments as a tourism product should be based on marketplace demands and the wise use of the cultural and social resources of the destination (Bramwell, 1998; Smith, 1994). Particularly, latent visitor surveys can explore the visitors' expectations and address the directions of festival planning.

Based on literature research, this chapter discusses the planning process of a particular festival and examines these process at a regional level. The purpose of this research is to develop a festival planning model as a tourism attraction and apply the model to a case study. It focuses on the process of researching consumer's needs by using a potential consumer survey and developing a consumer-oriented programme. In addition, this study evaluates the implications and effects of the festival.

Methodology

A questionnaire was designed to develop the festival model and programmes. In the project survey, the items were prepared to investigate consumer and expert groups' opinions on; (a) interesting festival programme elements; (b) the educational dimensions of a science festival for children; (c) the festival's impacts on the city; (d) the group type of latent visitors; and (e) respondents enthusiasm for attending the festival.

Study setting and data collection

The city of Daejeon gained recognition for successfully hosting the 1993 International Science Expo. Within Korea, Daejeon is a Mecca for advanced science and technology, and is the second administrative capital next to Seoul, the nation's capital. The mayor of Daejeon is the WTA (World Technology Association) chairperson. The city hosts the Daedok Research Complex, which is representative of about 60 national and commercial institutes of science and technology, KAIST, a higher science university, and the EXPO Science Park.

A sample of individuals was selected over an eleven-day period in Daejeon and Seoul in Korea, which are considered as main markets. A total of 603 individuals completed the questionnaire. Sampling was conducted as follows:

- 13th January 2000. – 23rd January 2000 (11 days).

- Latent visitors (251 samples from 5 districts in Daejeon and 210 samples from 5 districts in Seoul): 461.

- Experts (Scientists in Daedok Research Complex, Science teachers in middle & high schools): 142.

Analysis

Descriptive analysis was used to provide more basic information and to understand the context of preparing the festival. Data for analysis were based on responses from six hundred and three people (n = 603). The sample of experts tended to be male (78.2%), and relatively middle aged (71.1% were aged 31 to 50 years old). About two-thirds of the latent visitors lived in Seoul. Over two-thirds of the respondents were accompanied by other family members including children. Nearly fifteen percent of the respondents were with friends or colleagues.

Table 1   *Descriptive analysis results for the reponents' profile*

Items	Categories	Latent visitors		Experts	
		Frequency (n)	**Percent (%)**	**Frequency (n)**	**Percent (%)**
Gender	Male	192	41.6	111	78.2
	Female	266	57.7	29	20.4
	N/A(Missing)	3	0.7	2	1.4
Age	-30	43	9.3	24	16.9
	31-40	241	52.3	58	40.8
	41-50	150	32.5	43	30.3
	51-	22	4.8	11	7.8
	N/A(Missing)	5	1.1	6	4.2
Place	Daejeon City	173	37.5	-	-
	Seoul City & Other City	284	61.6	-	-
	N/A(Missing)	4	0.09	-	-

Note: Latent Visitors n= 461; Experts n=142

Table 2   *Descriptive analysis for group types (if latent visitors & experts will attend the festival*

Group type	Latent Visitors		Experts	
	Frequency (n)	Percent (%)	Frequency (n)	Percent (%)
Family with child(ren)	353	76.6	99	69.7
Friends/colleagues	63	13.7	21	14.8
Alone	7	1.5	-	-
Other	6	1.3	14	9.9
N/A(Missing)	32	6.9	8	5.6

Note: Latent Visitors n= 461; Experts n=142

Table 3   *Descriptive analysis results of educational subjects for children*

Educational subjects	Latent Visitors		Experts	
	Frequency (n)	Percent (%)	Frequency (n)	Percent (%)
Bio-engineering	115	24.9	47	33.1
Information Technology	193	41.9	56	39.4
Korean traditional science	15	3.3	7	4.9
Game & animation	43	9.3	13	9.2
Robot	34	7.4	8	5.6
Astronomy	51	11.1	7	4.9
Others	2	.4	-	-
N/A(Missing)	8	1.7	4	2.8

Note: Latent Visitors n= 461; Experts n=142

Table 4   *Descriptive analysis results for types of programs*

Types of programs	Latent Visitors	Experts
Practical participation (experiential) type	4.7	4.5
Science programs in daily life	4.4	4.3
Enjoyable interactive science type	4.3	4.1
Advanced technology type	4.0	4.0
Science in culture & arts	3.7	3.9
Overseas science programs	3.6	3.7
Korean traditional science	3.6	3.6
Competitive game type	3.2	3.4

Note: Latent Visitors n= 461; Experts n=142

Table 5   *Descriptive analysis results for willingness to attend the festival*

Intention to attend	Latent Visitors		Experts	
	Frequency (n)	**Percent (%)**	**Frequency (n)**	**Percent (%)**
1= Not at all likely	8	1.7	3	2.1
2	7	1.5	1	.7
3	22	4.8	3	2.1
4	151	32.8	27	19
5	87	18.9	25	17.6
6	99	21.5	52	36.6
7= Very likely	85	18.4	29	20.4
N/A(Missing)	2	.4	2	1.4

Note: Latent Visitors n= 461; Experts n=142

Among the science fields, two subjects are outstanding for children's education. Nearly forty percent of the respondents (latent visitors 41.9%; experts 39.4%) recommended information technology and about twenty-four (latent visitors) to thirty-three (experts) percent of the respondents suggested bio-engineering as educational subjects.

The overall evaluations of the expected festival programmes were mostly positive. Especially, the "practical participation programmes" was very high (latent visitors, mean = 4.7; experts, mean = 4.5). The "science programmes in daily life," question was also answered very positively (latent visitors, mean = 4.4; experts, mean=4.3). In addition, the evaluation of "enjoyable interactive science" was also high (latent visitors, mean = 4.3; experts, mean = 4.1).

When testing the willingness to attend the festival, about sixty percent of the respondents were willing to attend the festival (scale scores of 5 to 7). Less than seven percent of the respondents answered that they did not intend to visit the attractions (scale scores of 1 to 3).

Figure 1 *A model of festival development and planning*

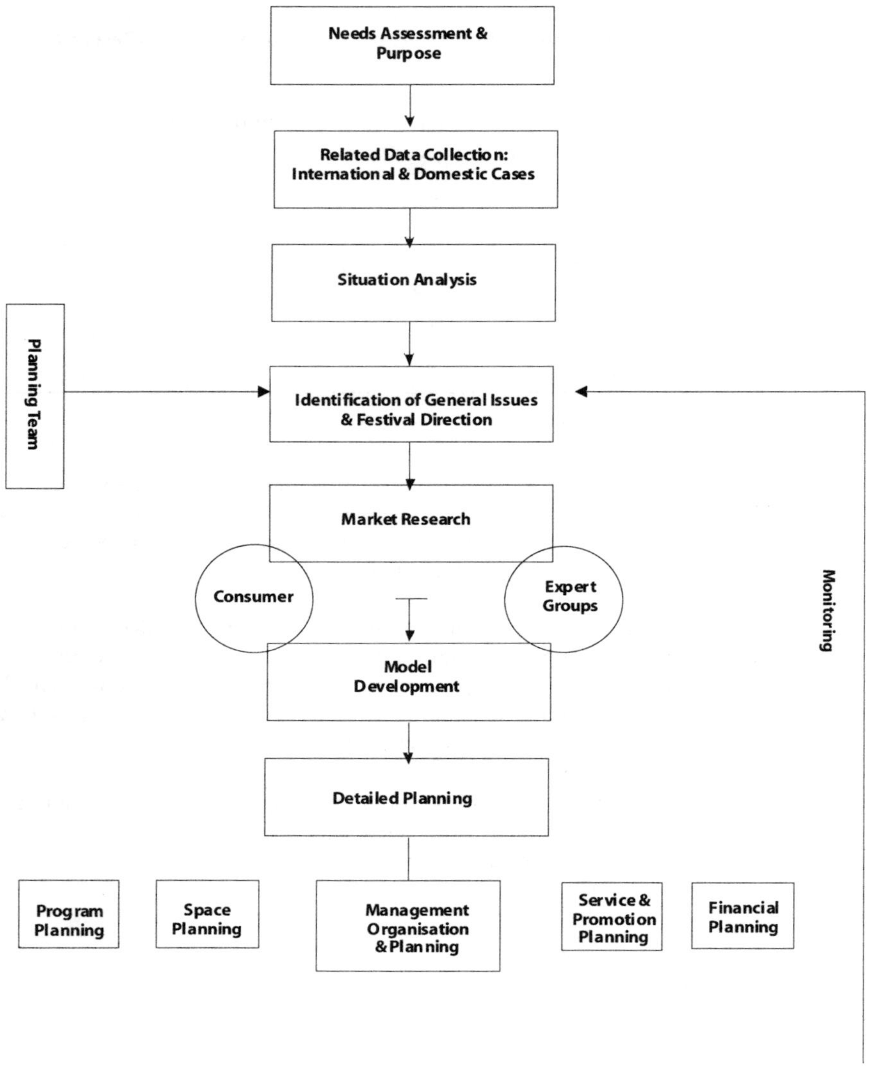

```
                    ┌─────────────────────┐
                    │  Needs Assessment & │
                    │      Purpose        │
                    └──────────┬──────────┘
                               │
                               ▼
                    ┌─────────────────────┐
                    │ Related Data Collection:│
                    │ International & Domestic Cases│
                    └──────────┬──────────┘
                               │
                               ▼
                    ┌─────────────────────┐
                    │  Situation Analysis │
                    └──────────┬──────────┘
                               │
     ┌──────────┐              ▼
     │ Planning │    ┌─────────────────────┐
     │   Team   │───▶│ Identification of General Issues│◀──┐
     └──────────┘    │   & Festival Direction │       │
                     └──────────┬──────────┘          │
                                │                       │
                                ▼                       │
                     ┌─────────────────────┐           │ Monitoring
                     │   Market Research    │           │
          ┌───────┐  ├──────────┬───────┐ ┌───────┐    │
          │Consumer│ │          │       │ │ Expert│    │
          └───────┘  │    Model         │ │ Groups│    │
                     │  Development     │ └───────┘    │
                     └──────────┬──────────┘           │
                                │                       │
                                ▼                       │
                     ┌─────────────────────┐           │
                     │  Detailed Planning   │           │
                     └──────────┬──────────┘           │
                                │                       │
 ┌────────┐ ┌────────┐ ┌────────────┐ ┌──────────┐ ┌────────┐
 │Program │ │ Space  │ │ Management │ │Service & │ │Financial│
 │Planning│ │Planning│ │Organisation│ │Promotion │ │Planning │
 └────────┘ └────────┘ │ & Planning │ │ Planning │ └────────┘
                       └────────────┘ └──────────┘
```

Developing the DSF2000 Model

This conceptual model, partially adopted from Getz's model (1997) and WTO (1998), proposes a seven-stage planning process. This is a logical process that repeats certain elements of the various stages.

Stage 1: Needs assessment & purpose

During the first stage, the regional (or national) needs should be understood first. Why should a festival or event be held here? What kinds of festivals or events are preferred? This stage is to provide festival or event organisers and planners with a firm foundation upon which vision and strategies can be built. Objectives must be realistic and attainable, and it is generally useful to build in steps by which results can be evaluated (Getz, 1997).

The basic purpose of the DSF2000 was to enhance Daejeon's image as an advanced science city and to provide an educational setting where advanced science events could be demonstrated to impart knowledge to the public and children. Additional purposes of introducing the festival were to promote regional tourism and attract economic benefits. The vision of the festival includes three notions; regional culture, science education, and tourism.

Stage 2: Related data collection

Before developing the festival concept, related data and information including domestic and international cases needs to be reviewed.

The International Science Festival in New Zealand was analysed in terms of the programmes, the destination, target market, promotion, and organisation. Also the 1999 Korean Science Exhibition was evaluated by two methods; observation and questionnaire survey. The research investigated the programme, visitor satisfaction, types and activities.

Stage 3: Situation analysis

To analyse the situation, the SWOT method was used. The analysis of the SWOT is as follows;

Table 6   *SWOT analysis of DSF 2000*

Strength	Opportunity
• the reputation of Daejeon as a science city	• Vacation season for students and family
• a lot of science institutes (KAIST, EXPO Science Park, Daedok Research Complex, and the National Science Museum)	• Linkage of KAIST 's Robot Olympiad
• Gaining the public name of 'National Cultural Tourism Festival' from Ministry of Culture & Tourism in 2000	• Student volunteers available
• Solid political support	
Weakness	**Threat**
• Brand new festival	• Competition of similar events (Korea Science Exhibition) in Seoul
• Weather condition(hot)	• Competition of other mega events (Millennium related events) in 2000
• Difficult theme(science)	• Conflicts between the National Science Museum and Expo Science Park

Stage 4: Identification of general issues and event direction

Arising from the situation analysis and related case studies, a number of issues were identified. General issues were stated as goals to achieve and suggested the direction of the event (Getz, 1997). The planning team developed initial concepts from the above three stages.

Four initial concepts:

- Publicity: public science education.

- Economics: increasing tourism.

- Popularity: interesting and enjoyable programme.

- Reliability: increasing the city's image and citizen attachment, especially scientists in Daejeon who are generally from other cities.

Stage 5: Market research

Getz (1997) suggested that market research is necessary in order to identify some essential questions which include: (a) customers' needs and motives (b) the role of events in creating/enhancing the destination theme, (c) the role of events in increasing the attractiveness of tourism resources, and so on.

The questionnaire survey was prepared for two groups. One was for customers who live in Daejeon and Seoul. The other was for expert groups who are scientists in the Deadok Research Complex, and middle and high school science teachers. The results are shown in tables 1 through 7.

Stage 6: Model development

From the survey results, the planning team prepared five principles of this festival model. The first principle is consumer-based programmes that included practical participation, science in daily life, and interactive science programmes. Information technology and bio-engineering were also highlighted. The second principle is public science education that was integrated into the Expo Science Park and research outcomes from the Research Institute in Daejeon.

The third principle is to enlarge the image of Daejeon and citizen attachment by the linkage of the Science-Belt which consists of the National Science Museum, the Daedok Research Complex, KAIST and so on. The fourth principle is the practical use of EXPO Science Park which has been stagnant since the 1993 EXPO. The final principle is to make the DSF2000 a major tourism attraction. For the domestic tourist, a Yusong spa tourism package, and for international tourists, a Korean Traditional Science programme package were designed.

Table 7   *Contents of festival model*

Principles		Contents	Zoning
Consumer-based program	Program	Practical participation (experts 90%, mean 4.5; latent visitors 90%, mean 4.7)	
		Popular Science program in common lifestyle (experts 85%, mean 4.3; latent visitors 85%, mean 4.4)	
		Enjoyable science play (experts 80%, 4.1; latent visitors 80%, mean 4.3)	
	Preferred science fields	Information Technology (experts 39%, latent visitors 42%)	Digital World (C Zone)
		Bio-engineering (experts 33%, latent visitors 25%)	Bio World (B Zone)
Public education of science	Exhibition of research outcomes	Research institutes in Daejeon	
	EXPO Science Park	Use facilities	
Enlarging image of city and citizen attachment	Science-Belt	National Science Museum, Daedok Research Complex, KAIST	Science-Belt
Practical use of EXPO Science Park	Hard-ware	Government Pavilion, Electric Energy Pavilion, Technopia Pavilion, Humans and Science Pavilion, Earth Pavilion, Imagination Pavilion	
	Soft-ware	IMAX Movies, 4DVR	
Development of tourism attractions	Domestic tourists	Package programs	Yusong area
	International tourists	Korean Traditional Science, ancient Korean inventions such as rain gauge, water clock, etc.	Time & Space World (D zone)

The theme of the festival was "Click! Scientopia." Scientopia is a combination of the words, science and utopia. There were four zones; the 'Scientopia Gate (A zone)', the 'Bio World (B zone)', the 'Digital World (C zone)', and the 'Time & Space World (D zone).'

Table 8   *The themes and the zones of the festival*

Category	A zone	B zone	C zone	D zone
Name	Scientopia Gate	Bio World	Digital World	Time & Space World
Science fields	-	Bio-engineering	Information technology, Advanced technology	Korean Traditional Science, Astronomy
Theme	Welcome to Scientopia	Green Breath	Future Scope	Time & Space Journey

Stage 7: Detailed planning

Based on the theme and model, more detailed plans were prepared such as program planning, space or zone planning, organisation and management planning, service and promotion planning, and financial planning. Each of these planning types was also designed to achieve the principles and purpose of the festival. The planning team diagrammed four zones for each science subject and sketched out the programmes for each zone. The planner also proposed blueprints for customer services and other detailed planning of the festival. In addition, the planning team adopted a hierarchical monitoring system for the purpose of modifying any problems.

Conclusions

Planning is necessary to develop and synthesise new products or functions in order to be an applicable tool for problem solving and problem prevention (Alipour, 1996). Even though planning of product development is required to satisfy visitor needs and enhance their attractions, there has been little research in the field of festival planning.

This paper introduces the planning process of the Daejeon Science Festival 2000. This study has also shown how measuring market research assists in the planning process before developing the model. It is helpful to survey the needs and opinions of latent visitors and experts, if the planning team wants to develop consumer-oriented festivals. The implications of these findings were evaluated for the model development of the DSF2000. Notably, the findings from a survey can assist the organisers in identifying priorities for preferred science fields, desired programmes, and a more appropriate target market.

The planning model of the festival was comprised of seven stages that were modified from Getz's strategic planning process (Getz, 1997) and WTO tourism planning process (WTO, 1998). It included needs assessment and purpose, related data collection, situation analysis of the festival, identification of general issues and direction, market research, model development, and detailed planning based on the systematic nature of the planning process. Five principles of the model were also proposed after considering results of the above stages: consumer-based programmes, science education, enhancing city image and citizenship attachment, practical use the of EXPO Science Park, and tourism attraction development. Additionally, festival theme and space zoning were projected for each festival programme.

The new festival was successful. In the post evaluation of the DSF2000 (see appendix 1), the inaugural year of the DSF2000 had an estimated visitor count of 208,000 over the 10 day period. The overall tourist ratio for the DSF2000 was 53.5%. A tourist is defined as those who reside outside of Deajeon City and its surrounding suburbs. The majority of tourists, 22%, came from the main market of Seoul and other cities within Kyounggi Province. The economic impact of tourist spending was estimated at US$ 4.1 million, the total resident and tourist figure being estimated at US$ 6.6 million. On average, visitors stayed 5.5 hours at the festival. This can be attributed to the large selection of event programmes, long waiting lines into the pavilion shows, hands-on experience programmes, and activities and programmes held outside the Expo Science Park site.

There was a 73% willingness to revisit the DSF2001 rate among visitors. The programme which includes other facilities around the "science town", is experience orientated which contributes to the high interest. Among our research statistics, 54% were very satisfied because of the educational nature of the festival. The programme of the festival is focused on hands-on experiences for children and accompanying adults. On a 7-point Likert scale, visitors responding to festival experience satisfaction, gave a 5.11 rating for hands-on experiences and a 4.83 rating for exhibitions and watching performances. For the educational programs, 25.5% most favoured bio-engineering, followed by 17.6% for traditional science, 13.1% for creative and investigative programmes, and 9.8% for scientific presentations (STMPU, 2000).

Many festivals and events, both old and new, have been developed in Korea. However, more information concerning the planning of festivals and events is needed. This study introduces the process of festival planning in the view of the latent visitor and expert groups. The proposed planning model in this case study needs to be tested against other festival case studies in order to generalise or modify the model.

References

Alipour, H., (1996), "Tourism development within planning paradigms: The case of Turkey", *Tourism Management*, 17 (3), 367-377.

Bramwell, W. M. (1998), "User satisfaction and product development in urban tourism", *Tourism Management*, 19 (1,) 35-47.

Burr, S. T. (1997), "Love the neighbor and prosper: Community festivals and events", *Parks & Recreation*, 32 (9), 106-118.

Chacko, Harsha E. & Schaffer, Jeffrey D. (1993), "The evolution of a festival: Creole Christmas in New Orleans", *Tourism Management*, December, 475-482.

Getz, D. (1997), *Event management & event tourism*, Elmsford, NY, Cognizant Communication Corporation.

Gunn, Clare A. (1994), *Tourism planning: Basics, concepts, cases*, Washington, DC: Taylor & Francis.

Hall, D. M. (1992), *Hallmark tourist events: Impacts, management & planning*, London, UK: Belhaven Press.

Handfield, R. B., Ragatz, G. L., Petersen, K. J., & Monczka, R. M. (1999), "Involving suppliers in new product development", *California Management Review*, 42 (1), 59-81.

McDonnell, I., Allen, J., & O'Toole, W. (1999), *Festival and Special Event Management*. John Wiley & Sons: Australia.

Smith, S. L. J. (1994), "The tourism product", *Annals of Tourism Research*, 21 (3), 582-595.

STMPU (2000), *The Evaluation of DSF2000*. School of Tourism Management, Paichai University. Daejeon, Korea, Expopark Corp.

Uysal, M. & Gitelson, R. (1994), "Assessment of economic impacts: Festivals and special events", *Festival Management & Event Tourism*, 1 (1), 5-10.

WTO (1998), *Guide for local authorities on developing sustainable tourism*. Madrid. World Tourism Organization.

Appendix 1

Post Evaluation of DSF2000

Items	Contents
Visitors	About 208,000 visitors
Rates of Tourists	53.5%
Economic impacts	Tourists: More than $ 4.1 million Total visitors including residents: More than $ 6.6 million
Average number of hours spent at DSF2000	5. 49 hours
Willingness to revisit	73.2%
Program	Highly evaluated program: Practical participation type Educational program: bio-engineering

Addressing Sensibilities: a rationale for an 'inclusive' approach to festival programming and promotion

Richard Voase

University of Lincoln, UK

Introduction

The landscape of marketing was transformed, in the last decade, by the proliferation of computer technology. Database marketing, the term used to refer to the collection, storage and manipulation of large volumes of multivariate customer data, emerged as a definitive innovation in marketing management from the 1990s. A revised philosophy of marketing, relationship marketing, owes much to the capability, offered by databases, to simulate personal relationships with customers.

There has been recent evidence of healthy critical reflection, by marketing practitioners, of the usefulness of database marketing (Croft 1997). However, the database in practice has become an integral component of the contemporary marketing approach. Pre-eminent is the usefulness of the database in its ability to differentiate groups customers by variables held in common. In other words, the attraction of the database is its ability to identify *difference.*

It will be argued that this ability to differentiate has led to a new scientific orthodoxy in marketing, which is not always helpful, and can be hazardous. The axiomatic assumption that the segmentation of customer markets by difference is *the* valid approach neglects a crucial fact: that any body of human consumers can be defined by similarities, as much as by differences. To rush toward market segmentation is to forget that humans enjoy a set of senses and sensibilities in common.

It will be suggested that a renewed focus on the collective rather than the segmented is particularly important in the programming and promotion of events and festivals. The nature of the audience experience will be examined; the results of as-yet-unpublished qualitative research will be considered. By way of practical conclusion, a rationale for 'inclusivity', that is an appeal to the collective through programming and promotion, will be proposed.

Orthodoxy in marketing discourse

It is important at this early stage to set out, in clear terms, the ways in which the application of database technology, and the new philosophy of marketing which has emerged from it, have become an orthodoxy which might benefit from critical reflection. Two everyday examples of orthodoxy-in-discourse will be presented, followed by critical comment from within the field of arts marketing.

The first example is taken from a local newspaper report regarding the proliferation of health-and-fitness centres in an English provincial town. A marketing lecturer from the local university's department of business and management had been asked to comment. He said this:

> "...with so many gyms to choose from, companies have to target consumers in order to get a slice of the market...the secret of success is for the gym companies to find a gap in the market...Companies must tailor their appeal to specific groups instead of being all things to all people..." (Gannon, cited in Atkins, 2002)

The soundness of such a strategy, in a context of multiple providers, cannot be doubted. In fact, the lecturer's words proved prophetic, in that one of the gyms chose to specialise in 'women only' weeks after the newspaper report appeared. What is interesting, however, is that the ensemble of health-and-fitness equipment - swimming pool, exercise equipment and so on - does not vary from gym to gym. Similarly, the customer's experience of using such equipment does not vary greatly in accordance with lifestage or socio-economic grouping.

In other words, what the commentator chooses to see, and with which we as readers readily concur, is *difference*. Objectively speaking, we could just as readily, in fact more easily, see similarity. This orthodoxy constitutes perhaps more than normative prescription: it is ideological in nature, potent through its invisibility, in which, in the words of St Paul adapted by Althusser, we 'live, move and have our being':

> "It is indeed a peculiarity of ideology that it imposes (without appearing to do so, since these are 'obviousnesses') obviousnesses as obviousnesses, which we cannot fail to recognise and before which we have inevitable and natural reaction of crying out (aloud or in the 'still, small voice of conscience'): 'That's obvious! That's right! That's true!'" (Althusser 1992: 54)

The second example of orthodoxy-in-discourse which has been chosen to illustrate the point, is found in a practitioner report, a Marketing and Interpretation Action Plan, prepared for one of England's major cathedrals. Respectively cited as a 'key principle', a 'marketing function' and as an item for the 'marketing action plan' are the following:

> "All marketing and promotional activity is to be clearly directed at identified target markets or market segments."

> "Understand and meet visitors' needs and expectations within target market sectors and promote better understanding through market research."

> "...develop databases of consumers to be targeted through direct mail and e-mail activity...this database would become a highly valuable marketing resource." (Lincoln Cathedral 2000: 3, 4, 6)

As with the first example, the orthodoxy of difference is present. Promotion is to be prefaced by identification of difference, and the creation of separate target markets. But like the equipment in the gymnasia, the object of visitation, the Cathedral, is identical regardless of the nature of the visitor. And like the experience of visiting the gymnasium, the physical act of visiting is identical for all classes: walking around.

In fact, the document also alluded to dimensions of the visitor experience which, if better understood, would reveal what actually does happen when human beings visit a Cathedral. The primary research undertaken by the author to uncover the nature of this experience, and some of the findings, will be discussed shortly.

For the present, this section will close with reference to matters much closer to the field of event and festival management, from practitioner circles within the field of arts marketing. Toward the end of the 1990s, in the UK, concern was being expressed that excessive reliance on database marketing was inhibiting the acquisition of new audiences (Hill & Whitehead 1998).

This concern was expressed most memorably by a senior arts marketeer who, pointing to an overall arts audience which was growing smaller and whose average age was rising, pointed the finger of blame at the very marketing orthodoxies whose worthiness, during the course of the 1990s, had become unquestioned:

> "I believe in our headlong rush to establish 1990s arts marketing as a science, we have forgotten how to create ballyhoo...I believe that we, in our area of marketing, are in danger of being so fixated by the science that we've neglected the art." (Doyle 1999)

So, assuming that we are indeed ideologically conditioned – 'fixated', if you like – to see difference rather than similarity; and driven by orthodoxy to promote to people on the basis of what group or lifestage they belong to, rather than how they will enjoy the experience on offer; what questions need to be asked to uncover what actually goes on when people visit a place, an event, or a festival. In short, what is the nature of the ballyhoo?

Senses and sensibilities

Humans experience the world by assimilating messages through a range of senses. Our current society tends to privilege the visual and the spectacular; but all will testify that, for example, the sight of the sea, for someone unaccustomed to it, is complemented by the sound of seabirds, the smell of seaweed, the touch of wet sand against the foot, the taste of salt spray. The experience of encountering the sea is multi-sensual. All humans possessed of a full set of senses can experience this.

Sensibilities are slightly different. Sensibility refers to the capacity to feel. Sensibilities, in contrast with the straightforward deployment of the senses, may indeed be in part the product of nurture as well as nature. For example, the extent to which a particular individual is open to emotional response to, for example, a painting, may depend to some extent on whether or not that individual has been encouraged to develop aesthetic sense.

Regrettably, in the world of the arts and the ability to appreciate them, there is a long history of looking at people and seeing differences rather than similarities. At a time when 'segment' meant little more than a piece of fruit, Molière portrayed his *Bourgeois Gentilhomme* as an innocent abroad, attempting to develop an aesthetic sense by purchasing the advice of a phalange of experts. His advisers, though mutually antagonistic, are united in an interest to maintain the myth that the purpose of aesthetic sense is to support personal distinction, rather than to enjoy oneself.

Similarly, the distinction between 'art' meaning 'high art', and what is now known as popular culture, first emerged in Britain during the 19th century (Pick 1986: ch 1). In terms of the theatre, what began as a divide between the officially-licensed theatre and unlicensed music hall has progressed to the present day in the form of the dichotomy between subsidised high art and commercial popular entertainment. When the twain meet, in the form of a subsidised theatre luminary directing a commercial musical, controversy is never far away.

These longstanding divisions within the arts have served to obfuscate the fact that sensibility can be as much to do with nature as with nurture. In a previous publication (Voase 2001), taking live drama as the subject, this author has proposed a theoretical framework for the audience experience at a theatre event: how live drama is 'consumed', if you wish. Three incremental dimensions of experience were proposed: the *inspirational*, the *collective*, and the *symbolic*. For the present purpose, these are summarised below.

The *inspirational* dimension relates to the effect of the drama on the personal sensibilities of the individual: how one person is emotionally or intellectually moved by what they see and hear. This may be a strictly personal experience, or shared later with confidant(e)s. Little may be visible, save perhaps being 'visibly moved'. Indeed, discursive terms such as 'rich' or 'moving' may be deployed, where the individual cannot or does not wish to articulate the details of the experience. Where the experience remains private, the term 'biopersonal' could be usefully deployed.

The second, the *collective* dimension, is by contrast much more visible. It is the kind of experience by which whatever is seen and heard from the stage elicits a common response from the audience, transcending status, class and lifestage barriers. For example, and in the words of John Godber, a much-produced British playwright, participating in a televised discussion, it concerns the satisfactions of having laughed at the same thing with four or five hundred other people: a 'feeling of aliveness'. Alan Ayckbourn, also much-produced and participating in the discussion, added that "it's that assertion of common humanity" (BBC 1993). Shared inspiration of this kind may be termed 'biosocial'.

The third, the *symbolic* dimension, is also social in character but is the opposite of the collective: this is where *difference* makes its appearance. The theatre publicist, Danny Newman, permitted himself a flight of fancy in one of his publications. He painted a picture of the kind of subscriber who kept themselves within the theatregoing community for symbolic reasons. The subscriber's sartorial style, reading matter and weekend pursuits spoke powerfully of an individual whose theatregoing supports membership of a subset, not a set, of humanity (Newman 1977: 268)

Whether we accept Bourdieu's verdict (1984) that cultural pursuits are a means of creating personal distinction by amassing cultural capital; or whether we prefer Baudrillard's interpretation, that of inexorable conformism (1998: 92), the symbolic dimension of experience does not necessarily involve enjoying oneself. The author recalls overhearing a conversation from within a sponsorship party during a previous career as an arts administrator. The conversation was not about how to enjoy the concert, which was about to start, but how to survive it.

Of course, for any one individual, the experience of watching and hearing live drama may involve elements of the first two, and perhaps all three, of these dimensions. But the point to be understood is that discourse of the arts has long induced us into thinking of a divide between the high and the low; and the discourse of marketing, in the last decade, inducts us into not just seeing differences, but actively promoting to those differences. The fact that arts audiences are moved by what they see and hear, on a basis of shared humanity, is at risk of being forgotten.

The following section reports the results of qualitative research which was designed to reveal what exactly happens, in terms of human experience, when people visit a cathedral. Although in the typology of vehicles for experiences, a cathedral is a static visitor attraction rather than an event or festival, the results arguably have significant implications for programmers and promoters of events and festivals.

The experience of visiting a Cathedral

At the request of the Dean and Chapter of Lincoln Cathedral, England, qualitative research was undertaken with the aim of providing information to inform promotional activity, and the future development of the Cathedral as a visitor attraction. As cited earlier, the Cathedral's marketing and interpretation strategy was already replete with explicit proposals regarding desirable approaches to marketing.

However, the aim of the strategy was to 'identify the scope for adding value to the rich experience' of visiting the Cathedral (Lincoln Cathedral 2000: 3). Preliminary discussion with the Cathedral's officers revealed that the precise nature of this 'rich' experience was unclear. It was thus agreed that the first stage of a programme of research should seek to reveal insights into the nature of the visitor experience.

It was further decided that the qualitative data required would be best secured by seeking out a negotiated or group view. This would offer the greatest potential for insight into the experience. Accordingly, a focus group of nine subjects was assembled. The criterion for participation was that each subject should have a memory of having visited an English Cathedral (not Lincoln) in recent years. Lifestage, gender and socio-economic class were felt to be unimportant in terms of the nature of the enquiry, but the group's profile was recorded for reference purposes (Table 1).

Table 1:   *Cathedral research: profiles of focus group subjects*

Subject	Gender	Age Range	Occupation	Socio-Ec. Group
1	Female	26-35	Local Govt. Officer	B
2	Male	26-35	Student (& office worker)	C1
3	Female	26-35	Student (& hairdresser)	C1
4	Male	36-45	University administrator	B
5	Female	36-45	Academic historian	A
6	Female	46-55	Student (formerly Chartered Accountant)	A
7	Male	46-55	Local Govt. Officer	B
8	Male	56-65	Technical Publisher (ret'd)	A
9	Male	56-65	Chartered Surveyor	A

The research covered a number of matters, not all of which are relevant to the purpose of this chapter. What is however of interest is what might be termed the 'mode of consumption' of the visitors. A commentary based on the results is summarised, below, in terms of what have been styled 'three phases of consumption'.

1. Phase one: arrival

References were made by subjects to the typical availability of two genres of literature, referred to as the 'handout' and the 'glossy'. The 'handout' was acquired typically on entry, the 'glossy' was to be acquired later, dependent upon the level of interest evoked during the visit. Both publications were felt to convey historical facts and observations: when and how the cathedral was built, etc.

2. Phase two: looking around

Subjects became significantly more animated when asked how they actually went about constructing their visit: 'consuming' the Cathedral, so to speak. The *modus operandi* of visitors had components in common: looking around, and sitting still, not necessarily in that order. The pace of 'looking around' varied with the individual.

Where subjects visited the cathedral in company, they would sometimes agree to separate from companions in order to look around at their preferred pace. The 'sitting still' element was regarded as a solitary pursuit, even if companions were seated adjacent. What were termed 'peripheral' areas – going up the tower, visiting the cellar, were interesting in a tantalising way, offering an experience of 'the Other'.

3. Phase three: post-hoc satisfactions

This phase was perhaps the most intriguing in terms of yielding insights, and the discursive terms used by subjects are relevant. One subject referred to a 'profound sense of emptiness', having wanted to experience a 'sense of human connectedness', a desire which somehow had been frustrated. The guide books, as vehicles for facts, appealed to the head rather than the heart, and did not meet the subject's need.

This response resonated with other subjects, two of whom referred to preparations for a popular music concert which had been underway as they left the building. This they regarded as 'memorable', offering a sense of 'human continuity'. Other subjects concurred with this desire for continuity and connection. Additionally, subjects referred to a sense of 'calm' acquired on entry, and which remained after exit.

Analysis

In terms of the incremental dimensions of experience theorised earlier, the experience of visiting a cathedral, as revealed by this research, appears to be located within the first, inspirational dimension. At the point of exit, subjects appear to find themselves located on the threshold of the collective dimension. In other words, that which has been experienced as inspiration has implications for collective experience, the nature of which remains unclear to the subject.

The words and phrases chosen by the subjects to articulate the nature of their experience bear close comparison with those used by playwrights Godber and Ayckbourn in the televised discussion, cited earlier. The difference between the theatre audience and the cathedral audience, however, is the absence of a mechanism, discursive or otherwise, to translate a profound experience of the inspirational into a sense of the connectedly collective.

Orthodoxy re-visited

This research represents, as mentioned earlier in this paper, the first phase of what is intended to be a wider programme of research. However, the results of this first phase would seem to indicate that the 'rich' experience of visiting a cathedral has little to do with lifestage, social class or other criteria into which the discourse of marketing inducts us. Conceivably therefore, Lincoln Cathedral's preliminary intention to view its visitors in terms of target markets and segments, and retain data based on such criteria, may benefit from re-consideration.

Interestingly, the results of this research received *prima facie* validation from the results of an undergraduate student project, conducted for the Cathedral (Anderson *et al*, 2002). The students' research included exit interviews with individual visitors, and included questions about the satisfactions of the visit. The results endorsed the 'heart' as opposed to 'head' nature of the satisfactions, and showed that the nature of the experience did not differ significantly with socio-economic class. It was an experience common to humanity: one could suggest the term, 'biosocial', to describe it.

Conclusion: and implications for festivals and events

This chapter has sought to expose a particular ideology which lies behind contemporary marketing thinking. Termed 'orthodoxy-as-discourse', it involves the sub-conscious choice to see difference rather than commonality. The vocabulary of 'targeting' and 'segmentation' offers a set of all-too-easy discursive vehicles for articulating this ideology, regardless of circumstance.

In order to understand the nature of the visitor experience at particular arts events, specifically the case of drama, theorised incremental dimensions of sensibilities were proposed, by which the event is 'consumed'. These dimensions are the inspirational, the collective, and the symbolic. It is only in the symbolic dimension that people are apt to regard themselves as members of sub-groups rather than of common humanity.

Inspiration which remains unshared may be termed 'biopersonal'. Inspiration which is shared amongst a collective may be termed, 'biosocial'. Research into the experience of cathedral-visiting suggests that the satisfactions of the visitor are of the inspirational (biopersonal) kind, with a desire, apparently unconsummated in the case of these particular subjects, to translate this experience into some kind of satisfactions related to human connectedness (collective, biosocial).

What, then, are the implications for the programming and promotion of events and festivals? The first observation is that they offer a rationale for the existing and typical programming and promotional approaches of many festivals. Typically, a festival will be centred around a set of major, keynote artistic events: these shall be termed the 'core': events from which personal inspiration can be derived.

Wrapped around the core are other smaller-scale events, such as talks, discussions, ironic or comic shows and the like, which typically invite a higher level of active audience involvement: an expression of the collective. Perhaps not part of the mainstream festival are a range of other events, aimed at minority audiences, subsets of the collective body: the fringe. At the fringe level, arguably, a segmented and arguably symbolic dimension is reached.

Expressed as a continuum, therefore, the nature of the experience moves from the core, to a periphery, to a fringe. Each festival-goer is presented with options to define their own place on the continuum: whether they see themselves present for biopersonal inspiration, biosocial collective experience, or as a subset of explorers/*aficionados* at the fringe. Festival organisers preside over a trajectory from the core to the fringe, via a periphery: from *inclusivity* to *selectivity*.

So if festival and event programmers are already presenting a range of experience opportunities which coincide with biopersonal, biosocial as well as subset needs, what is the message of this chapter? The message is quite simply this: the databases are on the march, and ideology is riding on their backs. The temptation offered by this technology, and the marketing orthodoxy which accompanies it, is to see every product or service as serving a subset, rather than common humanity. Emphatically, as this author understands it, that is neither the intention nor the nature of a festival.

Festival programmers, and promoters, should not be seduced. It is hoped that the insights offered in this paper provide a rationale for an 'inclusive' paradigm.

Even if particular festivals and events are themed on the works, say, of a particular artist, or a particular artform, it has never been the understanding of the present author that such events are solely intended to service the needs of the already-converted. Surely the point of a festival is to evangelise. Festivals are about celebration, about including a community in a biosocial experience by which their lives become richer. They are not vehicles for scientific marketing: they are about creating ballyhoo.

References

Althusser, L. (1992), Ideology and the ideological state apparatus, in Easthope, A. & McGowan, K. (eds) *A Critical and Cultural Theory Reader*, Buckingham, Open University Press, pp 50-58.

Anderson, D., Buxton, L-J., Murphy, L. & Risius, E. (2002), *Enquiries into the visitor experience at Lincoln Cathedral*, University of Lincoln undergraduate student project report, unpublished, used with permission.

Atkins, R. (2002), Can gym fix it to turn fat to fit? *Lincolnshire Echo*, 17 October, pp 14-15.

Baudrillard, J. (1998), The Consumer Society: Myths and Structures, London, Sage.

BBC TV (1993), *Close Up North*. Broadcast on BBC2, 16 December.

Bourdieu, P. (1984), Distinction: a social critique of the judgement of taste, London, Routledge.

Croft, M. (1997), Facts of life, *Marketing Week*, 1 May, pp 43-4.

Doyle, R. (1999), Where has all the ballyhoo gone? *Artsbusiness 22*, 15 March, p.17.

Hill, E. & Whitehead, B. (1998), Comment: hitting the spot, *Artsbusiness 9*, 31 August, p.2.

Lincoln Cathedral (2000), *Marketing and Interpretation Action Plans for Lincoln Cathedral*, Lincoln: Dean & Chapter of Lincoln, unpublished, used with permission.

Newman, D. (1977), Subscribe Now! Building arts audiences through dynamic subscription promotion, New York: Theatre Communications Group.

Pick, J. (1986), Managing the Arts? The British Experience, London: Rhinegold.

Voase, R. (2001), The imagination rediscovered: cultural consumption, post modernisation and the future for live drama, in Janssen, S., Halbertsma, M., Ijdens, T. & Ernst, K. (eds) *Trends and Strategies in the Arts and Cultural Industries*, Rotterdam, Barjesteh.

Section 2

Planning, Management and Operations

Event Management:
identifying key success factors for bidding

Lizl Steynberg

Pretoria Technikon, South Africa

Melville Saayman

University of Potchefstroom, South Africa

Introduction

Sporting events are rapidly increasing in popularity as a means of attracting attention to particular geographic (city) locations (Getz, 1998). Increasingly, cities are basing their marketing efforts around hallmark events (e.g. Manchester and the Commonwealth Games, Rotterdam and Euro 2000, Johannesburg and the World Summit on Sustainable Development), in order to maximise the benefits to be achieved from event-driven tourism, sponsorship, and media exposure. Countries like Australia and South Africa have identified events as one of their tourism drivers to increase tourist flow. Sporting events make up an important part of the overall hallmark event industry. A critical issue that has emerged from the attractiveness of sport is the reality that a limited number of hallmark sporting events exist. This has led to fierce competition among cities to be successful in winning the business of playing event host. In being successful to host an event, bidding plays an important role. Bidding can therefore be defined as the process of acquiring the right to host an event. Given the importance of the bid process in the context of managing events, it is surprising to note that very little research has been conducted in this area. The purpose of this chapter is to identify key success factors in order to present a successful bid. In order to achieve the above, aspects pertaining to the bid process will also be discussed.

Deciding to bid for an event

A group of organisations or individuals usually own the commercial and legal rights to an event. The event owners look for the most appropriate location and event management team to implement their event. Unless an event is independently conceived of and owned by an organisation, which then proceeds to organise it, a tendering process is usually put into motion, which allows any number of competitors to submit their proposals for consideration by the event owners. Owners of events which take place annually or every few years look for different venues or destinations around the country or internationally. The process of bidding for these events is established by the event owners and may vary in complexity, depending on the scale and frequency of the event.

As this scale and frequency grows, the benefits and commercial returns are perceived to increase and the process becomes more competitive. In the first instance, a decision must be made as to whether or not to bid for an event. For this decision to be made responsibly, and in order to compete successfully to host an event, a thorough understanding of the event requirements, the bidding timetable, the competitors and the benefits and risks, which may arise, is essential.

When deciding whether or not to submit a bid for an event, there are a number of questions which require consideration before any decision is made. Many of these questions relate to bidding for larger-scale events, but should be considered in any bidding process.

Key questions to be considered when deciding to bid for an event include the following:

- *Does the deadline set by the event owners for the submission of a proposal allow for preparation and submission of the documentation required to present the bid?*

  Timetables for bidding are established by the event owners and are strict and usually very demanding. Timetables should be considered and well-understood before any decision to bid is made, as there can be no extensions to the due dates. It is essential to consider what trade-offs and compromises will have to be made as well as what the implications of meeting the deadlines will be. In many instances, timetables for bidding leave little if no time for consultation with role players who would be involved in hosting the event. If the undertaking is an international event of large scale, the timetable should be addressed to determine whether any opportunities exist to host test events in the facilities to be used beforehand. This is particularly applicable to large sporting events.

- *Will the bid meet the event owner's macro geographical requirements?*

  It is important to consider the timing of a bid politically, geographically and historically in terms of the event owner's requirements, as event owners may be sensitive to the geographical spread of the event. An analysis of what other events are occurring over the same period should be considered. This applies especially to cities bidding to host international or national events that are held annually in different locations around the country or world. For instance, large sporting events such as World Championships move around the world each year. If the International Athletics World Championships were held in Johannesburg this year, there is little chance that South Africa or even Africa will be hosting the event next year. The same applies to large annual exhibitions and conferences.

- *Are the (First World) requirements of the event owner reconcilable with the socio-economic and political realities facing a developing country city?*

  The technical requirements for some major events are usually provided in documents made available to bidding entities by the organisation holding the rights to the event and are used to a large extent to standardise and facilitate their evaluation of different bidding cities. The technical requirements for a major event will cover the need for financial deposits, technical aspects, the degree of local support for hosting the event, and the provision of letters of support for the bid.

  In cases where event owners do not outline detailed descriptions of the technical requirements to be provided, a bidding entity should carefully analyse the submissions by other cities for previous events to ascertain the level of detail provided.

Developing cities or countries face considerable disadvantages compared with developed cities in bidding for events. They normally lack capacity in infrastructure and organisational skills. A bid by a developing city or country for the right to host a hallmark event will probably be made within a context of rapid growth and change and serious local deprivation experienced by the majority of the city's residents. The underlying approach of a bid must, therefore, seek to achieve some improvement to the lives of the most deprived inhabitants of a city. In a developing context, hosting an event must address the priority development needs of the poorest sectors of the population. The bidding entities have to ensure that infrastructure necessary for the event serves a vital purpose after the event in providing the most deprived of communities with critical facilities and services. A crucial question asked by an event owner will be whether the governance of the city is sufficiently established, and administratively competent, to provide the essential foundation for the bid if required. For a developing city bidding for an event, the challenge will always be to assess whether it can offer the event owners an event that achieves more than one objective.

- *Is the bid able to deliver a sufficiently saleable product to attract the private sector sponsors that will be essential?*

The hosting of a hallmark event entails the securing of both public and private sector sponsorships to fund its organisation. Sponsor support will depend on whether there is sufficient unequivocal, upfront political, private sector and public support for bidding for the event, and on the degree of media and public exposure offered in return. The degree of popular local and international interest that may be created for the event requires upfront consideration.

- *What will be the benefits of bidding for and hosting the event – locally, regionally and nationally – and to whom would they accrue?*

The benefits to a city and its region of hosting an event may be measured in a number of ways and feasibility studies to determine the impacts of the event should be conducted before proceeding to bid for an event. Determining the number of jobs created (part-time, full-time/skilled, unskilled/permanent or temporary) and the area and nature of land and facilities improved or redeveloped in a city as a result of event-related activity are two means of assessing this impact. There may also be a number of potential negative impacts and costs which have to be mitigated in the management of the event. These should be investigated and considered before deciding to bid for an event and monitored during the hosting phase if the bid proposal is successful.

- *Does the city in which the event would take place have the required transport infrastructure, facilities and accommodation?*

Air, sea, regional road and rail access to a venue/city in which the event may take place from elsewhere in the country or abroad must be addressed. A safe, reliable and efficient transport system providing movement between accommodation and venues is a prerequisite. The event owners will assess the state of the venues and infrastructure to be used and in most cases will look more favourably on bids indicating that all of these are in place and have hosted or have been utilised for similar events in the past. If all or any of the required venues and infrastructures do not exist, as may be the case in developing countries, the bidding entity must assess whether or not it will be practically and financially feasible to build them in time for the event and, more importantly, for what purpose they will be used for after the event.

- *How much public and private investment will be required, and will this be affordable in the light of other possible competing requirements?*

  The bidding process will be costly and its funding should be provided on a shared basis between public and private sectors. The financial costs of bidding need to be understood in advance and once the bid process is underway the required resources must be forthcoming and timely. Sponsorships and municipal facilities and services will be needed. A consideration will be how much outright funding from the private sector will be needed to prepare the bid proposal and how much value-in-kind assistance will be asked of the public sector.

- *Has the bid the blessing of any federations, associations or institutes whose active and ongoing support and involvement will be essential?*

  The technical preparation of an event plan, the technology and communication proposals, the transport plan, the environmental proposals and preparation of cost estimates for infrastructure that will be required by the event owners will all require the involvement – and often approval – of a variety of stakeholders and authorities. The complexity and time required to obtain these commitments and approvals should not be underestimated when considering the submission of a proposal to host an event.

- *Is the human capacity and skill to draw upon available in order to bid for and host the event?*

  Of all the considerations in deciding to bid, this is the most fundamental. While support is the critical starting point, without capacity and capability it is meaningless. It is essential to assess the capacity and capability of the key responsible stakeholders – public and private sectors and communities – to sustain and deliver a bid for an event. The bid entity will need to assess its needs for public sector capacity vis à vis the negotiated contributions of the private sectors. The evaluation of capacity must look ahead to the possibility that the bid will be successful and a crucial capacity question at the outset is the availability of the right kind of people to lead and direct the bid.

The bidding process

Surprisingly little research attention has been devoted to the process of bidding for the right to host an event. Ingerson and Westerbeek (2000) ascertained the importance of experience and knowledge in bid team structure, pointing out that, for successive bid attempts to stage the Olympics in Australia, some individuals were involved with more than one bid. Experience in the bid process enables bid team members to build relationships with event organisers over a period of time. As bid team members gain experience, they become better negotiators and are better able to show genuine commitment to hosting future hallmark events. Strong bid teams are able to develop effective internal and external networks, which assist them in building alliances and increasing their competencies.

Crockett (1994:13) recognised that cities bidding for events need to get smarter about the bidding process because of the limited supply of hallmark events that exist and the increased demand for events world-wide. Crockett (1994) identified six different considerations, namely: economic impact, regional promotion, financial returns, location decision, needs of decision-makers, and professional presentation, which a bid team must assess prior to entering a bidding process. However, there has been no empirical research to test the validity of these considerations. Swart (1999) argued the importance of strategic planning in bidding for hallmark events in South Africa and focused the discussion on the theoretical components of strategic planning (mission, objectives, external factors and internal resources, strategy formulation, implementation and control).

Qualitative research carried out by Ingerson and Westerbeek (2000) is one of the few empirical studies that have developed a comprehensive range of criteria that are important in relation to the bid process for hallmark sporting events. In their review of literature, Ingerson and Westerbeek (2000) found eight bid process criteria that consistently emerged as being of some significance. They classified these into primary and secondary criteria. Primary criteria were identified as being imperative to the formal application to host the event and included political, economic, media, infrastructure and technical. They pointed out that for a city to be considered a potential bidder it must meet these criteria as defined by the event owners. On the other hand, secondary criteria, such as socio-cultural impact, competitive and business support, not only had less research supporting their importance, they were considered less important, because they were deemed only to enhance the bid proposal, not to be fundamental to the success or failure of an event. Using these criteria as a guideline, six highly experienced bid campaigners from four countries were interviewed (semi-structured interviews). Resulting from these interviews, eight new criteria were identified that were perceived as significant (Table 1). Table 1 includes key features further describing elements of each criterion.

Table 1   *Key success criteria when attracting hallmark sporting events to a city*

Primary Criteria

Political	Processes, policies and government infrastructures Government support for bid Political stability of city
Economic	Potential economic impact Financial stability of the city Ability to fund event (public and private)
Media	Local media support Global media exposure access Portray positive image
Infrastructure	Location and accessibility Transport system Existence of facilities
Technical	Communication system Technical expertise
Socio-cultural	Image of the city Community support

New Primary Criteria

Building relations T	Identifying the individual needs of voting members or important influences Invest time and effort in human contact Access to people in key positions
Bidding brand equity T	Having established facilities, key target markets and visible power brokers Have a presence in the marketplace as a bidding organisation
Commitment T	Part-time versus full-time bidders Ability to start construction early (before announcement of the winning bid)
Guarantee added value T	Great product knowledge in order to show how value can be increased Ability to do primary and secondary research (viability, attitudes, characteristics)
Legacy	Ability to show where the tax money went Ability to generate goodwill for the event owner by showing the legacy
Bidding experience T	Having the established networks (internal) Having the established networks (external) Know what is considered important Awareness of timing and event-specific issues
Bid team composition	Mix of youth and experience Personal selling skills of the team (bidding people are marketers)
Creative statistics	To present those statistics the event owner wants to see Provide correct information but in a bid-favourable fashion

Secondary Criteria

Business environment	Ability to attract other businesses to the area
Competitive environment	Other city bid strategies Other events previously bid for Global competitors

Note T = critically time-dependent
Source: Ingerson and Westerbeek (2000)

In discussing the newly identified criteria it was found that some are specifically related to the bid team. Building relations, commitment, bidding experience and bid team composition reflect the need to recruit, train and develop individuals with specific bidding skills. Ingerson and Westerbeek (2000) noted, in this regard, that experienced bid members bring knowledge and networks to new bid committees. Building relations is supported by general relationship marketing theory that maintains that building and enhancing interactions with key stakeholders (decision-makers) can develop long-term satisfaction and mutually beneficial partnerships. The better the relationship marketing skills of bid team members, the greater the strength of relationships and the more likely that interactions will be favourable for both parties. Bid teams (cities) must show a commitment to the cause (event) either through continual bidding for a range of hallmark events, as Manchester has done at both Olympic and Commonwealth Games level, or with infrastructure and public support, as Melbourne has achieved by building a range of international standard facilities.

Building brand equity is best illustrated, 'if the bid organisation's name is immediately recognised, and brand identity can be leveraged' (Ingerson & Westerbeek, 2000:248). Given the competitive nature of hallmark event bidding, it is becoming more important that strategic practices like reputation building and branding are adopted. Part of the relationship marketing concept is the notion of adding value to the relationship. This prompted Ingerson and Westerbeek (2000) to identify guarantee added value and legacy as being important criteria for consideration. As part of the determination of the value they are offering, bid committees need to consider the perceived value from various stakeholder perspectives. Payne and Holt (1999:46) pointed out that the customer's perception of the value created should be determined and then taken into account when the organisation defines its offering. For example, the facilities, improved infrastructure, business opportunities or the development of sport, are common examples of the legacy and event delivered to the city's occupants. For the event owner, an attractive (popular) host city coupled with a successfully staged event will give the organisation prominence on the world stage and attract future (high quality) bids for their events. Finally, creative statistics support the ability of event bidders to present event (organising)-specific information (e.g. projected spectator numbers or potential profit) in a way that the bid and the benefits of hosting the event are placed in a favorable light.

Ingerson and Westerbeek (2000) noted that, while some of the new primary criteria presented in Table I may appear to be self-evident, there is little research evidence that they are considered to be important by event managers. They argued that excluding these criteria may lead to incomplete bid preparation and evaluation (Ingerson & Westerbeek, 2000:251). Of the new criteria described, at least six are recognised as being critically time-dependent or, in other words, the more time invested in these areas, the more these criteria will be developed by the bidding team to their advantage. This supports Crockett's (1994) and Swart's (1999) reasoning that event bidding is a process requiring the use of clever strategies and competitive positioning tactics and builds on the contention of Ingerson and Westerbeek (2000) that successful event bidding is a continuous and cyclical process.

If a community or organisation does not own the right to host an event, the rights may be sought from the event owner. Rights may be applied for via a bid (proposal) process. A bid outlines the steps intended to take and the services planned to provide to successfully stage the event. The event rights holder has specific requirements or information that must be addressed to their satisfaction in order to bid. If the event holder does not have a bid package, a proposal must be developed that highlights key operational areas and resources that the community will employ to ensure a successful event.

Firstly, all proper forms must be obtained or minimum requirements to be addressed from the event rights holder. Develop a strategic plan to secure and compile necessary information in a timely manner. The bid is the initial commitment made on behalf of the community to the event rights holder. It must accurately represent the community's resources, as many of the elements requested are vital to ensure the success of the event. If a community does not have a specific resource to meet the event requirements, information on how those requirements can be met must be included. The preparation of a formal bid and its presentation is the most important thing a community or organisation can do to win the rights to host an event. The bid should be imaginative as well as comprehensive. Each page should reveal the commitment that the community and organisation are undertaking.

As stated previously, the bidding process for an event depends to a large extent on the nature of the event. The phases in any bidding process are illustrated in Figure 1 and are discussed below.

Figure1   *Phases in the bidding process*

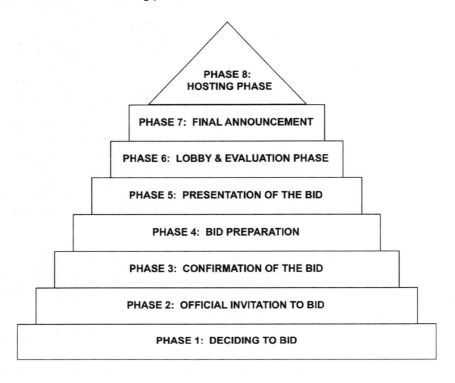

Phase 1 – Deciding to bid

The first step is to decide to bid and to consider the merits and risks of bidding before formally announcing the intention to bid. This may entail the election of a city, or a country, to bid for an event on its behalf, and the appointment of the necessary consultants to undertake cost-benefit analyses.

Phase 2 - Official invitation to bid

The event owner officially invites organisations or cities to bid and provides a detailed timetable for submission of proposals.

Phase 3 - Confirmation of the bid

Bidding organisations formally confirm and announce their intention to bid for an event. This announcement is usually supported by the necessary political and financial endorsements and may include the provision of a deposit to the event owners in the case of a hallmark event like the Olympic Games.

Phase 4 - Bid preparation

The bidding entity begins the preparation of a candidature file, bid document or proposal, either through the assistance of consultants or the formation of a legal bidding company or committee.

Phase 5 - Presentation of the bid

The bidding entities submit and present proposals to the event owner by a stipulated date.

Phase 6 - Lobby and evaluation phase

In the case of international events where the stakes are high, the event owners begin an evaluation of each bid submitted and the bidding entities, in turn, begin to lobby individual members of the event owners' organisation of the merits of their proposal and for votes in their favour.

Phase 7 - Final announcement

The event owners gather all the candidates and announce the successful bidding entity. In the case of a large-scale or hallmark event, the host city will be announced and a contract will be signed immediately after the announcement.

Phase 8 - Hosting phase

The successful bidding entity enters into a contract with the event owners and begins the preparation for the event.

Preparing a bid

Sparrow (1987) and Saayman *et al,* (2001) outlined key stages of the bidding process. First, is a conceptualisation of the event and how to get it, which then must be *sold* to the important authorities. Initial acceptance of the idea is likely to be based on at least a prefeasibility study, which assigns some preliminary numbers to the costs and benefits expected. Given a decision that the idea is viable and the risks acceptable, a formal commitment will be necessary. Subsequently, a bidding group, and perhaps a separate marketing group, must be established to make and sell the bid (Ueberroth, 1985). Competition for the event must be evaluated and countervailing strategies developed. A variety of formal and informal promotions can be used, including familiarisation tours for the decision makers, lobbying, and recruitment of influential people, especially prominent politicians, as spokespersons.

Finally, if the bid is accepted, a detailed feasibility study becomes essential and a full planning/marketing process must be established. Sparrow (1987) said that this stage requires the appointment of a key player (or committee) to steer the process, *imaging* the event to give it profile and to build support, intensive public and private sector collaboration (especially to mobilise the tourist industry), planning for impacts, and detailed market research.

If a formal bidding process is required, the bid documents should include the following:

- Personalised letter to the client, or sanctioning body.

- Letters of invitation/support from all important local organisations and officials (with attention to order, considering local protocols).

- Executive summary.

- Profile of the group making the bid and accepting responsibility for the event and its financing.

- Support already obtained for the bid.

- Summary of the event concept.

- Details of the plan: venue, facilities, investments, timing, scheduling, programming, meeting all the criteria.

- Forecast of attendance; marketing plan.

- Assertion of financial and economic feasibility, financial plan and budget.

- Forecast of impacts; contingency plans.

- Highlights of the legacy.

- Advantages over competitors for the event.

Planning and organising for bidding

While the hosting of an event may only take place over a few days, the actual preparations may take much longer – even years in the case of a hallmark event (Saayman *et al*, 2001). In bidding for a major event, a vision, goals, objectives and principles should be formulated which balance candidature and societal requirements. These will derive from the philosophy that has been developed for the bid and should form the basis of the manner in which the bid entity proposes to host the event if successful.

The broad spatial implications of meeting an event owner's requirements must be established as early as possible. A spatial plan should be prepared which meets the event owner's requirements as well as impacting positively on the city in which the event is planned. Explicit approaches should be prepared and adopted with respect to the operational and infrastructural aspects of hosting the event. The location of facilities (both competition and training), the location of specific uses, the provision of any required housing and other accommodation (for example hotels), the use of improvements to transport infrastructure, the identification of projects for immediate implementation and the achievement of environmental sustainability all require explicit approaches to be formulated.

Once the principles and a spatial plan have been agreed, the next step in developing the event plan is to test the applicability of various venues and infrastructure against the event owner's requirements. This may be done in terms of ownership, proximity to public transport, relationship to other facilities like accommodation and tourist attractions, and environmental impact.

The bidding process for an event is usually tight, extremely demanding, conducted by individuals from wide backgrounds or professions and does not allow for anything less than *getting it right first time round*. The complex and time-limited nature of the proceedings will necessitate a strict, professional and ruthless management process, prioritising all work requirements according to a work breakdown and leaving little room for mistakes. Precise and competent identification of what is required and how this work should be scheduled is imperative to avoid doing anything that is not absolutely necessary. Effective project management will, therefore, be at the heart of all the activities of a bid.

The design, provision and management of systems (that is, information storage, handling and communication, financial management, procedures, technology, etc.) will either facilitate or hinder the work of the bid. This will lead to the establishment of work patterns and communication within the bid and between the bid and outside; it will provide the mechanisms that enable people to work together effectively and can be a main contributor to the culture of the organisation.

Critical systems focus areas include:

- Information storage, retrieval, developing, processing, dissemination.

- Document management.

- Financial management: budget forecasting, cost controlling, creditor payment.

- Procedures that guide communication within and outside the bid: verbal, written, formal, informal.

- Choice of computer and telecommunications technology: hardware and software and its interlinking internally and externally (this is an important consideration for bidding cities in a developing country context which do not have well-developed communication networks).

- Control of the nature and flow of the work and its products.

- Employment and dismissal procedures, performance appraisal and remuneration.

- Employee development and human relations.

- Quality assurance.

The work breakdown should be prepared according to the event requirements – always making provision for prioritising work and formulating contingency plans for unexpected situations. Schedules for detailed planning, community consultation, design, construction, site making, and test events must be prepared in time, so that the event owners can be guaranteed of delivery on time and the local authorities and other groups involved in the planning and development of the sites can have a clear understanding of where they fit into the process and, therefore, the implications of delay on their part.

A job scheduling system such as a computerised project management package is useful in forcing individual managers to define their work responsibilities, products needed, resource requirements and deadlines.

Preconditions for a successful bid

The following suggested preconditions for the successful bidding and hosting of an event are made.

To win, a bid must have:

- *A collective vision* (national, regional and local) that hosting a hallmark event is a national priority; that it is within the capabilities of the city and country, and the total organisational and financial commitment is in place.

- *Societal and political consensus* to bidding and hosting, allied to sufficient, committed public and private sector capacities, capabilities and resources.

- *Very clear basic strategies* to orientate the entire process, based on the collectively shared vision, goals, objectives and principles.

- *A thorough understanding of precedent* – that is, the successes and failures of previous bids by other cities.

- *Capacity to organise and host the event* (infrastructural and organisational) and the event owner's confidence.

- *An understanding that the event owner's needs are paramount* and must remain so throughout the bid.

- *Political, absolute, up-front, publicly committed trust in and active support for the bid and the bidding organisation* on the part of all levels of government, most particularly those from the host city.

- *Broad stakeholder commitment* to and belief in the organisational structure of the bidding entity.

- *A clear understanding of the city's context* – the unique characteristics – to capitalise on the natural assets in a way that enhances, rather than detracts from any existing sense of place.

- *An absolutely clear event plan* – understandable (by non-professionals) and that is appropriate philosophically and technically in all of its dimensions to the event owner's requirements for hosting the event, and which reconciles those needs with the socio-economic, political and environmental realities of the city context within which the event will take place.

- *An understanding of respective roles,* by different players (for example by politicians) that they are support players to the bidding process and cannot win the bid on politics alone; that a bid has to be broken down into two phases: technical and lobbying, and that the first is where the public sector must play its role and the second is a function which should be directed by the bidding entity.

- *Very precise territorial and organisational objectives between the bid organisation and the politicians and officials* – that is, to know who is responsible for what, to know what to do, where to do it, including the sharing of the responsibility for the involvement of the public in the bid preparations.

- *Strong, consistent, charismatic leadership* within the bid entity and the management team.

- *A legally and financially empowered executive* for the bid to act with great authority.

- *Sufficient up-front financial resources* to properly complete the bidding process.

- *Satisfied sponsors* who are happy with a product that gives value to private sector processes.

- *A proactive and interventionist attitude* towards investing in facilities that will have both an effective short-term life and a long-term, post-event use of maximum benefit to the city and its residents.

- *Effective and thorough communication* of the event plan, financial integrity and benefits arising from the economic impacts of the bid.

- *Enthusiastic media support* for the bid, locally and nationally.

- *A jointly developed social contract* managed between bid entity, the responsible authorities and citizen-based organisations that leads to the community and citizens being informed and involved in the bid as creative, supportive partners.

- *A clear set of agreed ground rules* to provide the basis for a productive relationship between the bid and non-governmental organisations.

- *The means to achieve the confidence of the event owner* through lobbying and communication.

- *An exit strategy:* a carefully prepared, publicised and positive response to succeeding or failing the bid.

Key Success Factors (KSF) in the event-bidding process

There are a number of key success factors in the process of bidding for hallmark events, according to Westerbeek *et al*, (2002), Saayman *et al* (2001), Saayman *et al* (2002) and DEAT (2002). These key success factors (KSF) are listed and discussed below (Figure 2).

Accountability

Accountability represents the capacity of the event-organising team and the city or country to deliver high quality services to the event promoter and to the various stakeholders both in the community and in political circles. Accountability deals with the dependency relationship event bidders have with event owners and the public(s). It relates to the ability of event bidders to identify key target markets that are important to the event owners and their ability to generate goodwill for the event owner by showing the legacy the event leaves behind. Event bidders can prove that they will be accountable by showing that they have an established and recognised presence in the marketplace as a bidding organisation, a strong reputation (as a city) in hosting successful events and by show-casing a broad range of excellent facilities. Bidding organisations are accountable to the public in relation to the need to show where tax money has been spent and how the local community will benefit from the event being held in their city (Ernst & Young, 1992; McGeoch & Korporaal, 1995).

Political support

Not only is political support important from the perspective of securing vital resources (financial, physical, human resources) but also political and financial stability of the city and country are important in relation to the formulation of (longer-term) policies of government that will clearly contribute to the quality of the event. It obviously is important in this process for government representatives to be able to show the potential economic contribution of the event to the local economy, which will generate considerable community support for the event and increase the popularity of the politicians involved. The political support attributed to an event is considered important specifically with respect to the services provided to the event promoter and the community. The capacity of the event organiser to successfully involve the government in activities relevant to the bidding process is essential in enhancing the value of the event to the event promoter.

Relationship marketing

Relationship marketing deals with the power of the people on the bid committee (e.g. the involvement of political leaders) and the consequential influence this power base is able to generate among key decision makers pertaining to the bid outcome. Power not only leads to increased access to key decision makers, it also facilitates opportunities to invest in human contact with event owners, thereby increasing the likelihood that bid team members become *friends* with key decision-makers. Increased access creates opportunities to offer (event-related) gifts and host functions for event owners and key decision-makers. Because they become *friends,* their credibility is raised and they are less suspicious than when no personal relationship has been cultivated. The capacity to have good relationships with politicians and to have people with sufficient influence and positional power on-side to support the bid is a crucial influence. However, such relationships need to be balanced with the accountability and transparency requirements that are expected of politicians in democratic systems.

In relation to the above, communication and marketing issues come into play. The reputation of the city or country as a major tourist destination and the communication and IT systems that are in place, or have been obtained to run the event, will contribute to ensuring national and global media exposure of the event. Obviously widespread communication and exposure are important for both the event and the host city/country, both looking to increase brand equity and their properties. Therefore, marketing in all its forms plays an extremely important role.

Ability to organise the event/expertise

The ability to organise the event contains a number of items reflecting event organisation-and-management expertise that event owners have demanded traditionally from event organisers. The specific technical expertise and the event management (administration) expertise at hand (as part of the organising team) to run the event, the event equipment available (e.g. timing systems, audio-visual facilities), and the ability of the event organisers to fund the event (public and private) are all basic requirements that relate directly to the hosting of the actual event. The ability to organise an event is evidenced by having a solid track record in organising similar events. The technical expertise incorporated into the ability factor, reflecting equipment and staff knowledge, is seen as an important contributing element to the bid process. The event owner views the ability of the event-organising team as a critical service in the decision to award the bid team the right to host the event.

Infrastructure and suprastructure

Directly relating to the ability to organise is the infrastructure and suprastructure factors. The latter implies the structures that provides certain services to tourists, for example hotels, restaurants, and shopping centres. In this regard, location and accessibility (where situated in the city and how to get there by public transport) of the proposed event site are of importance. These issues are considered by event owners and organisers in conjunction with the visual (architectural) attractiveness of the (proposed) facilities, as described by NIEIR (1997). In relation to the location in particular it can be derived that population size in the catchment area of the event is of importance as well. Strong community support for the event in relation to a large population size ensures that the event will be visited by many people, especially in the event precinct area of the host city. Furthermore, infra- and suprastructure reflects on the ability of the event organiser to convince the event promoter that the host city has the necessary city infrastructure enabling the event to be successfully held in that city. This extends to the ability to deliver facilities, accommodation and transportation as well as community support for the event.

Figure 2 *Key success factors (KSF) in the event bidding process*

The existing facilities or suprastructure factor relates strongly to the criterion that was defined as legacy (Ingerson & Westerbeek, 2000). However, not from the perspective of what is left behind for the host community when the event is finished but much more from that of the existence of critical event facilities at the time of the bid. In other words, the pre-existence of established high quality facilities should have been facilitated by (hallmark) events that have been hosted by the city in the past. This will most likely also ensure the availability of overnight accommodation (for spectators) in the host city/region and with a range of established facilities it is likely that the host community is very capable of putting facilities to good use, in turn enabling governments to start construction of facilities early (before the announcement of the winning bid). It will be necessary to constantly improve and maintain facilities. While events will tend to be hosted in cities and regions with the best facilities, it will also be necessary to use events to kick-start developments in other regions.

Partnerships/funding/sponsorship

A proactive approach to partnerships between institutions is fundamental to the promotion of events. Strong alliances with the private sector assist in corporate fundraising/sponsorships and extend budgets beyond the limited contribution of government. It is necessary to develop and enhance strategic alliances with tourism and non-tourism industry partners to maximise the promotion of the hosting country internationally. Effective partnerships will require that responsibilities be clearly identified, clarified and allocated among agencies and associations within both the private and the public sectors. Hallmark events cannot take place without major sponsorships or some form of government contribution.

Community participation

Participation in the event and tourism planning needs to take into consideration the needs of the host community. There are excellent financial reasons for adopting a model of community participation for hallmark events (Hall, 1995). Community involvement encourages greater variation and local flavour in the nature of the tourist destination, assists in the protection of the tourist resources and reduces the opposition to tourism development.

Human resources

The success of an event is dependent on the quality of the people that are driving the process. These include city or country representatives, politicians, event organising committee, volunteers and other stakeholders, be it within the community or even the concessions. Their management skills and ability as well as their enthusiasm will determine if the event is going to be a success or not.

Image

Images are what make the host city/country different and identifiable. The higher the awareness of the destination, the greater is the potential to attract and build events. Natural beauty and amenities, restaurants, nightlife and cultural offerings are competitive draw cards at both a national and international level. A co-ordinated and innovative approach to marketing both cities and regions of that specific country as an event destination is a must. Dilution of resources and lack of prioritisation will not achieve a competitive advantage. Bidding countries must be positioned as fashionable, dynamic and beautiful if they are to achieve global advantage.

Safety and security

In a study done by du Plessis (2002) with regard to competitiveness, the study clearly showed that in order for any destination to remain or to become competitive internationally safety and security was rated as the most important factor. This aspect has far-reaching consequences in terms of image as well as whether supporters or tourists will visit the event. Safety and security should be guaranteed with regard to general crimes as well as terrorist attacks.

Cost

The relative weakness of certain countries' currency against first world currencies is a definite draw-card in attracting the international market to developing countries with a prerequisite that these countries must have the infrastructure to host the prestigious event. Organisers are facing increasing pressures to deliver high value produce on a budget, making the over-all cost of a destination a critical selection factor.

Timing

The timing of an event can also serve as a key success factor for bidding. Given the seasonality of the destination, events can be utilised to boost visitor arrivals in shoulder-season and off-peak periods. When approached to host an event in a city/country, negotiations can be made with event organisers to stage the event at a time that would result in the greatest economic impact to the city where the event will be hosted. Events must be beneficial in timing to both the visitor sector of the hosting countries' economy and to the countries' institutions with the facilities.

Organisational structure

It is necessary to have an established organisational structure and demonstrate up-front financial capability. To host major sporting and cultural events successfully, planning is key. Committees need to be set up to oversee the process and ensure that things run smoothly. The organisational structure will include departments such as Secretarial and Administrative; Human Resources; International Liaison; Information and Publicity; Sports; Market Development; and Technical.

Geographical location/climate

In the same way that the timing of an event can be negotiated to ensure maximum benefit to the city/country, so too, can the location of an event. Locations can be chosen based on their ease of access for visitors, but also to highlight areas of the city that want to be promoted as distinct product offerings. It is, therefore, important to work in partnership with event organisers to ensure that events take place at times and locations most suitable to a city or region. The accessibility includes the number of international and national aspects, and public transport, to name but a few. Accessibility and locality must be promoted through a commitment which ensures that no participant or spectator is excluded by high ticket prices, low wages and venues that exclude people with mobility problems.

Cost effectiveness, chance of success and degree of spin-offs in the bidding process also need to be considered. In addition to these factors, future bids for events, should also give consideration to the following:

- Complete synergy between the bid organisation, the national sport federation, business and government.

- The bid's credibility will be measured by the ability of the financial analysis and budgets to support these assumptions.

- Identify key interfaces with the public and get them right. The event belongs to the public of the host city, not the event organiser's nor the wider international community.

- No matter how important the technical aspects of bidding become, effective personal lobbying will still be the key to winning an event bid.

Conclusion and managerial implications

Although the research literature identifies many and various success criteria, 14 factors are of vital importance in the process of bidding for hallmark events. Because these factors constitute elements considered to be of importance in the context of bidding for the right to host an event, they need to be treated as the first point of reference when preparing to host a hallmark event in a city. Irrespective of the capacity of event organisers to host the event, event-owning organisations are looking for much more than organisational ability. It seems that event infrastructure and event management (including securing political support, safety and security) are the most important elements in the process of ensuring a successful hosting of the event. Factors like communication and exposure, accountability, bid team composition, and relationship marketing are, although still perceived as important, more likely to be supporting the vital factors. In other words, vital factors relate to the operational aspects of organising the event, whereas supporting factors relate to facilitating aspects of making the event successful. In this regard it can be assumed that, in most cases where cities are bidding for hallmark events, they will be equally competent and prepared in relation to the operational aspects of organising the event. The majority of issues relating to the vital factors are quite tangible in that physical proof of competence can be provided. Much of this physical evidence (i.e. event-organising skills, facilities, infrastructure) can be bought, given the availability of financial resources. However, pertaining to supporting factors, distinct competitive differences between event-bidding organisations can emerge. For example, the unique (and intangible) composition of the bid team will have great impact on establishing (intangible) networks with power brokers, relations with media, the reputation of the bidding organisation and the acceptance of hosting corporate functions in the process of attracting the event. Because the quality of the bid is likely to be on an even-par with other bidding organisations in relation to the vital factors (because they are easier to manage), the decision made over which of the bidding organisations will gain the right to host the event is likely to be the result of a competitive advantage in relation to one or more of the supporting factors. However, it needs to be noted that the importance ratings do not provide conclusive evidence on these matters and hence further research into potential significant differences in importance ratings between factors is required.

Finally, future research should be directed at distinguishing between the perspectives of the event owner and the event bidder. However, in order to identify whether the perceptions of those who offer the event-organising services (event bidder) are in line with those who will base their decision (event owner) on which organisation obtains the right to organise the event on the package of services that offers the best value, future research needs to determine whether both groups have similar views on what are key success factors in the bid process.

References

Crockett, S. (1994), *"Tourism sport – bidding for international events"*, *Journal of Sports Tourism*, 1 (4), 11-21.

DEAT (2002), *"Towards a national event strategy for South Africa"*, South African Tourism, Department of Environmental Affairs and Tourism, Pretoria, South Africa.

Ernst & Young (1992), *The complete guide to special event management: business insights, financial advice, and successful strategies from Ernst & Young. Advisors to the Olympics, the Emmy Awards, and the PGA Tour*, John Wiley & Sons, New York.

Forecast. (2001), *The 11th report of the tourism forecasting council*, Tourism Forecasting Council, February.

Getz, D. (1998), *"Trends, strategies and issues in sport-event tourism"*, *Sport Marketing Quarterly*, 7 (2), 8-13.

Hall, C. (1995), *Introduction to tourism in Australia: impacts, planning and development*, Vol 2, Longman, Australia.

Ingerson, L. & Westerbeek, H. (2000), *"Determining key success criteria for attracting hallmark sporting events"*, Pacific Tourism Review, 3 (4), 239-253.

McGeoch, R. & Korporaal, G. (1995), *"The bid: Australia's greatest marketing coup"*, Mandarin, Australia.

NIEIR (1997) *"The economic role of Australian cities"*, National Economic Review, 37 pp.8-36.

Payne, A. & Holt, S. (1999) *"A review of the 'value' literature and implications for relationship marketing"*, Australasian Marketing Journal, 7 (1), 41-51.

Saayman, M. (ed.). (2001), *An introduction to sports tourism and event management*, Institute for Tourism and Leisure Studies, Potchefstroom.

Saayman, M. (ed.). (2002), *Leisure, tourism and hospitality management*, Institute for Tourism and Leisure Studies, Potchefstroom.

Sparrow, M. (1987), "A planning model for hallmark events" in *Proceedings of the Conference on People and Physical Environment Research*, paper 87, Perth, Centre for Urban Research. University of Western Australia

Sport Business, (2001), *"Editorial"*, Sport Business pp. 55:50.

Swart, K. (1999) *"Strategic planning – implications for the bidding of sport events in South Africa"*, Journal of Sports Tourism, 5 pp. 2.

Ueberroth, P. (1985), *Made in America, his own story*, William Morrow, New York.

Westerbeek, H. M., Turner, P. & Ingerson, L. (2002), *"Key success factors in bidding for hallmark sporting events"*, International Marketing Review, 19 (3), 303-322.

Modelling cultural special events management in an Egyptian context

Galal Salem, Eleri Jones and Nigel Morgan

University of Wales Institute Cardiff, UK

Introduction

Special events are an important tool in the promotion of tourism products and are used to market particular products, areas or even entire countries. Special events can encourage long-term investment; create new permanent and/or temporary jobs; generate direct economic benefits for host communities through increasing visits, improving levels of visitor expenditure or minimising '*leakage of resident money from the economy*' (Long & Perdue, 1990: 10). Events can be used to encourage local participation, to increase awareness of a venue, occasion, tradition or socio-cultural value; increase 'civic' pride; heighten an area's profile; satisfy the needs of special interest groups or conserve local heritage. Events may galvanise particular segments of society strengthening volunteerism, co-operation and intercultural interaction (Getz, 1997). Events can be used at '*both the macro- and micro-political level*' (Hall, 1992: 88) to enhance image and ideology or strengthen the position of elites within local or regional power structures (Hall, 1992). Macro-politically, events create or enhance international images of a county or regime (Hall, 1992). Micro-politically, events can be '*policy tools*' (Getz, 1997: 34) – for example, arts and music festivals promoting cultural development, ethnic and multicultural events reducing social or racial tensions, fostering inter-group understanding, and preserving traditions. In recent years there has been an exponential growth of 'special events' (Getz, 1997; Hall, 1992).

In 1992, the Egyptian Tourism Ministry (ETM) established an annual special events agenda comprising approximately twenty-five special events, and including at least four cultural events, with the aim of improving the image of Egypt as a tourist destination and enriching the Egyptian tourist product. Over a ten-year period, these events have experienced varying degrees of success. Some events (e.g. Aida Opera Performances; Pharaoh's Rally; Ismailia International Folklore Festival) have not managed to achieve their projected schedules and have run some years and been cancelled others. Others (e.g. the Nile Bounty Festival, Abu Simbel Festival; Tourism and Shopping Festival) have managed to run according to schedule but have failed to achieve their objectives. The variable success has been attributed to management issues. Moreover, various doubts have been expressed in the Egyptian press; for example, about the financial losses associated with the Aida Opera Performances and whether the promotional and prestigious benefits could justify such losses. Similarly, comments have been expressed about lack of co-ordination between the joint organisers of Ismailia International Folklore Festival and funding shortages in the Nile Bounty Festival. A good practice model of special events management applicable to the Egyptian context is notably lacking. Some research (e.g. Sa'ad, 2000; Hagag and Hamoud 2002) has focused on specific aspects of special events management, notably: planning including marketing, funding and event product definition.

This chapter is part of a larger study to develop a good practice model for cultural special events management in an Egyptian context. The research has resulted to date in an extensive literature review culminating in the development of a unified model of special events management based on a modified performance management cycle (Salem *et al*, 2003). The unified model comprises four stages: decision; planning; implementation; evaluation, which are used in this paper as an organising framework to inform the analysis and presentation of multiple case studies of three Egyptian cultural special events (the Nile Bounty Festival, the Ismailia International Folklore Festival and the Aida Opera Concerts) and to facilitate comparison between events, identifying issues for ongoing research. The chapter presents first the unified model and then the multiple case studies.

A unified model of cultural special events management

Salem *et al*, (2003) developed a systematic phased model of event management from the literature on special events management to provide an overview of event management practice applicable to festivals and cultural events to facilitate discussions with event managers. The model adapts a performance management model for use as a framework for the systematic identification and deconstruction of four major stages of event development, namely: decision; detailed planning; implementation; evaluation (see Figure 1). In practice the model is not necessarily linear and may be iterative, e.g. redefining the event product in the light of a detailed financial study or market research. Activities do not take place in series but are broken down to facilitate parallelism and the involvement of different groups, whether employed directly by the event or sub-contracted. The four phases of the model are described briefly on the next page.

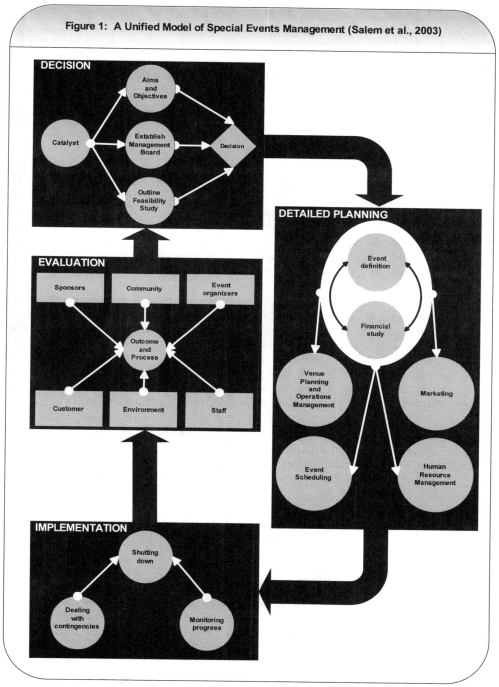

Figure 1   *A unified model of special events management (Salem et al, 2003)*

The decision phase

The decision phase initiates the process and determines ultimately whether the event goes ahead or not. At its most complex, the decision phase comprises five distinct activities: catalysis; specifying the event aims and objectives; establishing the management board; outline feasibility study including market research and an initial financial study; decision-making.

- Catalysis relates to the source of the idea for the event and may result from the public (government, local authority or agency), private (corporation, firm or individual) or voluntary sector.

- Event aims and objectives are crucial and must be resolved early as they impact on many aspects of the event and may fall into one of three main categories: economic, social and cultural, political. Most events have economic aims although these might not be the over-riding priority and may be indirect rather than direct. Event aims are ideally broken down into 'SMART' objectives (Specific to the event, Measurable quantitatively, Agreed (or achievable) by those involved, Realistic (or relevant) to the resources available, Timed (around the event schedule) to help identify performance targets for the event, which facilitate the later evaluation of the event.

- A management board is usually formed to progress the event and may comprise one or more people who plan, implement and evaluate the event. The board needs to reflect a diverse range of skills and expertise, which may be vested in one or more individuals, and typically comprises: an event manager who is appropriately skilled to lead the event through all its different phases; a financial advisor to predict income and expenditure, establish cash flow forecasts, set and monitor budgets and undertake financial reporting; a marketing advisor resolves marketing issues and works closely with the financial advisor; a legal advisor deals with all contractual issues.

- An outline feasibility study checks that the event 'stacks up' and provides a broad indication of success or failure, although for larger events with more risk associated with event failure more detailed research may be required to enable a decision to be made. The initial feasibility study tends to focus on market research and an initial financial study.

- Decision-making requires the board to have collected enough information to decide whether the event should progress to the detailed planning stage.

The detailed planning phase

The detailed planning stage follows the decision phase and is the essence of managing the event. Detailed planning initially involves event product definition and development of a detailed financial study, which usually focuses on three issues: anticipated income and expenditure, budgeting and cash flow. Product definition and the financial study can form an iterative cycle. Detailed planning then moves onto development of strategies relating to venue planning/operations management, marketing, human resource management and event scheduling.

Event product definition results in the unique blend of activities that comprise the event and are the tools for achieving the overall event aims and satisfying customer needs. Considerations include: theme; venue considerations including size and capacity; facilities; visibility, centrality and clustering; cost and history; date (allowing enough lead-time for event organisation) and timing (down to the hour); ticket pricing. Event design should aim to create a mix that satisfies the largest number of potential customers and avoid product orientation, i.e. trying to sell the event *'with little or no regard for what potential customers need, want, and will pay for'* Getz (1997: 251). The earlier the features are specified the better, although *'events are organic and will evolve all the way through the event itself'* (Armstrong, 2001: 49). For a mega event product definition may take place over a period of several years leading up to the event.

Event marketing

Event marketing has three important objectives - *'read their* [customer] *needs and motivations, develop products that meet these needs, and build a communication programme which expresses the event's purpose and objectives'* Hall (1992: 136). Market research, although not always utilised, can help understand customer motivations. *'You may have the best quality event product, but unless you have a strategic plan for promoting this product it will remain the best-kept secret in the world'* (Goldblatt, 1997: 230). Promotional techniques include advertising, publicity (*'securing…free space in printed media or free time in broadcast media'* (Davidoff and Davidoff, 1994:197)), public relations and merchandising. The timing of marketing activities is critical to event success.

Venue planning and operations management

The venue planning process allows the event organisers to plan how the event will fit into the venue and how facilities, staff, equipment services, etc, will be distributed. Important considerations include: signage, crowd management and crowd control.

Human resource management

Human resource management is a key element of the event experience and differs between one-off events, events with a permanent home and peripatetic events. The human resource strategy flows from an initial analysis of which elements are to be delivered by the event organisers and which are to be sub-contracted to other organisations, resulting in a staffing structure and a plan for event delivery. Several different categories of staff are likely to be involved – a professional core comprising full-time and part-time permanent and/or temporary staff supplemented by specialist consultants, hourly-paid staff employed directly by the event or indirectly through contracts and unpaid volunteers. Assessment of labour demand is complex and requires analysis of the requirements of each event element. Volunteers are particularly important in the implementation of festivals and cultural events and can work in most roles, including the organising committees. A major issue for events is that there is no precise tool for forecasting productivity rates of volunteers so an over-estimation of volunteer numbers is required. Sources of volunteers include: sponsors; universities, schools and colleges; service, social and sport clubs; special interest groups; previous volunteers; religious groups; professional organisations and unions. A volunteer recruitment plan should be developed, although Ernst & Young *et al,* (1992) optimistically argue that once news of the event is out people will volunteer immediately which may be true for mega-events where to have 'been there' is an important motivation.

Event scheduling

Event scheduling enables monitoring of event progress providing an evaluation tool. Event schedules usually identify date, time, action, location and responsibility and are annotated with explanatory notes. For complex events a master schedule may co-ordinate the major elements, with each manager producing a separate schedule for his/her crew.

Implementation

The Salem *et al,* (2003) model considers three issues under implementation: monitoring event progress, dealing with contingencies and shutting down activities.

1. Monitoring event progress

The detailed planning phase will ensure that the event opens with a confirmed management plan identifying key activities, which can be monitored to ensure that the event is going to plan and, where necessary, corrective actions taken. Where the plan is modified it must be communicated effectively to all staff.

2. Dealing with contingencies

Whilst unexpected happenings are generally out of the control of the event organisers event organisers need to ask *'What if…?'* and rehearse solutions. There are *'two good defences against most problems: well-prepared leadership and a strong set of contingency plans'*, although they *'cannot possibly cover every conceivable occurrence'* (Armstrong 2001: 152). Well-trained staff members able to deal with most expected contingencies are vital, although staff must also know what to do in the case of emergencies.

3. Shutting down activities

Shutting down post-event includes two tasks: dismantling and selling or removing the equipment and cleaning up. A timetable for suppliers to dismantle and remove hired equipment should be identified in the hire contract. Cleaning up should not be confined just to the cleaning of the venue but should extend beyond the event and include the removal, and ideally recycling, of promotional materials and special signage.

Evaluation

The purpose of evaluation is to learn from experience how the event could have been done better. Evaluation can be divided into outcome and process evaluation. Five different stakeholder perspectives are important – the event organisation, volunteers and other staff, event sponsors, customers and the host community. Performance indicators for evaluating outcomes for the event organiser and the sponsors are likely to be derived from the original SMART objectives set for the event in the decision phase. Environmental impact objectives may be included in these.

Data for outcome evaluation, e.g. final profit, numbers of tickets sold, emerges after the event. Process evaluation requires feedback from event staff and customers, although timing is critical as dispersal happens quickly after the event. Staff debriefing sessions, e.g. in focus groups using visual records, e.g. video footage, photographs and media coverage, as tools to ask staff to reflect on the event, are useful for collecting data. Customer feedback can be obtained in various ways, including informal (customer comments, complaints and suggestions) and formal feedback (involving questionnaire surveys providing data on customer profiles, motives for attending and spending patterns or other tools, such as interviews and focus groups).

After data collation and analysis a formal evaluation session is invaluable so that event managers can *'constantly learn, and improve management'* (Getz, 1997: 331). In this session all stages of the process must be reviewed including the initial objectives, e.g. for ticket sales or profit, which may not have been achieved because they were not feasible or other reasons, e.g. the promotional campaign running late. However, evaluation can also be used to enhance activities that went well during the event.

Methodology

The Salem *et al* model is used as an organising framework for case studies of three Egyptian special events, which were identified using the Egyptian Ministry of Tourism list of special events taking place in 2002 as a comprehensive reference. The 2002 list includes twenty-six special events classified into three categories: sport events (thirteen events), tourist events (four events) and cultural events (nine events). From this list special events were selected for detailed study. Selection criteria include:

- Cultural special events: i.e. special events associated with a cultural theme as "the principle idea of the event".

- Organised entirely or partly by governmental bodies.

- Non-financial targets are the prior goals (e.g. social or cultural goals), whereas financial targets are secondary goals, or not considered at all.

- Repeated events (i.e. not one-off events).

Three cultural special events met these criteria – the Nile Bounty Festival, the Ismailia International Folklore Festival and the Aida Opera Performances at the Pyramids. The three cases were examined between the 12th of November 2002 and the 7th of January 2003 through an investigation of the documents related to each event. Document analysis was supplemented with semi-structured interviews with the event organisers. For the Ismailia International Folklore Festival all the documents were obtained from a single source, while for the other two cases documents were traced to several government departments. In all three cases, the documentation provided details of the managerial procedures used for organising the events, including dates. The dates facilitated the development of a chronological model of events.

Results

Case 1 – The Nile Bounty Festival (see Figure 2)

Pre-event activities

The Nile Bounty Festival (NBF) was re-established in 1992 when the Ministry of Tourism *(the catalyst)* suggested restoring the old celebration of the Nile flood *(the initial idea)* to offer free entertainment to Egyptian citizens and to enrich the international tourism programme *(the strategic aims)*. The annual organisation of the event was passed to the Cairo Governorate *(the responsible body)* through the Regional Association for Tourist Promotion, Cairo (RATPC).

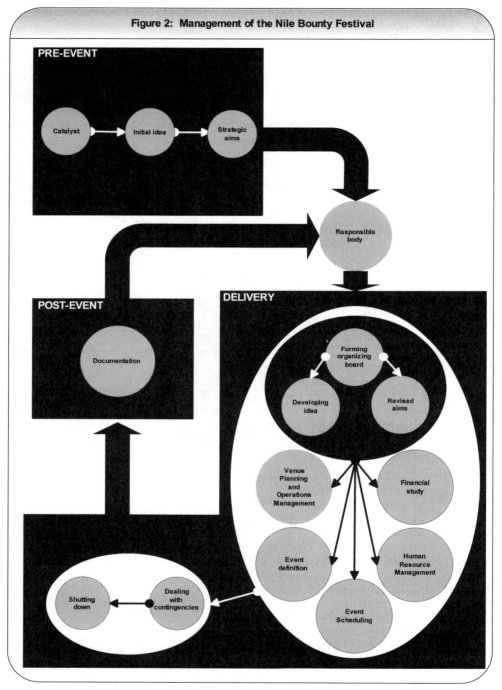

Figure 2 *Management of the Nile Bounty Festival*

Delivery phase

The first task RATPC undertook was establishing the festival organising board, which had an initial duty of developing the initial idea and revising the aims. The organising board then proceeded to undertake common planning phase activities: event definition; event scheduling; financial study; venue planning and operations management; marketing, in parallel, and immediately on to implementation activities – dealing with contingencies and shutting down. There was no evidence of temporal distinction between the planning phase and the implementation phase, comprising dealing with contingencies and shutting down which is why in Figure 2 the detailed planning and implementation phases have been merged into one delivery phase.

Post-Event

The event culminated post-event in the collation of documentation from the event, which was submitted to RAPTC for official storage. There was no evidence of any evaluation.

Thus, document analysis reveals a three-phase managerial model.

Case 2 – The Ismailia International Folklore Festival (see Figure 3)

Pre-event activities

The Ismailia International Folklore Festival (IIFF) was developed in 1985 when the manager of the National Folklore Team in the Ministry of Culture *(the catalyst)* suggested organising an international festival for folklore dance groups *(the idea)* with the aim of offering free entertainment to Egyptian citizens and encouraging tourists to visit new destinations *(strategic aims)* - an idea which was encouraged by the Ismailia Governor who suggested hosting the festival in El-Ismailia City *(event definition)*. Accordingly, since 1985 (except from 1990-1994 when the festival was cancelled), the Cultural Palaces Organisation and El-Ismailia Governorate *(the responsible body)* have shared responsibility for the festival.

Planning phase

Relying entirely on the financial support of the Ministry of Culture, the planning phase began with a financial study *(financial study)* aiming to determine the budget required to establish the festival. The Ministry of Culture agreed to provide the budget and established the organising board *(organising board)*, which undertook venue planning and operations management, marketing and event scheduling in parallel.

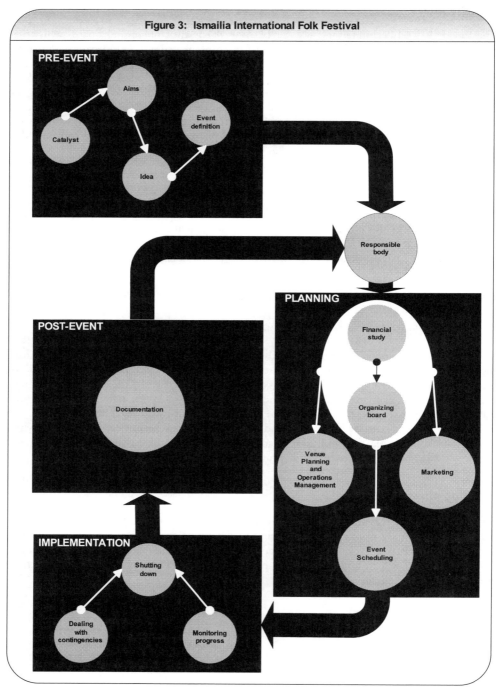

Figure 3 *Ismailia International Folk Festival*

Implementation phase

Moving to the implementation phase, three tasks (*monitoring progress, dealing with contingencies and shutting down*) identified in implementation stage of the unified model were apparent.

Post-event activities

Again, as in the case of NBF, all the data resulting from the festival were documented for official usage in a limited sense, i.e. for organisation of the next annual festival. There was no evidence of any evaluation in the documentation.

Thus, the managerial model comprises four stages.

Case 3 – Aida Opera Performances (see Figure 4)

Pre-event activities

The opera Aida is based on a story written by the Egyptologist August Mariette and composed by Verdi, inspired by Pharaonic history at its height and was first performed in 1869. In 1994 the Ministry of Tourism *(the catalyst)* suggested recreating the traditional Aida concert using Egyptian monuments (i.e. the Pyramids or Luxor Temples) as backdrops for the show *(the idea)* – the Aida Opera Performance (AOP). The strategic aims of the concert were to improve the image of Egypt as a secure tourist destination, promote Egypt as a cultural destination, and achieve a profit or at least break-even financially *(the strategic aims)*. To get the best outcome, the Ministry of Tourism agreed to finance the performances, which were to be organised by the Egyptian Opera House *(the responsible body)*.

Planning phase

An initial financial study was conducted with the intention of costing the performances and this was followed by revision of the aims and financial objectives of the event. Following approval of the financial position and the financial objectives by the Egyptian Opera House, an organising board was established to carry out the work. In similar fashion to the unified model the organising board undertook five parallel detailed planning activities: event definition, marketing, detailed financial study, human resource management, venue planning and operations management.

Implementation phase

The implementation phase similarly included the three steps identified in the unified model, i.e. monitoring progress, dealing with contingencies and shutting down.

Post-event activities

The financial objectives resulted in the conducting of a financial evaluation. However, no other evaluation activities are conducted. All the documents resulting from the event were collated for later official usage, again to be used in a limited fashion for organisation of subsequent events.

Thus, analysis of AOP reveals a four-phase managerial model.

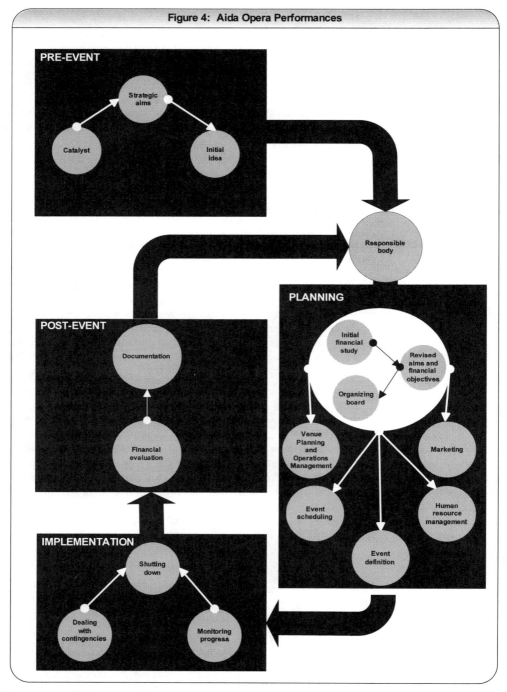

Figure 4   *Aida Opera Performances*

Discussion

Six distinct points can be drawn from the three case studies as identified below:

- There is no decision phase. The pre-event activities are better labelled 'pre-event'. There is some variation in the number of activities involved in the pre-event phase, which takes place at a very high governmental level and culminates in each case is the passing of responsibility to a responsible body generally at governorate level.

- Neither feasibility studies nor market research are evidenced in the planning process.

- No event management expertise/experience is involved in this initial phase. The mode of establishment of the organising body does not maximise the involvement of persons with event management expertise in the organisation of the event.

- The temporal separation of, and distinction between, the detailed planning and implementation phases is not as marked as suggested in the unified model and in one case, i.e. NBF, these phases merge into one phase labelled 'delivery'.

- The lead-time for organisation of the event does not give sufficient time for the effective marketing of the event.

- SMART objectives are not developed and thus there are no clear performance indicators to drive an evaluation process.

- The only evidence of evaluation is in relation to the evaluation of AOP, an evaluation restricted to a financial evaluation. Lack of stakeholder, especially customer, evaluations is a major shortcoming.

- There is no formal model of good practice in event management used to co-ordinate the event management process although this is not unusual.

- The financial models employed do not utilise financial targets to drive ticket sales or involve sponsorship.

Conclusions

The benefits of special events in the promotion of tourism products are undeniable. Events are used in Egypt both as macro-political and micro-political tools. The events examined here have enhancement of international images of Egypt as a secure destination and a cultural destination identified in their aims. These same events were also being used micro-politically to provide free entertainment for host communities and to promote cultural development and preserve traditions.

However, to maximise the benefits of such events there are a number of management issues that need consideration, notably the development of a model of good practice that could be incrementally enhanced in the light of experience in the Egyptian context and could codify knowledge and experience gained from the delivery of Egyptian special events to inform future practice. Such a model might focus on incorporating a feasibility study early in the planning process, maximising the lead-time for effective marketing, using SMART objectives to drive performance indicators for the evaluation of the event, involving stakeholder feedback to inform future practice; utilising an alternative financial model and thus removing the reliance on public funding through exploration of sponsorship opportunities and maximising income streams.

References

Armstrong, J. (2001), *Planning special events.* San-Francisco, Jossey- Bass.

Davidoff, P. G. and Davidoff, D. S. (1994), *Sales and marketing for travel and tourism* (2nd ed.). Englewood Cliffs, Prentice Hall.

Ernst & Young, Catherwood, D. W. and Van Kirk, R. L. (1992), *The Complete Guide to Special Event Management: Business Insights, Financial Advice, and Successful Strategies from Ernst & Young, Advisors to the Olympics, the Emmy Awards and the PGA Tour.* New York, John Wiley & Sons.

Getz, D. (1997), *Event management and event tourism.* New York, Cognizant Communication Corporation.

Goldblatt, J. J. (1997), *Best practices in modern event management* (2nd ed.). New York, John Wiley & Sons.

Hagag, M. and Hamoud, G. (2002), *Special event management.* Cairo, Helwan University.

Hall, C. M. (1992), *Hallmark tourist events – impacts, management and planning.* London, Belhaven Press.

Long, P. T. and Perdue, R. R. (1990), The economic impact of rural festivals and special events: assessing the spatial distribution of expenditure. *Journal of Travel Research,* 28 (4), 10-14.

Sa'ad, A. (2000), *Organising and managing special events in Egypt and their role in tourist development.* PhD thesis, Helwan University, Cairo.

Salem, G., Jones, E. and Morgan, N. (In Press), *An Overview of Special Events Management.* In: Festivals and Cultural Special Events. London, John Wiley and Sons.

The 30 second tourism event – a total eclipse of the sun in outback Australia

Linley C. Hartmann and Graham Brown

University of South Australia

Introduction

The total eclipse of the sun is an event that has fascinated people through the ages because of its association with forces affecting our environment and our psyche that seem beyond the power of humankind. Temporary, celestial events, visible to the naked eye, "animated the night and sometimes the daytime sky, and ...created an 'otherworld' for virtually all cultural groups (which)...together played a critical role in the artistic, intellectual, and political development of early civilisations" (Masse, 1995:463.) Major monuments of the Aztecs in Mexico have been identified as images related to the Total Eclipse of the Sun (Milbrath, 1995.) At the beginning of the twenty-first century, modern travel provides access to most eclipse sites within a day or two of any part of the globe, and modern technology provides access to simultaneous viewing (wherever computer technology is accessible) and, to those who can afford it, their own personal telescopic and digital camera recording of the event.

This event moves location across the globe independent of the control of governments, promoters and tourist preferences and a growing number of followers are prepared to travel to wherever it will be visible. The event has many facets, from the scientific to the mystical, and attracts a diverse range of onlookers although it is subject to uncertainty depending on weather conditions for the brief time span of its occurrence. For the Aztecs, the Total Eclipse was a festival and similarly present day eclipse experiences have the potential to engage some observers beyond passive participation and to create a social and cultural process. The 2002 eclipse lasted approximately 40 seconds and for most observers this was in the context of a new landscape, a new night sky, different food, new companions, and the culture of the Outback. The chapter draws upon ideas about the importance of multiple genre and group processes to examine the activities and behaviours of one particular eclipse tour. The chapter begins by reviewing the nature of the Total Eclipse of the sun and some reported experiences which highlight some of the rituals of the event, before examining the cultural characteristics of the South Australian location and how a range of activities were used by one 'amateur' tour organizer to extend the tour experience of one group based at Arkaroola in the Outback. It then presents observations about the actual course of the event and participants responses to these.

The Total Eclipse of the Sun

The total eclipse of the sun is an event that occurs approximately every 18 months somewhere in the world and lasts from a fraction of a second to a maximum of seven and on half minutes. The total solar eclipse in 2003 touched only Antarctica and tours were offered to view this eclipse from aircraft and ships. The next total solar eclipse to be visible from land will be in March 2006 in West Africa, Turkey and Mongolia. The total eclipse of the Sun is ...

"arguably the most awesome sight in all of nature. Day is suddenly replaced with an eerie twilight and the Sun's brilliant disk is blocked by the dark Moon. Only then is the Sun's glorious corona revealed to all. This incredible spectacle is visible once every year or two when the Moon's small dark umbral shadow races across our planet's surface. A partial eclipse may be seen from a large fraction of the earth, but only those lucky enough to be within the umbra's track will witness the corona and totality." (Espenak and Naeye, 2002).

The peculiarity of the Total Solar Eclipse is that the Moon blocks out the Sun's light thereby darkening the sky so the rim of the sun is just visible and this rim provides a backdrop to the dark rim of the Moon, both rims thereby becoming visible when this is not normally so. The eclipse of the sun usually includes a wide band of partial eclipse and a narrow path of totality (where the moon completely covers the sun,) which, on December 4, 2002, began in the South Atlantic, crossed South Africa, the Southern Indian Ocean and ended in Southern Central Australia. Here, the total eclipse path was about 32 kilometres wide and 800 kilometres long and within this band the dark shadow of the sun in full eclipse, (the Umbra,) moved across the ground at a speed of 3,000 kilometres per hour beginning at 1940:10 in Ceduna and ending at 1941:33 at Lyndhurst. (See the map in Appendix One.)

The weather is a major factor in a successful viewing of the Total Eclipse of the Sun. To help assess the risks, NASA's Goddard Space Flight Centre prepared an official bulletin for the internet detailing predictions, tables, maps, and weather prospects (Espenak and Naeye, 2001). In South Australia, the weather prospects along the entire eclipse track indicated a 70% chance for clear skies during the eclipse. However, the low altitude of the sun was an extra hazard that would magnify the effects of cloudiness, and hot summer temperatures would increase the possibility of dusty whirlwinds. The coastal location of Ceduna, the largest town, was also disadvantaged by the possibility of wind and cloud and a 10% lower chance of clear sky.

Despite these risks, the experience of totality, even for 30 seconds, is considered worth the risk by many Total Eclipse followers. One such follower explained himself this way:

"My plan is to take about six or seven pictures during those precious moments … (of totality) .. and then throw my head back and gawk at the sky. …Even if your trip ends in a clouded out event, you still have a lot to enjoy … and don't lose heart and don't give up – cloud often disappears at the final moment…" Harris (2002).

The clearing of the sky at the last minute is a well-recognised phenomena for which eclipse watchers hope. Below is a summary of a description of the situation at the 2002 annular eclipse in North America, that shows the effort people will make to reach a good viewing site:

'At 9am we started the bus journey to the site in Mexico and arrived at 7pm where more than 200 people were waiting. Clouds prevented them seeing the beginning of the eclipse at 7.35pm and gradually people left as they gave up hope. At 8.34 at the time of sunset and just as annularity arrived, still all we could see were clouds. Just as I was about to resign myself to the fact that I would not be able to see the eclipse, a miracle happened. In that very thin line free of clouds, where the sky touches the sea, the eclipse suddenly became visible. Everyone screamed and clapped their hands. The few who had their cameras ready began to shoot very fast, getting as many photos as possible, because that sight lasted only two minutes. The clouds then swallowed the sun…' (Cuellar, 2002).

Special event issues in a total eclipse of the sun

Shone (2001) argued that special events in the form of festivals, carnivals and holy days that break up the routine of daily lives continue to play an important role in human society, as they have in the past, with the added purpose of attracting tourists to a particular place. Shone (2001:4) developed an inclusive definition of a special event as:

> "that phenomenon arising from non-routine occasions which have leisure, cultural, personal and organizational objectives set apart from the normal activity of daily life whose purpose is to enlighten, celebrate, entertain or challenge the experience of a group of people."

Within each of the four categories of special event objectives mentioned above, Shone (2001) acknowledges that there is great variation in the size and in the complexity and uncertainty associated with them. Complexity varies with purpose, size, and the range of people involved whereas uncertainty refers to doubts about matters such as cost, timing and technical requirements.

An increasingly widespread view is that special events include a number of genres and common processes. Getz and Cheyne (1997) cite the ideas of MacAloon (1984) and of Falassi (1987) to help explain the multiple nature of events and how common processes may be used to achieve multiple goals. MacAloon (1984) argued that single genre events are not common and more frequently events include a mix of spectacle, festival, ritual, and games. Aspects of spectacle bring out the larger than life aspects of a visual performance; aspects of festival bring out celebration and joy; aspects of ritual evoke spiritual and social transformations; and games bring a sense of play, and humour and possibly competition to social interactions. An example of this is the way sports events are increasingly incorporating other elements of festival activities. Falassi (1987) suggested that as participants experience a series of processes together, these free them from their usual routine and help them enter a special spatial and temporal environment: These processes were identified as valorization, (a ritual that modifies the usual function of the location and acknowledges the event,) which is followed by any number of rites concerned with such issues as purification, passage, ritual dramas, exchange and competition; and finally when the event is over, a devalorization ritual that provides closure to the event. Involvement in these social and cultural processes, therefore, builds a sense of community and shared values, and fosters a sense of joy and in some circumstances unruly behaviour.

These issues need to be considered within the context of individual responses. Getz and Cheyne (1997) point out that for modern travellers the motivation to travel is closely linked to a search for authenticity or a genuine cultural experience. How visitors respond when their expectations are not met may also vary. Getz and Cheyne (1997) cite Ryan's (1994) argument that tourists' desire for a successful experience can become a determinant of their behaviour such that they will focus on positive aspects that are congruent with their wishes and play down negative aspects. In accordance with this argument, Eclipse watchers who found themselves in a culturally inauthentic situation would, therefore, be likely to minimise these activities so as not to detract from their overall experience of the eclipse. In addition, the cultural authenticity of an experience may be reduced by, for example, the establishment of a street market or a music festival that is not normally part of the local culture. However, cultural authenticity may be more important for international visitors than regional or local visitors who may regard an additional range of activities as an exciting complement to an otherwise humdrum setting.

The randomness of timing and location of the Total Eclipse of the Sun means that it is an uncontrollable event around which tour operators and the local community must use their ingenuity. Special events usually occur over more than one day and certainly more than a few minutes, as happens with the Total Eclipse of the Sun. The need for activities in the surrounding days that enhance the significance of the Total Eclipse as an event, and/or provide a culturally relevant experience, and/or provide a range of unrelated activities will need to be considered for different groups, as will the need to compensate for a non-event due to weather conditions. An eclipse view is not restricted to a stadium, a harbour, or an opera house. It is much more difficult to control access to viewing sites and more difficult to predict how many people, with which expectations, will be present. For moderately affluent, international travellers, a Total Eclipse experience can be an extra-ordinary scientific and cultural event, to be shared with like-minded people. For local, non-eclipse followers, the meaning of the Eclipse as an event is likely to be less clear and perhaps incidental to other activities. Before examining activities and processes of a South Australian Eclipse tour that included all these interests, this paper will now outline details of the South Australian setting.

Location of the Total Eclipse in South Australia

The special characteristics of the Total Eclipse of the Sun can be viewed only within a narrow pathway thereby attracting observers away from more readily accessible sites, near population centres, where it would be possible to observe an eclipse covering, for example, of 85% of the sun. This was the situation for December 2002 when the Far North of South Australia became a tourist destination for the Total Solar Eclipse event.

The three maps in Appendix One show the general location of the eclipse path within Australia, within South Australia, and then at the Northern End of the Eclipse path. The following description of the path of the eclipse was taken from *Astronomy*, 2002.

> The umbral shadow ... comes ashore at the small town of Ceduna... From there it moves northeast, crossing the immense salt pan of Lake Gairdner and then the south eastern corner of the Woomera Prohibited Area, a former weapon testing site still used for rocket launches. It next heads just south of the uranium mining town of Roxby Downs and on past the northern tip of the Flinders Ranges. The umbral shadow briefly kisses the north western corner of New South Wales before ending its 7,500-mile-long run in Queensland. (Talcott, 2002)

This description provides some clues as to the nature of the country. Ceduna, with a population of 4,000, is a coastal fishing, acquaculture and agricultural centre, a gateway for tourists and for transports travelling overland to Western Australia and the west coast of South Australia. Aquaculture is now a major industry, with more than 20 million Pacific Oysters grown each year. After crossing the coast, the eclipse path moves across remote and sparsely inhabited desert country. The inland rainfall in the twelve months preceding the Eclipse ranged from 100 to 200 millilitres, reflecting the drought conditions prevalent across Australia. Extremes of temperature that can be experienced are indicated by the maximum temperatures above 39 degrees Celsius and minimums as low as six at night, recorded in November 2002. Road conditions limit access to the full extent of the eclipse path, much of which is only accessible by dirt road or 4 wheel-drive vehicle. There are only three metal roads across the area – one to Ceduna, one to Leigh Creek, a mining town at the northern edge of the Flinders Ranges, and one through to the Northern Territory and Alice Springs. The public sites on the path of eclipse totality that were accessible from these roads were Ceduna, the Stuart highway, Woomera and Roxby Downs, and Farina near Lyndhurst, north of Leigh Creek.

The inland economy is based on mining and pastoral activities, a rocket launch base, and tourists travelling to the 'Outback'. Part of the prohibited area of Woomera Rocket Range was opened to the public for the eclipse and the town has recently become better known as the site of an internment camp for refugees. In contrast to Ceduna, Roxby Downs, (population 3,000) is located in red sand dune country, 564 kilometres from Adelaide. It was built in 1987 to service the Olympic Dam copper-uranium mine, the largest mineral ore body of its kind in the world. With approximately 200 kilometres of underground roadway and fully remote underground trains, the mine currently produces more than nine million tonnes of ore annually. In contrast, Lyndhurst is an historical outback 'town' just North-West of the Flinders Ranges, with a population of just 10 people that serves the surrounding pastoral districts and travellers.

Information available from the Astronomical Society of South Australia (ASSA) web page shows how the edge and centre of the Total Eclipse path and the magnitude of the eclipse (that is, how much of the Sun's diameter is eclipsed,) are precisely defined. At Andamooka, a short distance from Roxby Downs (a major viewing site,) only a partial eclipse was visible because the northern limit of the eclipse path was eight kilometres south-south-east of the Post Office there. Mount Hopeless homestead, a few kilometres off the Strezlecki track in the North East was identified as a place where the eclipse would last for 22 seconds but one that would be inaccessible after any significant rainfall. However, with a magnitude reading of 1.002 this was one of the 'private' locations where the total eclipse could be viewed. It was near here that the Arkaroola Tour observed the Eclipse. In comparison, the magnitude at Ceduna was 1.004 and at Lyndhurst it was 1.003 but at Andamooka it was 'only' 0.997.

Except for Ceduna, the setting of the Eclipse path was in the area called the 'Outback', which has both mystical and treacherous qualities for most urban Australians. Summer heat has caused the death of many tourists who have become stranded in their vehicles; and at night, animals on the road make driving hazardous. The Astronomical Society of South Australia web page advised motorists that:

> "...although thousands of Outback journeys are completed without trouble, be aware that lack of preparation and ignorance have killed people before. The Outback is not a hostile place, it is simply indifferent to human life. Plan on spending the night in the Outback right after the eclipse." (ASSA, 2000)

Within this setting a number of initiatives were undertaken by the South Australian Tourism Authority and private individuals to create a memorable, and extended Total Eclipse experience. Local community based events were designed to attract individual participants and to encourage tour operators in developing a package of activities involving a longer stay in the state. Ceduna's community attempted to lengthen visitor stay time with a two day 'Solar-bration by the sea' to include a street party, open air markets, food, art and street theatre, indigenous and contemporary entertainment and fireworks. Similarly, in Leigh Creek, the largest town near to the eclipse path in the north, a five day Eclipse festival included street parties and food stalls while at Roxby Downs, Woomera and bush barbecues were organised. At Lyndhurst, an area of one square kilometre was set aside for viewing and a Music Festival complemented the Bush barbecue.

Overall, the attendance of visitors to the Total Eclipse left the local communities very happy. On December 3 The Australian (2002a) national newspaper reported that towns were bracing themselves for "a brief tourism tidal wave, as more than 45,000 people position themselves for tomorrow's solar eclipse". Subsequently, newspapers reported that in those few days approximately £2,000,000 (The Times, 2002) was injected into the economy of Ceduna and $AUS200,000 into that of Lyndhurst (The Australian, 2002b).

Genres and processes on the Arkaroola Tour

Arkaroola has not so far been mentioned as a location within the path of totality or close to it. It is shown on the map in Appendix One to the right of Leigh Creek. It is about a two and one half hour drive from Lyndhurst on a good dirt road, and seven hours from Adelaide. The South Australia Tourism web page 'Welcome to the Flinders Ranges and Outback' indicates that since 1968, Arkaroola has been a privately operated 60,000 hectare Wildlife Sanctuary which provides motel and caravan/camping accommodation and the opportunity to see old mining sites, waterholes, stone arrangements, pastoral history and radioactive Paralana Hot Springs. Located 660 kilometres north of Adelaide it specialises in science and nature based tours with 4 wheel-drive guided tours, scenic flights and hiking, although only limited access is allowed to the local roads. There are two observatories, one with a 360mm (14.5 inch) telescope.

There are some things the web page does not mention. There is no mobile phone connection and the area is an isolated and spectacular range of old mountains, rich in minerals and closely explored by mineral companies which have constructed an extensive range of access tracks across the tops of the ridges. Some of these have now become the site of the 'Ridgetop Tour', a four hour, un-airconditioned, 4 wheel-drive trip across spectacular country, that most visitors undertake. It is rough and bumpy, although much more comfortable than 20 years ago, and after six years without any worthwhile rain, (as in 2002,) the country can seem harsh and dry to those unaccustomed to it. After rain, it blooms with life and colour, with flowing creeks, and with washed out roads. It is an area of ancient geology and rich indigenous heritage. In contrast to the flat, almost treeless, red plains surrounding the ranges, the setting is spectacular and the Arkaroola resort an oasis of modern civilisation lying under a generally clear and cloudless, starry night sky.

Organisation of the Arkaroola Tour

This tour was organised using minimal resources, as a not-for-profit venture, by a local, semi-retired, Total Eclipse enthusiast with no tourism business experience, and without professional assistance, who captured an international and domestic market of 130 scientists and eclipse followers. Having participated in several previous eclipses and been involved in local astronomical activities, he possessed a range of experience that gave him insight into the organisational detail associated with Eclipse tours.

He first conceived the idea of organising an event for the Total Eclipse in 2002 during a visit to Arkaroola in 1999 when the resort's management agreed to take a booking for the whole of the resort for a five day period. The 2002 SOLAR ECLIPSE TOUR AT ARKAROOLA was identified as a "five day package for astronomy and natural science lovers ... based on the outback tourist resort of Arkaroola." Tour details were provided in October 2001, at a special weekend seminar regarding the eclipse of the sun organised by the Astronomical Society of South Australia and on a web-page constructed by the tour organiser.

At this time, details of the complementary activities were provided. These included expert lectures from a geologist, an anthropologist, and astronomers; contact with an indigenous cultural centre, bush tucker tours with Aboriginal guides and tours of the local area including the ridge top tour. The main event, the viewing of the Total Eclipse, was to be at a spectacular location just outside Lyndhurst with a backdrop of Ochre cliffs that would change colour with the light (comparable to the way Uluru changes colour.) Buses used to transport visitors from Adelaide would also be used to travel to the site and the Arkaroola resort would provide all the facilities for an eclipse barbecue.

The organiser considered that a number of features differentiated this Tour from other eclipse opportunities. First was the location in the magnificent Arkaroola/Mt Painter region of the North

West Flinders Ranges of South Australia where high quality accommodation could be offered at the Arkaroola Resort, which includes a swimming pool, a good dining room, an observatory, fabulous walks and a ridge-top tour across the old mining exploration tracks. Other towns closer to the Total Eclipse Path had very limited accommodation. Second was the input of expert key speakers on local Aboriginal heritage, on the geological features of the distinctive environment, and, on astronomy and the eclipse of the sun itself. Third was the organisation of transport to the location. The two buses met the needs of visitors from overseas, interstate, and South Australian who did not want to drive for seven hours over unfamiliar, and in some places, unsealed roads. In addition, at the viewing site, the buses would provide useful facilities and reduce the number of private vehicles crossing environmentally fragile paddocks. The seven-hour bus trip to Arkaroola from Adelaide was organised to provide stops at which the experts introduced visitors to the features of the countryside. The first of these was at the entrance to the lower Flinders Ranges, where the origins of the formations rising out of the plains would be explained. The second was at the Yurambulla caves where an explanation would be given of the importance of these caves in Aboriginal culture and of the rock art dating back several thousands of years.

The organiser discovered that people often assess the practicalities of an activity after paying their deposit. One US visitor cancelled his booking when he discovered that he did not have sufficient frequent flyer points for the trip to Australia and could not afford the fare because he had just built a 14 inch telescope in his back yard. Another UK visitor decided to continue with plans to undertake the tour in a rental car even though his wife decided not to accompany him when her elderly mother became ill. First, he discovered that he could not read a road map, his wife having always 'navigated' their travels at other times; then he discovered that he could not drive from Adelaide to Alice Springs in one day (a distance of approximately 1200 kilometres,) and lastly he found that travelling alone was no fun for him and so he returned to the UK!

The organiser was clearly following a traditional pattern for Eclipse tours for a group with scientific and environmental interests. For example, The Astronomical Society of the Pacific organised a two week tour of Australia, including an "excellent viewing location" at Roxby Downs, tours of Sydney, Canberra, (with visits to Observatories and a sheep station,) and Adamooka (an opal mining town,) and Alice Springs and Uluru (for views of Aboriginal cave paintings, arts and crafts and Henbury Meteor Craters,) followed by Cairns (with a full day on the barrier reef.) A team of three Astronomical experts provided lectures during the tour, which was led by the Executive Director of the Society. This combination of activities was on a grander scale than the Arkaroola tour but the same elements were present. The ritual requirement of an isolated viewing site was also present but not the extended and potentially uncomfortable travel to the site, although perhaps this was incorporated into the air trip to Australia.

This then was the basic framework of activities and the cultural setting in which the organiser of the Arkaroola planned the Total Eclipse activities. With two on-site observatories and a strong contingent of participants with an international and scientific background, the stage was set for some serious tour networking. This next section of the paper reports on the researcher's observations of the key purpose of the tour – viewing the eclipse. Several aspects were evident. First, the viewing Tour did not go as planned but was a great success. Second, the group wanted the trip to be successful and tried to establish a positive atmosphere. The group themselves initiated a range of genres into the activity through their different types of interactions. Third, the organisers managed to bring a strong closure to the tour.

Nothing can go wrong, go wrong....

For dedicated eclipse followers part of the eclipse ritual often may be a long trip to reach a suitably isolated location and there to face the uncertainty of a clear viewing. On this journey there was talk about previous eclipse experiences for those new to the experience and the experienced watchers. Similarly, the return journey provided a time for closure that included discussion of the experience and was followed later by a sharing of the experience and resultant photos on public web pages.

When the organiser described the Eclipse viewing site in his tour information, he was describing a *potential* viewing site and there were two issues that needed to be addressed: the permission of the pastoralist-leaseholder which had been obtained, and the permission of the Aboriginal community. The degree of control by the local community in determining access to sites was unclear as was the view of the different local Aboriginal communities. The approval of the local Aboriginal community was one way to ensure access to the site by his group and to a certain extent his "sovereignty" over this preferred patch of ground. It was of some concern to him when two months before the event this detail had not yet been conclusively resolved.

On the first morning of the tour, it was announced that the proposed viewing site was not available due to the costs of third party insurance. (In South Australia over the previous six months this had become a major issue for event managers.) It was not clear whether there were other issues but this was the explanation. At a time when the success of the whole exercise was in jeopardy, the organiser and the Resort Manager assured the tour that efforts were underway to organise an alternative site that would provide clear and private viewing, far superior to the 'dogs breakfast' of Lyndhurst public areas. In other words this would be an authentic setting, removed from music festivals and inexperienced Eclipse watchers. Their credibility and commitment were enhanced by their own very clear desire to observe the eclipse.

We were told that the proposed site on Murnpeowie Station to the North East would provide excellent viewing but the condition of the roads was uncertain. After six years of drought, 50mls. of rain had fallen in the week before the Eclipse and some of the roads were washed out as the creeks flowed. The duration of the trip could be two hours or five hours depending on the road. Once there, the group would barbecue organic beef from Murnpeowie after setting up their equipment. We, who were driving our own cars, decided that we should consider going in the Arkaroola bus.

Generally, people seemed fairly relaxed about this uncertainty and there were some mumbled expressions of irritation as a very assertive voice questioned the timing and the certainty of these arrangements. However, the tour organiser maintained an air of calm, assuring everyone that the very best efforts were being made to make sure that the Total Eclipse experience would be memorable. When one person grumbled that it would have been better if everyone had been informed earlier, another commented that this would just make people nervous and clearly the organiser was doing his best. This goodwill was even more memorable as, at the time, the daytime weather was characterised by intermittent cloud that seemed to threaten rain.

Nevertheless, Wednesday dawned hot and clear as the two large touring buses, a smaller (un-airconditioned) Arkaroola bus, and support vehicles departed at 9.30. Instead of a two hour drive to Lyndhurst, the drive was to be four hours. The country to the east of the Flinders ranges is flat, except where creek beds have eroded and small dunes have developed. The occasional kangaroo and emu were observed but mainly scrub and creek lines, and as the road passed across the lowest part of the plain the temperature rose noticeably in our un-airconditioned coach. Nevertheless there was a palpable sense of adventure. Most people were going somewhere they had not been before, across a dry, sparse landscape, and even those of us who had been there before still felt this excitement.

Not much went wrong. The Arkaroola bus did not see the other buses camped under a shady tree where lunch was being served and so we passed by for another hour. Fortunately communication between the buses was possible and eventually lunch caught up with us. The second tour bus developed radiator problems but after an hour or so a few makeshift materials were used to create an alternative mechanism. During this time the bus passengers rested under trees in a creek bed – hoping.

The viewing site was a bit of a shock. In the middle of a red gibber (stone) plain, with hardly a blade of grass, the buses pulled up so as to create a shade line in which folding chairs could be lined up. The eclipse was due to commence at 18.40. The salad was prepared in a mobile kitchen and the organic beef was cooked on several portable barbecues. The food was to be served at 17.30 so there was plenty of time after 15.30 for drinking cold beer and other liquids. But the real task was deciding where to position one's telescope. Should it be just behind the buses, or 20 metres away in the scrub, or next to the 'powered' van? Solar screens had to be checked, sun spots observed and speculation exchanged about whether low level cloud would form at sunset. Earlier in the afternoon a slight breeze meant that a shimmer of red sand was moving at a low level across the plain and across our feet.

More sunscreen was freely applied; umbrellas and chairs were shared as people waited for the shadows to lengthen. There was much discussion between strangers about telescopes, digital cameras and previous eclipses. Men and women who worked on the Hubble telescope connected with people who knew other people working in Boulder, in Sydney and London; people who were physicists, geologists, teachers of Physics, physicians and engineers. In true 'conference' mode the group mixed and shared their common interests.

The Researcher's observation was that the group climate was one of patient acceptance and the hope that nothing would go wrong and the evening would end successfully. And it did. The organic beef and salads were simple but superb. The champagne that had been too hot to drink all afternoon was served chilled to set the right mood just before the Eclipse started. As we all lined up facing the sunset, people wandered from telescope to telescope sharing the views. Digital photos were compared as the partial eclipse commenced; and a cry of ecstasy spontaneously erupted as the total eclipse began. Thirty seconds later it was all over. People talked excitedly, continuing to observe and photograph as the partial eclipse continued and the sun sank beneath the horizon.

Packing up was quickly done but before buses set off there was an extended ceremony of closure. The whole exercise had seemed as though it could become a disaster at any minute and spontaneously the Organisers shared their gratitude to all parties that this had not happened. As this process continued more people voluntarily expressed their feelings. Dominant among these was a view that the Arkaroola Resort Owner and the staff had contributed mightily. In darkness, the buses set off for the four hour return trip which was successfully completed by all on board but sadly had a negative impact on one or two kangaroos.

Conclusions

There are a number of implications that arise from this case study that have relevance for the planning of similar events and these will now be outlined briefly as they relate to the nature of the special event, the expectations of tour groups such as this and the role of the organisers. The benefits of participant observation research will also be discussed.

Unlike many special events, the key focus of this event was beyond the control of the organisers, though as it has occurred many times before, the organizer and many of the participants were well informed about its nature. An important feature of the event is that in many instances visibility of the sun becomes clear at the time of the eclipse and clouds dissipate. Knowledge of this and other features affecting visibility enabled them to plan around local conditions such as rain affected roads and heat.

The standard format for Total Eclipse tours has many commonalities with other tours in offering a distinctive focus plus a range of cultural activities specific to the environment within which it is present. In addition, the standard of amenities was high but also limited by the remoteness of the setting and for some guests this required some adjustment to their usual daily expectations. In the final analysis, it was the totality of the experience and how this was influenced by the interactions between people that made the occasion a success and helped reduce the impact of other inconveniences, such as heat, flies, and lengthy periods sitting in a bus. This suggests that one purpose for having a range of activities (as discussed by Getz and Cheyne, 1997) may be to create a variety of experiences within which these interactions can occur and thereby enable people to recognise their common interests and make connections.

Third, a key factor in this was how the 'perceived' competence of the organisers to deal with the environment and to understand the nature of the Total Eclipse created a sense of goodwill and low stress among the group that made the experience fun. Added to this was the clear commitment of staff to the enterprise and their matter-of-fact way of dealing with issues that created a calm atmosphere and sense of trust. This was highlighted in the concluding 'ceremony' in which the mutual contribution of all players, including the guests, was acknowledged and further developed the rapport established within the group.

This suggests that 'closure' of an event is particularly important in fixing a positive experience in the minds of participants.

This case study was prepared using participant observation as the primary research method and highlighted two issues. One was the need for good knowledge about the nature of special events. In order to more fully understand the nature of the special event under study, a web based data search was also undertaken. This search provided access to information about the total eclipse and experiences of it that would not have been possible ten years ago. The process of participant observation was greatly enhanced by this additional knowledge. The other source of information was the organizer of the tour who provided information about the planning and format of the tour. His information would not have made as much sense to the researcher without the knowledge provided by the internet search and both freed the researcher to focus on processes rather than the structure of the event when making observations.

The second issue was the usefulness of observation. The purpose was to obtain 'observed' rather than 'reported' data in order to understand how the different processes together created the special event experience. Participant observation has much to offer the researcher on festivals and events. However, methodological questions such as biases do need to be addressed in future studies that use observational approaches.

This chapter has briefly explored the organisation of one tour to view the Total Eclipse of the Sun to provide a range of special experiences for people with a shared interest in astronomy. It shows the efforts that were made to create an authentic experience for the group within the traditional parameters of an Eclipse tour for the seriously interested. It also attempts to provide some insight into how a group such as this 'managed' their interactions to create a positive climate for success and it illustrates how the Tour and Resort organisers in expressing their own sense of relief and gratitude that all had gone well, created a climate of closure for the whole tour.

References

Anon (2002a), Outback towns over the moon about the eclipse, *The Australian*, Dec 3.

Anon (2002), Australia celebrates 32 seconds of darkness, *The Times* Dec 5.

Anon (2002b), We stand in awe over our universe, *The Australian* Dec 5.

Cuellar, J. L. (2002), The last-minute eclipse, *Astronomy*, October Vol 30, 10.

Espenak, F. Naeye, R. (2002), Australia's 2002 Total Eclipse of the Sun, *Mercury*, Vol 31,2.

Getz, D. and Cheyne, J. (1997), Special event motivations and behaviour. In *The Tourist Experience: A New Introduction*, Ryan, C. (Ed) Cassell, London.

Harris, J. (2002), Fade to black, *Astronomy*, Nov Vol 30, 11.

Masse, W. B. (1995), The Celestial Basis of Civilisation, *Vistas in Astronomy*, Volume 39, No. 4, 463-477.

Milbrath, S. (1995), Eclipse Imagery in Mexica Sculpture of Central Mexico, *Vistas in Astronomy*, Volume 39, Issue 4, 479-502.

Shone, A. (2001), *Successful event management: A practical handbook*, Continuum, London.

Talcott, R. (2002), Quenching the Sun's fire, *Astronomy*, Vol 30, 4.

Appendix 1: Map of Australia and of the Total Eclipse Path 2002

Total Solar Eclipse of 2002 December 04

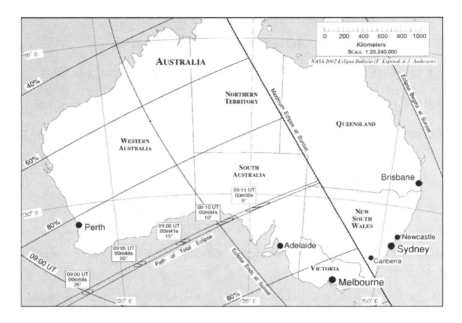

Source: http://astro.iinet.net.au/eclipse/solar/ceduna2002/aust_map1.gif

Total Solar Eclipse of 2002 December 04

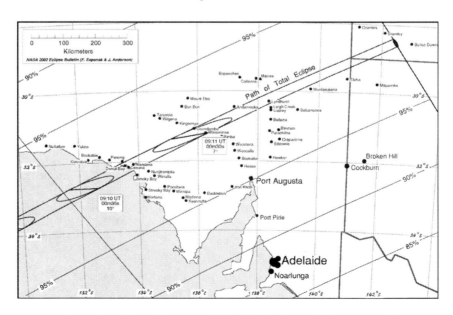

Source: http://astro.iinet.net.au/eclipse/solar/ceduna2002/aust_map2.gif

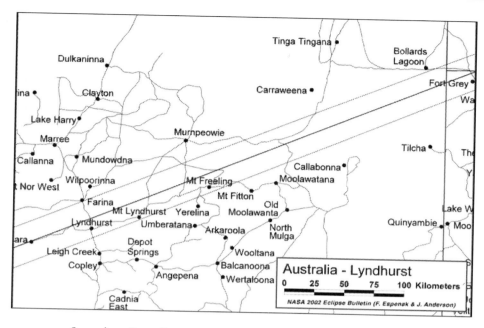

Source: http://astro.iinet.net.au/eclipse/solar/ceduna2002/aust_map5.gif

Rock Festivals and Tourist Safety: Regulation in the European Union

Susanne Storm

University of Southern Denmark

Introduction

Since the 1960s and 1970s rock festivals have become a youth phenomenon particularly in the Scandinavian countries, in the UK and the USA. They have also become popular in eastern European countries after the fall of the Soviet Union. In a certain way rock festivals can aptly be described as the visible sign of youth rebellion against authority in its many forms such as parental – public – or religious authority. To this can be added that rock festivals represent some kind of physical challenge in our modern, western society in which an increasingly heavy emphasis is put on the obtaining of knowledge and the ability to communicate rather than on physical efforts at least in the work context. Young people now find the physical challenges they seek at, for example, rock concerts and –festivals in their many variations. At these events young people find an outlet for their need for physical exertion and display which in many ways can be compared to the participation in dangerous sports such as parachute and bungee jumping, free diving and mountain climbing. The behaviour patterns of the young audience at rock festivals are often dangerous, a traditional ingredient being that the members of the audience further back from the stage press forward to get as close to the stage as they possibly can. In the ensuing crush those in front are deprived of escape routes and they risk being trapped should an emergency arise. The close physical contact between members of the audience establishes a kind of corporate collective, which again opens up possibilities for further dangerous behaviour such as stage diving and crowd surfing. Stage diving consists of individual members of the audience climbing on to the stage from which they throw themselves down on the closely packed audience immediately in front of the stage so that the stage-diver is caught in the air and carried aloft on the heads and shoulders of the standing audience. If a young person finds himself right at the back of the audience, he will try to get to the front by crowd surfing in which case he climbs on to the heads and shoulders of the audience in front and is carried forward in this way. Another traditional way of behaving is a violent dance performed by smaller groups in the audience in which the participants hurtle themselves against the bodies of the other participants. The pain caused in this way is part of the experience: The individual risks his life but gets the much coveted experience of letting himself go (it is mostly young men who indulge in this type of behaviour).

How dangerous this type of behaviour really is, was proved in the summer of 2000 when a very serious accident in which nine young men lost their lives took place at the Roskilde Festival in Denmark.

The Roskilde Festival is a rock festival, which takes place in June each year for the last thirty years. There are several other festivals held annually in Denmark, but the Roskilde Festival is the biggest and best known of these attractions. The capacity of the festival is roughly 100,000 persons including staff, performers and visitors. The number of visitors dropped by 10,000 at the 2001

Festival possibly as a result of the accident at the 2000 festival. Some 150 groups perform on the Festival's seven stages, the biggest of which is the Orange stage, which covers an area of 30,000 square metres and accommodates an audience of 60,000. The Festival employs some 18,000 members of staff, some of whom are salaried, while others work as volunteers. Of these, 170 are directly responsible for the running of the Festival itself. The Festival lasts for a week, and visitors are allowed to arrive a day early to pitch their tents. The Roskilde Festival is non-profit making, its income is donated each year by the Roskilde Charity Fund, which also administers the Festival, to humanitarian and cultural purposes as well as to charity work for the benefit of children and young people world-wide.

The accident happened on the 30 June 2000 at about half past eleven p.m. at the Orange Stage at which an audience numbering some 50,000 had gathered for a concert by the rock band "Pearl Jam". The concert started at half past ten in the normal fashion, but the night was rainy, cold and windy and the audience very tightly packed. Right from the beginning the stewards close to the stage were kept busy at the front barrier removing fans from the area immediately in front of the stage. The crowd kept pushing from behind and others crowd-surfed towards the front barrier. At some stage fans close to the front barrier fell or were knocked over, others stumbled over those lying prostrate and prevented them from getting up. A number of crowd surfers fell into the gap of people already lying on the ground and those standing next to them either did not or could not help. Those standing further off took no notice of what was happening. All the stewards could see was that a gap had opened in the crowd but not what had caused it. The dark night, the bad weather conditions and steaming condensation from the excited crowd in front of the stage all contributed towards making it very difficult to see what was actually happening and it took time before anybody reacted. Finally lifeless fans began to be lifted over the front barrier. The police and the Roskilde Fire and Ambulance service were alerted and a large-scale rescue operation was set in motion. Most of the fans suffered no lasting harm, but eight young men who had collapsed in front of the stage died of suffocation at the concert and a ninth died of his injuries a few days later without regaining consciousness.[1]

The accident gave rise to some soul searching both by the organisers of the Roskilde Festival itself but also by the Roskilde Police Force, who had granted the annual permission to hold the festival in accordance with the local police regulations.[2] The government in power at that time (a social democratic minority government) appointed a Committee under the Ministries of Culture and Justice to consider what should be done to prevent similar accidents from happening in the future.

The Public Prosecutor published a report in which the possibility of criminal liability was considered, but he concluded, that there was no criminal liability, neither for the Festival organisers nor for anybody else.[3] The Festival organisers had already covered all expenses in

---

[1] The introductory section with the description of the Roskilde Festival and the accident which took place there is based upon information provided by the Head of Security of the Roskilde Festival, Mr. Henrik Nielsen at an interview which took place on 27 November 2001. This section is also based upon reports in the press, when the accident happened and on the home page of the Roskilde Festival, http://www.roskilde-festival.dk. The description of the behaviour of young people at festivals is based on the description given by the Working Group set up by the Danish Government to study safety aspects of Music Festivals in their report published on 19 February 2001. The report is published on the home page of the Danish Ministry of Culture: http://www.kum.dk/uk/con-3.

[2] Report of Roskilde Police on the Accident at the Roskilde Festival on 30 June 2000, published 19 DEUember 2000 (in both a Danish and an English version). The report can be found at the following website: http://www.politi.dk/PUBL/roskildefestival_ulykke_redeg/Index_til_RoskildeFestival_redegoerelse.htm.

[3] Report of the Public Prosecutor with the results of his investigation into the accident at the Roskilde Festival on 30 June 2000, published 11 June 2002. The report can be found – but unfortunately only in Danish – at the same website as the one given above.

do not primarily concern tourism policy. In the Union's Green Paper of 1995 on the significance of the European Union for tourism, the Union gives an overview of the policies hitherto pursued by the Community and of what has been achieved. The Union points out that tourism is of vital interest for all citizens of the Union and must be considered an inalienable social right. Considerations of tourists in their role as consumers must also be awarded a central position in the Community's policy for tourism.[14] Later on labour market issues came to the fore when the Union considered the Community's tourism policy, which is not surprising as a great number of citizens work in the tourism industry in one capacity or other.[15] Thus the Community's tourism policy not only survives, it actually flourishes - not as a policy in its own right but as a so-called "flanking policy". It supplements and supports the Community's other policies, for example in the areas of consumer protection or labour market issues. This is probably the reason why the Nice Treaty contains no new provisions on the Community's tourism policy even though the Union in its report in 1996 had recommended the introduction of such rules in the enlarged Community. The Union made the point then that the requirement of unanimity in Article 308 would be particularly difficult to fulfil in an enlarged Community, but so far to no avail.[16]

To conclude these considerations and referring to the point at issue here, namely safety regulations for rock festivals, it will perhaps not be too drastic to state that it is highly doubtful that there is sufficient legal authority to be found in the Treaty's provisions on the Community's cultural policy. The provisions in the Treaty's consumer protection Title are better suited, but the problem is that safety provisions must be laid down either as harmonisation measures in the internal market or as supplementary provisions to help Member States implement already existing policies in this area.

The most appropriate solution would therefore be for the Community to adopt rules in the context of the Community's tourism policy – perhaps combining them with provisions for consumer protection. These possibilities will be discussed immediately below in the next section.

EU Safety Regulations for Tourists

The European Court of Justice decided in 1984 that tourists enjoy free movement rights not as service providers according to the Treaty's Articles 49-55 but as recipients of services.[17] At the same time considerations for the safety of tourists were first seen in a Council resolution, which deals with the whole question of a Community policy for tourism.[18] In this Resolution the Council invites the Union to put forward proposals in the area of tourism after consultations with the Member States and with respect to their distinctive national characters and international obligations. The Council recommends that many areas should be regulated, and in fact rules have been introduced for the purpose of protecting tourists, such as for example the abolition of border controls, the introduction of a European health insurance for tourists, harmonisation of the provisions for liability insurance of motor vehicles, provisions prohibiting misleading advertising of package holidays to mention but a few. The Council also mentions that the Union should make proposals to guard against safety risks during overnight stays at hotels. This resulted in a

---

[14] Union Green Paper "The Significance of the European Union for Tourism" of 4 April 1995 COM (95) 97 final.

[15] Report from the Union to the European Parliament, the Council. The Economic and Social Committee and the Committee of the Regions, "Community measures affecting Tourism (1997/99)" of 28 March 2001 COM (2001) 171 final. This is the most rEUent report in the area.

[16] Treaty of Nice, (2001/C 80/1) OJ C 80/1 10 March 2001.

[17] Luisi and Carbone *v* Ministero del Tesoro [194] EUR 377, [1985] CMLR 52.

[18] Council Resolution on a Community policy for tourism of 10 April 1984, OJ C 115, 30 April 1984, pp. 2 – 27.

Recommendation from the Union on fire safety in hotels, which was passed unanimously by the Council under Article 308 of the EU Treaty. In the preamble of the recommendation reference is made to the fact that many Member States at that time had no safety provisions at all, whereas other Member States did have provisions in their national legislation, but these were far from complete. The aim of the rules was to protect tourists and business travellers during overnight stays in hotels in the host country by defining technical minimum safety standards in case of fire.[19]

The question of the safety of tourists was debated a second time in 1991, when a member of the European Parliament raised the question if appliances such as swings, merry-go-rounds, ferris wheels, big dippers, which are provided for the entertainment of the public by travelling funfairs and amusement parks were sufficiently safe for the public to use. The Union replied to the question by referring to a proposal for a Council Directive which had been under preparation for the purpose of regulating the free movement of appliances such as merry-go-rounds, swings and the like which are provided by amusement parks in the internal market. Had the proposal, which quoted the harmonisation provision in Article 100a (now 95), been passed, it would have meant, that such appliances would be safe for the public to use. Unfortunately, the European Council decided at the Edinburgh summit that this question should be dealt with according to the principle of subsidiarity. Accordingly there was no need to regulate this question at Community level. Therefore the proposal was abandoned.[20]

The question was raised again in 1998, this time by another member of the European Parliament. The Union was asked, if it had any plans for introducing EU-wide standards for the health and safety of tourists on tourist sites such as campsites, caravan sites and other similar tourist facilities – which could include festival sites. The Union replied in the negative, as it considered that the establishment of specific standards for health and safety of the public on tourist sites to be primarily a matter for the Member States to deal with. Furthermore, the tourist industry itself had a role to play in raising the quality and safety of tourist sites to the highest possible standards. Finally, the Union said: "Effective dissemination of information to the tourist on minimum health and safety requirements on tourist sites is an essential element in raising standards. In that context, the Union will seek to encourage the dissemination of information and best practice in the case of innovative measures taken in Member States in this area. This will be a priority issue in the case of future work programmes dealing with the promotion of tourists' interests".[21]

The questions raised by the two members of the European Parliament have this in common: They both contain direct or indirect references to the principle of subsidiarity, which is found in Article 5(2) of the EU Treaty. According to this principle, which was introduced by an amendment in 1992 by the Treaty on European Union, the Community shall take action only if and insofar as the objectives of the proposed action cannot be sufficiently achieved by the Member States and can therefore be better achieved by the Community. The principle applies only in areas, which do not fall within the Community's exclusive competence, i.e. only in areas of shared competence between the Community institutions and the Member States. The tourism policy of the Community is precisely such an area, since it constitutes a so-called "flanking-policy" as mentioned above. The legal authority for taking action is contained in Article 308 of the Treaty combined with Article 3(1)(u). This elastic legal authority does definitely not fall within the area of

---

[19] Council Recommendation 86/666/EEU 22 DEUember 1986 on fire safety in existing hotels, OJ 1986 L 384/60-68. The Union has published a report about the implementation of the REUommendation by the Member States and the need for further regulation of the question at Community level: COM (2001) 348 final.

[20] Union Staff Working Paper on Community Actions AffEUting Tourism 1995/96 SEU (97) 1419 – 11, July 1997, p. 37 in the section on consumer health and safety.

[21] OJ C 354, 19 November 1998, p. 127.

the Community's exclusive competence – unlike, for example, the provisions on free movement of goods, persons, services and capital in Articles 25-31 and 39-60, the equal pay for male and female workers provision in Article 141 and the competition rules in Articles 81 and 82. The Union replies to the questions of the two Parliamentarians by suggesting that action undertaken for the purpose of protecting the safety of tourists is better achieved by the Member States than by the Community. Not only that, the Union goes further by saying that private undertakings, i.e. the tourism industry itself, ought to play an active role in improving quality and safety standards at tourist attractions. As examples, the Union mentions effective distribution of information leaflets and introduction of guide - lines on "good practice" as initiatives, which could be taken easily both by the Member States and the tourism industry itself (as a form of self-regulation).

The Union maintains that the principle of subsidiarity points to the Member States when the question is raised of introducing safety provisions for the protection of tourists when they are staying at sites categorised as tourist attractions, which includes rock concerts and festival sites. The question, which will be looked at below, is: to what extent, have the Member States lived up to the Union's expectations? Also: To what extent have the festival organisers done so?

Safety Regulations and Festivals in the Member States

It is probably correct to say that in the Community no country has gone further than the UK in working out guide lines for so-called "crowd management" of the audiences at rock festivals and rock concerts. The reason for this is probably an accident at Castle Donnington which happened in 1988: during an outdoor rock festival with performances by some of the world's then leading hard rock and heavy metal bands two young men were crushed to death by the pressure from behind as they were standing right in front of the stage. The accident caused the British Home Office to take the initiative to elaborate an "Events Safety guide". It was the result of collaboration between the Home Office, the British Health and Safety Council and representatives of the concert and festival industry itself. It was published first in 1993 and was immediately nicknamed the "Pop-code". It was published again in 1999 in a revised edition.

The Events Safety Guide does not lay down specific rules with safety standards and safety provisions for rock festivals and similar events. On the contrary, it provides a list of possible risk factors at such events, which the festival organisers can go through to see if one or more of them apply to the festival they are planning to organise. If they find out that several of them do in fact apply, the Guide then lists a number of safety measures from among which, the organisers can choose those which will be most suited for implementation at that particular festival. Risk factors are for example the sizeable crowd and its behaviour: swaying, crushing trampling and other forms of more aggressive and violent behaviour. Also the physical surroundings such as the stage itself and the enclosures in front of the stage, even the weather represents a safety risk if the festival is an open-air event. This became evident at the open-air Jean Michel Jarre windmill concert in Hjørring in the north of Denmark, which took place on 8 September 2002. Torrential rain on the preceding Saturday had converted the festival site to a mud bath. The audience numbered 35,000 but many were unable to get to the site as roads were churned up by the traffic. The ambulance service was called 17 times to broken arms and legs and once to a woman in labour, a thousand cars were stuck in the mud and had to be salvaged by the fire brigade. The authorities had given permission to hold the concert, but nobody had taken the weather into consideration and there were no provisions taken to deal with this risk factor. Accordingly the event deteriorated and became chaotic. If the festival organisers (a charity: the muscular atrophy fund) had taken the risk of bad weather into consideration, they would perhaps not have held the event in a mere field without proper access roads.[22]

In Sweden a Committee appointed by the Swedish Ministry of Culture with members representing the music and concert industry are working on guide-lines for festival and concert goers' safety. In this case it was also an accident, which caused the Committee to be appointed. The accident took place at the Hultsfred Festival on 17 June 1999. A young woman was crushed to death by a very animated audience. The performing band on the stage, "The Holes" had encouraged the audience to take their clothes off and the female leader of the band had already done so, which caused the pressure from behind towards the stage and those standing right in front of it to increase.[23]

In Denmark initiatives were first taken to consider risk factors and audience safety in 1995 in connection with the accident at Vejle football stadium. A Committee appointed by the Danish Ministry of Culture published a report on safety at Danish sports stadiums and concluded that standing room was among the highest risk factors for the audience at football matches. At that time the European Football association (UEFA) decided that standing room should be abolished, all members of the audience should be seated and that all seats should be provided with backrests. This was duly implemented for the 1998/99 season.[24]

After the accident at the Roskilde festival, the organisers of the Festival took several initiatives to make the festival safer to attend. These initiatives were based on an extensive risk assessment. One of the most important initiatives was the introduction of audience-sections so that the crushing and pushing was minimised. The sections were partitioned off with passages in between where guards could supply water and paper mugs for those in the audience who may be in need of it. Better communication lines were established between the guards present among the audience and the central security manager. Big screens were placed at vital spots, which allowed security messages to be passed immediately to the audience. A new training programme for the festival staff was developed in collaboration with the Roskilde School of Commerce on crowd safety and crowd management. Before the 2001 Festival opened, the organisers issued a Festival guide with the title "You and the Festival crowd – Enjoyment and Safety at Festivals" containing – among other things – recommendations on how to behave in dangerous situations so that members of the audience would have a better understanding of the potential dangers which could arise in crowds of the size which habitually attend the Roskilde Festival. Both the 2001 and the 2002 Festivals took place without mishap.[25]

Immediately after the accident in June 2000, the Danish Ministry of Culture appointed a working group of eight members representing the Ministries of Culture, Justice and Home Affairs, the Danish Music Council, the Roskilde Police Department, a group of major festival organisers and the Association of Local Authorities in Denmark. The Committee published its report in February 2001. The main conclusion of the report is that audience safety was in great need of improvement at these events – particularly as concerns the safe handling of large crowds. Thus a much tougher

---

[22] The Event Safety Guide: A Guide to Health, Safety and Welfare at Music and Similar Events. HSG 195 Health & Safety Executive Books 1999. The description of the Jean Michel Jarre windmill concert is taken from descriptions in the press at the time.

[23] Both the Castle Donnington and the Hultsfred accident have been described in the report published 19 February 2001 by the Danish working group set up by the Danish Government on 20 July 2000 to study safety aspects of music festivals on pp. 12 - 13. This report will be referred to again below.

[24] The Report of the Danish working group of 19 February 2001, p. 13.

[25] The information about new initiatives taken by the festival organisers of the Roskilde Festival has been provided by Mr. Henrik Nielsen as mentioned in note a).

control of audience behaviour should be introduced but should be balanced so as not to disturb the enjoyment of the crowd and change the festival's character. An improvement of the physical surroundings was also needed and a strengthening of the communication lines between security personnel was required. Finally the working group recommended that a Danish "Events Safety Guide" like the British counterpart, should be elaborated containing a thorough description of risk factors and leaving to some extent for the organisers to determine which safety measures should be taken and which would best serve the purposes of each festival. In this way the working group has confirmed the approach of not fixing detailed rules applying to all festivals but a more individualised and flexible approach, which will be based on the present Danish system of individual police permissions for each festival. Whether this approach is sufficient only time will show.[26]

Conclusions

The question is now whether these initiatives, which have been taken in some Member States with England as their model, are sufficient. It is also a question if the Union by referring to the principle of subsidiarity perhaps has seen fit to choose the easy way out. It is a well-known fact that improvements to a dangerous road crossing typically follow one or more accidents and somehow one gets the sneaking suspicion that perhaps the same mechanism applies here. It is a fact that both the Roskilde Festival and other European festivals, some of which have a long tradition behind them, have been held without any accidents having happened, until the accident does in fact happen. The improved safety measures taken by the Festival organisers themselves are of course necessary to prevent repetitions but the question is: is this enough? Similarly the Events Safety Guides, which are seemingly on their way in Denmark and Sweden, may be too locally specific. The proposal for a Danish Events Safety Guide, which has been elaborated by the working group, has not been published yet and its publication is not likely to have happened by the time of writing.[27] Is there not a good argument for introducing an Events Safety Guide at the European level so as to avoid more tragic accidents of the same sort? Undoubtedly the principle of subsidiarity applies as long as the treaty contains no explicit rules on tourism, but does not the principle point in the opposite direction: not to the Member States - as maintained by the Union, - but to the Community? A case can be made for a better solution of the problem of audience safety at rock festivals at the Community level and this is the main conclusion here.

---

[26] The Report of the Danish working group of 19 February 2001, pp. 27 - 30.

[27] Information from the secretary of the working group, Mr. Peter Navntoft, who is a senior civil servant of the Ministry of Culture.

References

Books and articles

Dejemeppe, P., "Les Droits du Touriste Européen", *Journal des Tribunaux Droit Européen*, 10:16 (1994).

Kapteyn, P. J. G. and VerLoren van Themaat, P. (1998), *Introduction to the Law of the European Communities* third edition, Kluwer Law International, London.

Niedobitek, M. (1997), *The Cultural Dimension in EU Law*, Kluwer Law International: London.

The Event Safety Guide: A Guide to Health, Safety and Welfare at Music and Similar Events. HSG 195 Health & Safety Executive Books 1999.

The Report of the Danish working group on safety at rock festivals of 19 February 2001

Van Kray, F. (1993), *Tourism and the Hotel and Catering Industries in the EU*, European Law Series, the Athlone Press, London.

Weatherill, S. (1997), *EU Consumer Law and Policy*, European Law Series Longman: Harlow.

Wouters, J., "La Libre Circulation des Touristes dans la Jurisprudence de la Cour de Justice C.E," *Journal des Tribunaux Droit Européen*, 10:16 (1994).

EU material

Union Green Paper "The Significance of the European Union for Tourism" of 4 April 1995 COM (95) 97 final.

Union Report on Civil Protection, Tourism and Energy of 3 April 1996. EU-Bull. 4-1996, I, the Intergovernmental Conference.

Union Report on the Implementation of the Recommendation on Fire Safety in Existing Hotels, COM (2001) 348 final.

Council Recommendation 86/666/EEU 22 DEUember 1986 on fire safety in existing hotels, OJ 1986 L 384/60-68.

Council Resolution on a Community policy for tourism of 10 April 1984, OJ C 115, 30 April 1984.

Council Resolution 89/46/EEU, OJ L 17/53.

Council Resolution 92/421/EEU, OJ L 231/26-32.

Union Staff Working Paper on Community Actions Affecting Tourism 1995/96 SEU (97) 1419 11, July 1997.

Declaration No. 1 to the Maastricht Treaty.

EU-Bull. 9-1990.

EU-Bull. 6-1991.

Europe Documents No. 1722/1723, 5 July 1991.

Luisi and Carbone *v* Ministero del Tesoro [194] EUR 377, [1985] CMLR 52.

Report from the Union to the European Parliament, the Council. The Economic and Social Committee and the Committee of the Regions, "Community measures affecting Tourism (1997/99)" of 28 March 2001 COM (2001) 171 final.

Treaty of Nice, (2001/C 80/1) OJ C 80/1 10 March 2001.

Material from the internet

http://www.kum.dk/uk/con-3

http://www.politi.dk/PUBL/roskildefestival_ulykke_redeg/Index_til_RoskildeFestival_redegoerelse.htm

http://www.roskilde-festival.dk

Safety at Cultural Festivals and Events: legal implications of a soft law approach

Jan Timmermann Pedersen

University of Southern Denmark

Introduction

When tragedies such as the one at the Roskilde Festival, Denmark 2000 occur, where nine young men lost their lives in the crowd in front of the stage, there is public demand for regulation. There is a saying in law that 'cases make bad law', meaning, that legal regulation based on single events is usually not a good approach. Inherent in this saying lies one of the major conflicts in legal regulation namely the problem of establishing a good connection between the general rule (statutory law) and the specific case (in this instance, granting a permit or not).

This chapter seeks to examine the legal activity in connection with regulation of public safety at cultural events. The main focus will be on activities in Danish law. The chapter briefly examines the present Danish regulatory system, and emphasises some of its legal aspects, and the regulation likely to emerge regarding safety at cultural events. Generally, this chapter focuses on the use of 'soft law' as a way to control behaviour, and on the connection between soft law/non binding law and the general binding law.

Cultural events play a significant role in modern tourism. This draws the attention of the legal scholar to the need for and level of protection for the consumer/tourist. The main questions relate to how to increase the protection of the participants and what means are available to do this? As with all aspects of regulation the aim should be to find a balance between the need for regulation and the need for freedom. As cultural events are in constant movement, regulation in this area faces special problems. Or, as the American rock singer and pianist Jerry Lee Lewis stated in the late 1950s: "It is impossible to play rock and roll with the lights on!"

The chapter also focuses on how the authorities, through different forms of regulation are able to, directly or indirectly control the behaviour of the organisers of cultural events. The chapter points out problems with different forms of regulation. In this respect the paper follows up some of the problems pointed out by the Working Group instituted by the Danish government after the Roskilde Accident (Rock Festival Safety, 2000). In statutory law the effect on behaviour is more or less given. But with other forms of regulation the controlling effect is more indirect. The regulation chosen in Danish law, with non-binding rules, will, in connection with the rules of liability and the general rules of public law, result in some controlling effect on the behaviour of the organisers of cultural events. In connection with the expected Danish ruling the chapter points out the areas in which regulation has the best chance of resulting in practical rules.

The expected Danish rules governing the area of safety at cultural events will be non-binding rules. The word 'expected' is used, because the work has come to an unexpected halt due to the election and a new government, otherwise a Danish safety guide of some sort was expected to come out in the spring of 2000. On the basis of the preliminary work it is expected that the regulation will only seek to regulate the behaviour of the organisers and the public authorities, but will not involve any direct liability rules. However, the mere existence of some sort of rules in connection with the general legal system of granting permits and tort law is bound to have a considerable effect on safety at large cultural events.

The report (Rock Festival Safety, December 2000) from the Working Group established after Roskilde 2000 recommends instituting Danish or Nordic guidelines in line with the English Event Safety Guide (1999). The group points out that it should be adjusted to Danish conditions. The group emphasises the need for improvements in the guide with regards to crowd management, chain of command, decision making competence and communications with the public. This is in line with the investigations made by the Danish police and three reports they published in connection with the Roskilde Accident. The first report was published on November 6, 2000, the second (and only one available in English) on December 19, 2000, and the third was published on June 11, 2002 (www.politi.dk/PUBL, 2002).

Scope of the chapter

The scope of this chapter and the scope of regulation are the same. Thus the problems in connection with defining the scope are the same, namely that an exact definition of a cultural event is very difficult.

One way of defining cultural events with regards to their regulation could be to focus on issues of size and capacity, where the main problem lies in how to handle a large number of people gathered at a given space. Regulation is thus brought into play where a gathering is not regulated by other general regulations such as building regulations or special regulations for theatres, discos, camping sites etc. An important question is, however, whether it is possible to precisely define the scope for regulations that shall include such a wide variety of events. Danish cultural events range from small exhibitions in a gallery, local city markets held once a year, to concerts with up to 100.000 people. At the Roskilde Festival in the year 2000 the attendance was approximately 75,000 and the number of people attending as part of their official duty in different categories such as control, food service, cleaners, etc. was approximately 25,000. Categorising these various events and legislating for each category is a huge, if not impossible, task.

The difficulty in defining the precise scope of regulation is a key reason why the area of safety at cultural events calls for a form of regulation other than the usual instruments of statutory law. Given these difficulties, the form of regulation due to the nature of the case has to be non-binding. It is interesting from a legal perspective to see how this soft law regulation will work in connection with the general legal system. This will be important for the regulators in two ways. First, it may assist the regulators in their effort to find the best form of regulation, and second, it may guide the users of the regulations (tourists/consumers or organisers) to benefit from them in the best possible way.

Ways of regulating festivals

From a legal perspective there are several ways of controlling the behaviour of the citizen at cultural events. The primary way is through statutory law; instituted at an international or a national level. Another way of controlling the behaviour of organisers is through binding rules designed to regulate in interaction with local authorities. The way to do this is by giving the local authorities discretionary powers and then through using the hierarchical system order the local authorities to act in a given way. A third way is by influencing the behaviour of the organisers indirectly. This can be done either through the local administration as mentioned above or by a direct soft law approach, where the aim is to regulate the behaviour of the organisers directly. Yet another way is to leave the problem of regulation to the parties involved. Regulation in this way seems to have equity between the parties involved as a prerequisite. This is not the case with festival organisers and their guests.

The Danish group appointed to come up with a proposal for regulations in this area was chaired by a member from the Ministry of Culture and a member from the Ministry of Justice. Other members were from various public authorities with an interest in cultural events and one member was from the festival side. The conclusion from the Working Group was unanimous. The proposal was a soft law approach based on 'The English Event Safety Guide' with some improvements and adjustments to Danish traditions. Each part of the group had their own motives for reaching this conclusion.

The organisers did not want to have rigid rules making it very expensive and difficult to run festivals. The public side of the working group did not want rules instituted that would in any way, enable the organisers to avoid final responsibility in case of an accident, picturing the possible liability of the public as a problem that could arise from statutory law. This is not a major problem in Danish law given that failing public control usually does not lead to legal responsibility for the public. If, for instance, food control fails, and people subsequently fall ill, this will in most cases not lead to legal responsibility for the public according to Danish law.

The appointed group saw music festivals for young people as the most problematic events with regards to safety. This coincides with the comprehension of the Roskilde accident as being the result of 'crowd-surfing' and other special forms of behaviour of the crowd at music festivals. The group saw the Roskilde Accident as a result of a special youth culture, which only takes place at very few festivals and saw no reason to over-react and institute massive regulation for all festivals on basis of the accident. The group tried to find a balance between freedom and the need for regulation (Rock Festival Safety 2000). This point of view could be considered a little narrow given that the number of accidents involving large crowds is not just connected to youth culture. The report itself mentions the Christina Nilsson accident in 1885 and the accidents with Hajj crowds gathering at Mecca, though in both cases 'crowd-surfing', indeed the idea of youth culture, were neither factors nor concepts.

In this respect it is interesting that the recommendations of the group seem to build solely on knowledge gathered on the basis of accidents at music events. Accidents at sporting, particularly football, events are only mentioned in passing (p. 10) even though accidents at this kind of event have lead to massive regulations by different football associations. The focus on the English Event Safety Guide seems narrow considering that there are good recommendations in the FIFA technical regulation from 1995 (www.fifa.com) and from the UEFA regulations on safety (www.uefa.com/uefa).

The Roskilde Accident in 2000 led to an inquiry into the role of the public authorities, and the role of the organisers. Focal points in connection with the public authorities have been their role in the granting of permits (prior regulation) and the actions taken in connection with the actual accident. Focal points in connection with the organisers have been the issues surrounding the 'chain of command' and decision making competences. It took some time before the accident was discovered, and that it then took too long before the music was stopped and proper announcements were made to the crowd. Another focal point has been the necessary processes of communication between the different authorities and the organisers of the festival. In this respect it is interesting to note that the above mentioned football regulations (instituted long before Roskilde 2000) take into account most of these problems.

The Danish authorities appear to favour a non-binding or a soft law approach to the regulation of festivals in line with the propositions of the Working Group. This soft law is meant to work together with the general legal system and the specific public system of granting permits and thus increase safety at large cultural events. However, as will be argued non-binding or soft law regulation concerning safety at cultural events has a tendency to develop into binding rules, either directly or indirectly.

The state of national regulation

In Denmark, and in several countries around Europe, there are some national rules, which regulate certain parts of cultural events. These rules are not designed to regulate cultural events as such, but regulate other activities - camping regulations, general fire safety rules etc. - that can overlap with cultural events.

In Denmark to date there has been no real need for extensive statutory regulation in the area of cultural events. The only statutory rule that regulates this area is the Standard Police Regulation, which is legally binding pursuant to the Police Act of 1871. Section 48 of this Act states that public entertainment, including concerts, cannot be held without police authorisation. Pursuant to section 50 those who have received authorisation to hold public entertainments must comply with any orders laid down by the police. These rules, or the basis of these rules, were made in 1871. The main purpose was to give the King (or his men) the power to "regulate" the political meetings of the opposition (the liberals and the social democrats).

Thus the Police Act of 1871 is the primary general statutory regulation of cultural events in Denmark. This provision places much discretion into the hands of the local police, which combined with the fact that the local police may be a small police station with perhaps 3 or 4 policemen emphasises the need for some sort of general regulation in connection with large cultural events.

The report from the Roskilde group recommended that the power to grant permits should stay with the police. But the group also pointed out that the police ought to institute a small national group inside the police, in order to gather information and be in a position to provide advice to the local police on the issue of the granting of permits to the organisers of large cultural events.

Problems with regulation

Regulation, with great discretionary powers in the hands of local police, may lead to very different levels of security in connection with cultural events. Even within a small country like Denmark it is possible that the rules for staging large cultural events may vary significantly. If the main rules regulating security at a given cultural event are in fact set by local authorities on the basis of a general competence, there is no certainty that the local authorities, even if they work together with experts such as the local fire brigade, have the knowledge or ability to assess security.

Another problem with the present Danish regulation, which is closely connected to the legal form, is that the general discretionary provisions were laid down in a period when it was common practice for the police to work on the basis of such wide discretionary rules. The public at that time did not challenge the basis of a given order as much as they do today. Since then the use of discretionary power by the public authorities has been reduced. This, and the increasing focus on the principle of legality, has lead to a more frequent questioning of the competence of the authorities. Both have perhaps led to a reduction in the real discretionary power of the authorities. Thus the demand for other ways to regulate has increased.

A third problem arising from regulating by giving local authorities discretionary power lies in the problem of knowledge. Today the organisation of cultural events is very complex and demands a great deal of knowledge. Not every local police station has the knowledge/information required or the ability to control large cultural events. These problems may be solved in various ways. For instance, nationwide cooperation between authorities may set common security standards. This, however, cannot ensure the level of protection and cooperation will only guarantee common standards. Generally the setting of standards is left to the cooperation of local authorities, many of which will have little or no interest in the case before the problem arises in their jurisdiction.

A fourth and perhaps greater legal problem with leaving wide discretionary power to the local authorities lies in the principle of legality to which all public authorities are bound. An important part of the principle of legality is that the more restrictive a regulation is, the more well-founded or higher ranked the basis of the regulation must be. The denial to give permission for staging a cultural event is by nature a restrictive measure. A wide discretionary power by local authorities means that the major part of the legal basis for denial (the restrictive measure) is very uncertain and will be at a very low level. It may be very difficult for a local authority to impose severe, and perhaps very costly, restrictions on a local organiser of a cultural event, when the only legal base is a general clause and some reference to common sense. In such cases the real basis for restrictions can, and will be, common sense. The local organiser will of course state that a high level of security is not needed. Given that accidents such as Roskilde 2000 are fortunately not that frequent, the danger appears to be theoretical.

A fifth problem with leaving matters to local authorities to demand a certain level of security is the scale of the event and hence the importance to the local community. In several small Danish towns the local festival is a way of gathering money for community groups - the football club, youth club, etc. This means that every new demand for increased security from the local police will result in less money for local work. Given the connection between the local police and other local authorities such as municipalities it must be very difficult to demand costly safety measures.

Regulating by general rules of competence with a high level of discretion left to the local authorities seems to be an insufficient way to regulate safety at cultural events in modern society. If the main problem is knowledge/ability, and if the competence is to stay with the local authorities, a form of regulation must be developed which guarantees sufficient local knowledge, and still leaves sufficient discretionary power to take into account the many differences of cultural events.

In summary, leaving it solely to the discretion of local authorities to take care of the security and safety at cultural events would seem not to be effective, particularly if the local authorities' only basis for control is a general clause of power leaving all or the major part of the security assessment to the local authorities themselves. Considering the general wish not to create statutory law, this leaves the government with two, more or less, conflicting problems. On the one hand there is an obvious call for, and a need for, common regulation, while on the other hand, the area is diffuse and under constant development, so that statutory law is no real option for the government.

Effects of a given regulation

If the setting of standards at a local level is the major problem, and there is a wish to institute common rules, how then should we regulate? There are various ways to minimise the problem with local standards but regulation may be at national or at international level. The tourism element of cultural events suggests regulation at an international level.

Statutory law

The obvious way to secure a certain standard of safety/security at cultural events is through statutory law at national or international level. But, to regulate behaviour of the organisers of cultural events by statutory law is very difficult. As pointed out above, the term cultural festivals and events covers a wide variety of activities. To create general rules that directly cover security problems at every kind of event seems impossible. Moreover, statutory law has another problem because of the retrospective element. It is impossible to foresee the future and inherent in cultural events is development encouraging even greater variety in the future.

Another negative effect of using statutory law is that it might take away the final responsibility from the organisers and to a certain extent also make the local authorities passive to the real issues. It would perhaps develop into a system where permission must be granted if the organisers meet certain standards. A situation where common sense is left out is not a good idea in an area such as cultural events. Furthermore, the authorities have no interest in taking on the responsibility for safety.

Strict liability and insurance

One way of regulating the behaviour of organisers of cultural events by statutory law, without going into detailed regulation of security, could be to regulate the area though the rules of tort. Establishing strict liability in the area may be an option since this form of regulation is not a direct regulation of the behaviour by detailed statutory law in the area of security. The primary aim of strict liability is to move the risk of damages from the individual to a group. Usually, attaching a mandatory requirement for insuring the strict liability replaces the risk. The risk is moved from the individual to the group with the insurance company as an intermediary. The rules of strict liability are often used in areas, in which there is a risk of severe damage to the individual but where society in general accepts this risk.

The replacement of the risk is the general aim of statutory based strict liability. However, strict liability with an obligation to take out insurance could have some regulatory effect on the organisers. The insurance company will assess the risk and try to minimise it and may force their customers (organisers of cultural events) to take initiatives to reduce the risk of claims for damages. This form of regulation will leave much of the actual regulating to private initiative. It will reduce the role of the public authorities to mere control if the organisers meet the requirements of insurance.

However, there are some problems with introducing strict liability for organisers of cultural events. One problem lies in the fact that not all cultural events have an economic aspect. To move risks from the individual to a group is a good solution where the mass is very homogenous and has a certain critical mass or financial backing as in the motoring sector, railroads, nuclear plants etc. Festival organisers on the other hand represent great variety. and variable economic performance so that regulation through strict liability and compulsory insurance is therefore not appropriate.

Circulars

Another, and perhaps more feasible, way to regulate the security at cultural events is to use a hierarchic system to impose standards for permissions granted by the local authorities. This will have, as its effect, that no permission can be given, if the standards set through the circular are not met by the organisers. A regulation of this kind has an indirect effect on the behaviour of the organisers and also has the advantage that it makes it possible to take into account the vast variety of cultural events. It also enables the local authorities, through leaving them with enough discretionary power, to take into account the specific nature of the cultural event when granting permission.

The problem with regulation by circular however, is that the information is given to the authorities and thus the organisers have no direct access to this causing a knowledge gap. If the purpose of regulating the area is to secure the guests at festivals by enhancing the organizers knowledge, regulation by circular is not the best instrument.

Soft law

Issuing a guide to the organisers and the local authorities and making sure that this guide is common knowledge for both parties is set to close the knowledge gap and is the approach favoured by the Danish authorities - a typical soft law approach.

The most important soft law regulation that deals with the security of festivals is 'The Events Safety Guide' (1999). This safety guide is not a binding (mandatory) regulation and can only be seen as a recommendation to organisers of cultural events. However, the construction of the legal system has the effect that regulations in the form of soft law can and often will regulate behaviour in a way that gives the rules the character of being binding. Soft law has a tendency over time to become hard or mandatory law in two ways.

The first way is that the public authorities, before giving a permit to an event, will use the guide as a checklist and see if the application complies with the guide. If the application does not fulfil the requirements recommended in the guide the authorities will not give the permit. This has the ultimate effect that an application in all circumstances must comply with the soft law regulation. No legally approved event will take place if it does not comply with the guide. The Danish authorities are planning to uphold the general rule of leaving it to the local police to give a permit. The power of the local police is not going to be changed. Thus the binding legal framework is the same as described above.

The second way is more indirect and by way of the rules of tort. If an organiser does not comply with the events safety guide, the organiser risks being rendered negligent and may have to pay damages. Legally there is no excuse for organisers staging an event and claiming not to be aware of the existence of the guide. The organiser has taken up practice in a professional area and is as such subject to the rules governing this profession. If the guide is common knowledge among professionals this will set a standard for the definition of faults.

These two ways of giving an event safety guide a form of mandatory power will ultimately have as a result that the non-binding rules of a guide will have serious impact on the behaviour of organisers of cultural events. Thus the form may be used as an efficient way to control the behaviour of an organiser of a large cultural event and thereby increase security.

Tort law

Mandatory law and soft law are not the only ways to control behaviour in a modern society. Tort law controls an important part of behaviour as well. Given the fact that most people do not want to be subject to claims of damages they will try to behave accordingly.

To avoid claims one must avoid being found guilty of negligence. If there are regulations in a given area that constitutes strict liability, it is impossible for the person being subject to claims of damages to avoid claims by controlling their own behaviour. This leads to the question whether strict liability, if connected with compulsory insurance, will not lead to carelessness. The person will in any case be liable, and if the damages are then paid by an insurance company the liability will have little or no effect as a behavioural control. Giving the insurance company the right to recourse in certain situations usually solves the problem.

In the area of cultural events there is no statutory law stating strict liability. Thus you would expect claims of damages to be based on negligence. However, in Danish law this is not the case, and strict liability may develop from a judge-made law. One of the areas in which strict liability or almost strict liability has been developed is in the area of personal injury by participation at amusements. The leading case is from 1957 (UfR 1957 p. 109). In this case the Supreme Court stated strict liability in a case where an amusement park had to pay damages to a girl who fell out of a ride. The effect of this case is that personal injury deriving from participation in a rock festival may be expected to lead to a high level of liability, if not strict liability for the organisers. This of course raises the question whether or not insurance should be mandatory, which it is not for the time being, and a further question of whether or not the insurance is sufficient. The Roskilde Festival had insurance to cover as many as ten people (providers) being seriously injured.

For the security of the guests, should claims of damages should arise, it is of course very important that the organiser is able to meet their demands. Being injured is in itself a problem, not being able to claim damages only adds to the problem.

If every organiser is forced to take out insurance the problem with behavioural control arises. In Danish law the right of recourse solves this problem. If the negligence is gross the insurance company has the right of recourse against the organiser. Gross negligence is when you have set aside clear demands as to conduct. In this respect ignoring obvious relevant parts of an event guide may lead to the courts stating gross negligence and then placing the final costs of damages on the organiser. Even with strict liability and an obligation to have insurance, there is still some behavioural control possible in the system. In such cases an event guide will be of importance for the control of behaviour.

Conclusion

The problem with security and safety at cultural festivals such as Roskilde will be solved. A Danish Event Safety Guide, taking into account the special Danish systems and improving on key issues, was to be issued in early spring 2002 but was delayed due to the election and a change in government. Its emergence is still awaited from the Ministry of Culture, but in the meantime the tragedy of Roskilde 2000 is no longer front page material. If a guide is issued it will soon become important for all organisers of cultural events and will, even though the form of soft law is chosen by the government, set standards for organisers.

An event guide has several advantages compared to traditional regulatory methods. Perhaps regulation through soft law will be developed in the future as a way to solve complex issues. As described above, the effect of soft law and the reason it is a possible way of regulation is highly connected with the functioning of the mandatory legal system. Thus the use of soft law will in no way render the present and well-known legal system neither useless nor unnecessary. On the contrary, working in parallel with the traditional legal system a Danish Event Safety Guide will play an important role in the protection of locals and tourists at cultural events.

Given that Denmark is clearly not the only country with large cultural events, and given the general desire to protect the safety and security of all citizens in the EU, a guide for every country could be a way of addressing the issue at EU-level. But as pointed out at the beginning of the chapter , the soft law approach is not unfamiliar to the EU itself and the production of a common EU Event Safety Guide could be a useful way forward. At the very least the EU could incentivise member states to solve the problem according to their tradition of regulation. Given the obvious international element of large cultural events the EU-competence for regulation in the area could also be linked to consumer/tourist protection. A general guide, or a set of common minimum standards, seems to be a good way of taking into account the differences at local level. Such a guide could be expected to play a major role in securing the safety of participants in large cultural events, especially in countries that have not yet felt the need for such a regulation, and without compromising the diversity and spontaneity of cultural festivals that attract visitors in the first place.

Section 3

Impacts and Evaluations

Economic Impact of Festivals in the United States:
a case study of the Scottish Highland Games

Deepak Chhabra

University of Northern Iowa

Introduction

Economic development and diversification are concerns for many communities, especially those that have relied heavily on one industry for their well-being. In response to the need for diversification, many regions have attempted to develop their tourism industry as a complement to their traditional economic base (Lickorish & Jenkins, 1997; Long & Perdue, 1996). Short-term events and festivals contribute to the tourism industry since they can stimulate tourism demand in quiet periods, help generate positive images of a location, and create opportunities for community action. In doing so, they generate employment and income opportunities for various sectors of the tourist industry. This study discusses the economic impact of festivals in the United States with the use of the USDA (United States Development Authority) Forest Service's IMPLAN model. The festivals discussed are two highland games held in the State of North Carolina. These are the Grandfather Mountain Highland Games (GMHG) and the Flora Macdonald Highland Games (FMHG).

Grandfather Mountain Highland Games are the oldest and most well known of the Games in the state. They are held annually on MacRae Meadow, high on the slopes of a mountain called Grandfather Mountain in Linville (Avery County) where the setting closely resembles Scotland. The history of GMHG can be traced to 1892. The MacRae (Highland Scots) family founded the resort town of Linville beneath the towering presence of Grandfather Mountain which they owned. Dedicated to her Scottish heritage, Mrs Morton envisioned a Highland Games on the mountain. In 1956, she founded the Grandfather Mountain Highland Games along with a reporter, Donald F. Macdonald (Ray, 1998).

The Flora Macdonald Highland Games (FMHG) is held in Red Springs (Robeson County) in North Carolina near the heart of the 18th century Highland Settlement (Donaldson, 1986). It involves many descendants of Highlander immigrants. They are named in honour of the Scottish heroine Flora Macdonald who saved the life of Prince Charles Edward Stuart. Prince Charles Stuart had plotted to overthrow the King of England in 1746 (Donaldson, 1986). In 1774, along with her husband, Flora joined the Scottish migration to North Carolina's Cape Fear Region. They settled near Fayetteville and were soon caught up in the Revolutionary War. Flora's husband joined the Scottish loyalists. He was captured and returned to Scotland. Flora joined her husband in Scotland after staying in North Carolina for five years. FMHG was established in 1980.

In 1997, GMHG drew around 30,000 visitors and in 1999 the total number of visitors was estimated to be 40,000 (GMHG Office, 1999). These numbers show the increasing popularity of the games. FMHG has also witnessed increased visitation during the last decade. Besides, each of these Games is run by non-profit organisations with very strong Scottish roots. They share the same basic format. However, each offers a somewhat different sense of community through its size, origin of the attendees, length of events and its respective emphases (Ray, 1998).

This study uses the tourism expenditures from the above mentioned Games to determine their economic impact upon the host regions. Most of the economic impacts of short-term events in tourism are measured in terms of output, total value added, and income (Kim *et al.*, 1998; Burgan & Mules, 1992; Var & Quayson, 1985; Crompton, 2000). Except for very large sporting events or mega festivals, the employment multiplier is not recommended. Such a multiplier assumes a fixed relationship between output and employment. Since festivals are short term, it is highly unlikely that any permanent jobs are created. The Adelaide Grand Prix Study (Burns *et al*, 1986) found that despite the event resulting in over $20 million in income, businesses did not employ significantly extra staff. Restaurants, hotels, car rental firms all reported that they responded to the short term increase in demand by working existing staff longer hours, extra rosters, overtime etc (Burns *et al*, 1986). Besides, the main visitor expenditures analysed for the economic impact of short-term events are incurred on meals, food and beverage, lodging, retail shopping and auto related expenses. Even though admission and registration constitute an important percentage of total visitor spending at the events, they have either been excluded or included to determine direct expenditures. The event organisers do not readily offer information on the use of revenue obtained from admission and registration fees.

Further, while determining the total visitor expenditures, it is important to segregate expenditures incurred by local people. "This question of isolating visitor and local expenditure arises because most of the local spending would have occurred anyway" (David & Schaffer, 1980:14). People are defined as visitors not only because their residence lies outside the impact region, but, more basically, because they are bringing in dollars that are usually spent elsewhere (Davidson & Schaffer, 1980; Brokensha & Tinks, 1985). At the same time, eliminating all local expenditures can eliminate locals who spend money because of the event. Local expenditures can be divided into retained and displaced expenditures (Ryan, 1998). Retained expenditures belong to those residents for whom the event is important and who would not have spent the money elsewhere. Displaced expenditures are not additional expenditures incurred by the locals and are a substitute for spending that would have taken place elsewhere if the event were not happening.

Another aspect that merits attention is the purchase from vendors who sell products or souvenirs at festivals. Vendors residing outside the festival region take their gross revenue with them when they leave. Thus, their pattern of input purchases and factor income may differ from the typical retail profile in IMPLAN. According to Grado *et al*, (1998), both the residence of the visitors and that of the vendors should be taken into account when regional expenditures are being determined. Long & Perdue (1990) found in their study on festivals that failure to account for non-local spending could significantly overestimate the economic benefits to the host community.

Based upon a literature review of short-term events, two commonly used techniques are identified (Fletcher, 1989; Heng & Low, 1990; Kottke, 1988; Wagner, 1997). These are the regional Input/Output (I/O) model and the Social Accounting Matrix (SAM). I/O analysis attempts to quantify, at a point in time, the economic interdependencies in an economy, such as a nation, a state or a county. In this analysis, all economic activity is assigned to one of two types of sectors: production or final demand. The SAM model is similar to the I/O analysis except that the households are considered endogenous to the model. This model has been used traditionally to examine the structures of larger regions and national economies (Pyatt and Round, 1985). It can also be developed for rural economies that are characterised by simple production activities. SAM includes a more comprehensive view of the circular flow of income than a standard I/O model. Other methods that have been used are the inventory/budget method, economic base analysis, and benefit cost analysis (Kottke, 1988). This study uses the I/O model using IMPLAN software to determine the economic impact of highland games upon the host region.

IMPLAN (1996) makes use of I/O analysis with SAM, Social Accounting Matrix (Pyatt & Round, 1985). It has three advantages (Thorbecke, 1985): First, it describes the structure of an economy in terms of the links between production, income distribution, and demand within a region's economy. Second, regional economic data are often gathered by different governmental agencies and stored in different formats, and SAM provides a concise framework for synthesising and displaying the data on a region's economy. Third, it allows for the calculation of regional economic multipliers for estimating the impacts of tourism on production, income distribution, and demand, given the existing structure of the economy.

As with all models, IMPLAN has limitations, particularly in its dependence on fixed historical economic relationships among industries and resource owners. The main assumptions behind IMPLAN (MIG, 1999) are:

1. The production function (an industry's list of expenditures) is assumed to have constant returns to scale. Constant returns to scale means the production functions are linear; if additional output is required, all inputs will increase proportionately.

2   Supplies are unlimited. An industry has unlimited access to raw materials and labour and its output is limited only by the demand for its products.

3. Price changes do not cause a firm to buy substitute goods. A fixed commodity input structure assumes that changes in the economy will affect the industry's output but not the mix of commodities and services it requires to make its products.

4. The proportions of all the commodities produced by that industry remain the same, regardless of total output or change in demand. An industry would not increase the output of one product without proportionately increasing the output of all its other products. In other words, in I/O models such as IMPLAN, an industry or a sector is defined as producing only one output. Thus, one such output could actually be several products produced in fixed proportions.

5. The industry uses the same technology to produce all its products. This assumption applies when data is collected on an industry by commodity basis and then converted to industry matrices. However, IMPLAN offers the advantage of providing comprehensive measures of direct, indirect and induced effects of changes in a complex economy. It develops regional multipliers that can be applied to all the tourism sectors.

The multiplier concept in economic impact studies summarises the economic activity stimulated by visitors, creating additional business transactions, personal income, employment and government revenue in the host community. Output, value added, personal (labour) income and employment are commonly used multipliers in short-term event studies. The use of the employment multiplier is controversial. Since events occur over a short duration, it is unlikely that the industries involved in the event will employ more workers. Rather, current employers work overtime to meet the additional demand for goods and services. In this study, Type I and SAM (Social Accounting Matrix) multipliers are used to determine output, value added and labour income impacts of the GMHG and FMHG visitor expenditures.

The output multiplier represents the value of production required from all sectors for a particular sector to deliver $1 worth of output to final demand. The larger the output multiplier, the greater the dependence of the sector on the rest of the regional economy and the more a dollar turns over in an economy before it leaks out to another sector or region. Value added multiplier estimates the effect on value added generated from the production of $1 of output for final demand. "Value added represents the costs added to the intermediate costs of producing goods and services to form the producer price" (Aruna *et al.*, 1998). The four components of value added are: employee compensation; proprietary income; other property type income; and indirect business taxes. Employee compensation and proprietary income together represent the labour income. Hence Labour income is a component of value added.

Methodology

The tourism expenditures at Grandfather Mountain Highland Games (GMHG) and Flora Macdonald Highland Games (FMHG) are estimated from visitor surveys. The self-administered on-site surveys included specific questions on expenditures associated with the Games visit. The survey at the Grandfather Mountain Highland Games (a four-day event) was conducted in July 1997. The estimated number of entrees over the four-day period was 22,390 (GMHG Office, 1999). Approximately 5000 surveys were distributed over four days and the response rate was 28%. The survey at the FMHG was conducted in October 2000. Estimated total number of visitors was 6800 (FMHG Office, 2000). Approximately 500 surveys were distributed randomly and the response rate was 24%.

The study area for Grandfather Mountain Highland Games region comprises of ten counties: Yancey, Avery, Ashe, Watauga, Burke, McDowell, Caldwell, Catawba, Wilkes and Mitchell. The main reason for this spread seems to be the lack of accommodation offered to the visitors in the Avery County and expensive accommodation rates in the Watauga County which is the next closely involved county because of its wide range of restaurants. Because of the magnitude of the event, the Avery County is not able to meet this demand for accommodation and restaurants. The study area for Flora Macdonald Highland Games region comprises of one county: Robeson.

Based upon the zip code information given by the survey respondents, local and non-local tourism expenditures were identified. The total number of local returns for the GMHG was 24.6% (4208 visitors) and the total number of local visitors at the FMHG was 39.8% (2706 visitors). Expenditures incurred by these people were excluded. Information on vendors was obtained from the Highland Games organisers. All the vendors selling Scottish goods had their residence outside the GMHG and FMHG regions. Hence the visitor expenditures incurred on Scottish goods were dropped from the economic impact. Besides, for lack of detailed information, the admission and registration expenditures were also excluded.

Findings

Total direct visitor expenditures generated at FMHG were $106,075.54. Total revenue generated by the event was $.06 million. GMHG generated $1.8 million in direct expenditures. Visitors spent approximately $.2 million and $.03 million on goods provided by the GMHG and FMHG vendors respectively. These were excluded from the impact. Overall, approximately $.5 million are taken out of the GMHG expenditures. For FMHG, $.04 million are excluded.

To interpret the visitor expenditures as changes in final demand, they were categorised into the following industries in IMPLAN:

1.   Eating and drinking.

2.   Lodging.

3.   Food stores.

4.   Vehicle repair.

5.   Refined petroleum.

6.   Miscellaneous retail.

In IMPLAN these sectors are aggregated into eating and drinking; lodging; food stores; vehicle repair; gas and miscellaneous retail based on the underlying assumption that each sector represents a homogenous production function. The Standard Industrial Classification codes were used when aggregating schemes.

As mentioned earlier, most of the economic impacts in tourism studies have been measured in terms of output, total value added, employment and income. The total output and value added at the GMHG event from the industries studied was $1.6 million and $.8 million respectively. Total labour income was $.57 million. This means that GMHG generated $.57 million in employee compensation and proprietary income. Also, if the GMHG were not to happen, the final demand in the GMHG region would have fallen by .04%. In other words the GMHG region would have lost $1.1 million. The total output and value added at the FMHG event from industries studied was $.08 million and $.04 million respectively. Total labour income generated due to the FMHG event was $.02 million. If the Flora McDonald Highland Games were not to happen, the final demand in the FMHG region would fall by .001%. In other words, the loss would be $.5 million.

Besides conducting an economic impact on the non-local visitor expenditures, a sensitivity analysis is conducted by adding 50% local expenditures to the non-local visitor expenditures. This analysis is based upon the assumption that not all local expenditures are displaced. The output, value added and labour income generated by this group is used for sensitivity analysis.

The output generated at GMHG by including 50% local expenditure was $2,107,703 as compared to $1,600,581 that excluded all local expenditures. The value added was $1,205,503 (inclusive of 50% local expenditures) versus $880,816 (exclusive of all local expenditures). Finally, the personal income including 50% local expenditures was $747,984 versus $569,019, which excluded the local expenditures completely. For the FMHG region, the output inclusive of 50% local expenditure was $86,034 as compared to $82,590 that excluded all local expenditures. The value added was $41,926 (inclusive of 50% local expenditures) versus $37,787 (exclusive of all local expenditures). Finally, the personal income including 50% local expenditures was $26,949 versus $24,566, which excluded the local expenditures completely.

Sensitivity analysis shows that the economic impact increased for both the regions with the inclusion of 50% local expenditures. Excluding all local expenditures has underestimated the economic impact of the visitor expenditures at the GMHG. However, the study did not filter displaced expenditures of the local visitors. The percentage used for retained expenditures (50%) is an assumption; hence the economic impact is based upon non-local expenditures.

Two types of output and value added multipliers were used in this study: Type I and SAM. Type I and SAM multipliers represent the value of production required from all sectors by a particular sector to deliver $1 million worth of output to final demand. Final demand is the ultimate consumption of commodities, including both goods and services. The size of the multiplier does not represent the importance of a given industry for the economy (Aruna *et al*, 1998). It provides an estimate of the impact created if that industry's sales to final demand change. Hence, it is an indicator that can be used to measure the interdependence of sectors.

For the FMHG region, the Type I output multipliers and Type SAM multipliers ranged from 1.07 to 1.27 and 1.29 to 1.42 respectively. The range of the Type I labour income multipliers and Type SAM labour income multipliers was from 1.03 to 1.32 and 1.19 to 1.51 respectively. Finally, Type I value added multipliers ranged from 1.04 to 1.38 and Type SAM value added multipliers were from 1.21 to 1.59.

For the GMHG region, the Type I output multiplier ranged from 1.09 to 1.31 and the Type SAM output multipliers ranged from 1.40 to 1.55. The range of the Type I labour income multipliers and Type SAM multipliers was from 1.03 to 1.32 and 1.26 to 1.61 respectively. Finally, Type I value added multipliers and Type SAM value added multipliers ranged from 1.06 to 1.36 and from 1.30 to 1.61.

Discussion

Approximately 13.5% of total expenditures in admission & registration were lost while determining the economic impact of visitor expenditures at the GMHG. In the case of FMHG, nearly 15.5% were lost. Detailed information is required from the Highland Games organisers to include these expenditures in the economic impact. However, it is important to note that the admission and registration revenues calculated from the on-site surveys were very close to the total revenue figure provided by the GMHG office. This indicates that the sample used for the onsite surveys was random and accurate information was obtained from the visitors. However, the figures did not match for the FMHG. This discrepancy could be due to the inaccurate expenditures listed by the visitors. Another reason could be that the FMHG office overestimated the revenue obtained through ticket sales. Despite these discrepancies, the study provides reliable and important information on the economic impact generated by the GMHG and FMHG.

Even though most of the economic impact studies in tourism have excluded local expenditures, a few studies have questioned the validity of the assumption that the local tourism expenditures are displaced expenditures i.e., expenditures which would probably have occurred in the region on other items (Adelaide Grand Prix, 1986; Ryan, 1998). However, from the tourism industry perspective, any net switching to tourism is relevant, and from an individual tourism perspective both transfer and switching expenditures are relevant because they represent a potential source of business. "As a result, the rational for exclusion of certain types of expenditures is related to the decision maker's frame of inference" (Adelaide Grand Prix, 1986: 12). This study tries to address this issue by conducting a sensitivity analysis since there is a possibility that the tourism spending at the Highland Games is understated. As expected the sensitivity analysis shows an increase in the total visitor spending after 50% of the local expenditures were included.

Further studies should carefully analyse local expenditures. The displaced expenditures of local residents need to be taken into account to reduce the probability of the assumption that all local expenditures are retained. Ryan (1998) talks about retained expenditures incurred by the residents attending the event in their town. They attend because the event is important to them. In this case, their expenditure can be regarded as 'retained' expenditure because it takes place because of the event. By ignoring these expenditures there is a likelihood that the total economic impact is underestimated. This can be avoided by including a question in the survey for the local residents: "If the Highland Games were not happening would you have spent the money elsewhere?" Since the study did not include such a question in the survey to deal with retained expenditures, the total economic impact is underestimated for the GMHG and the FMHG. However, probability of this impact is obtained under the 50% assumption. The comparison shows that assuming 50% local expenditures are retained expenditures the economic impact is underestimated by excluding them.

The issue of detained expenditures also requires attention. Gartner & Holecek (1983) included all local expenditures while asserting that a unique event cannot be a substitute for another local activity and the money spent here could not have been spent elsewhere. However, in this case, the risk of overestimating the economic impact cannot be ignored. Detained or substitute expenditures form an important section of local expenditures and take place irrespective of the event being unique.

Another important issue is the vendor. Vendors residing outside the event region take their money with them. Their revenue is a leakage for the community and hence not included in the economic impact. Scottish goods generated a considerable amount of revenue for the Highland Games. Since all the vendors selling these Scottish goods were from outside the region, their money was lost ($280,196.28 from the GMHG region and $26,651.94 from the FMHG region). Industries manufacturing Scottish goods should be set up in the GMHG and FMHG regions to reduce the influx of non-resident vendors.

The revenue figures calculated for both the Highland Games in this study are comparable with revenue figures acquired for short-term events across the world. Ryan (1998) studied seven short-term events in New Zealand. The total direct spending for these events ranged from $2,200 to $240,000 (Ryan, 1998). Total direct spending for a nine-day tourism exposition in Michigan was estimated to be $1.03 million by local residents (Gartner & Holecek, 1983). Both of the above studies excluded local expenditures from their total spending. However, the multiplier effect is missing in both the studies while this study takes the multiplier effects into account in this study (only the direct expenditures were discussed). It was revealed that the output, value added and labour multipliers are low across both the Highland Games indicating high leakage. The main reason is the low interaction between the various sectors in the host region. However, the SAM multipliers were found to be larger than the Type I multiplier especially for the GMHG region. The magnitude of a multiplier depends upon the degree to which the regional economy is able to retain as income the money spent by visitors. "The smaller the size of the region's economic base, and the fewer the intra-regional linkages, the more goods and services will have to be brought into the region from outside" (Pigram & Cooper, 1980: 19).

Also, previous studies on short-term events indicate that the output impacts are not very important to the host region. The community is more concerned with the impact upon their personal income. In such studies since such effect is not as high as the output impact they are not highlighted in economic impact reports under the assumption that showing greater impacts will create more government support.

In conclusion, Highland Games generate direct, indirect and induced tourism expenditures in the rural regions of North Carolina. However, the multipliers generated by the GMHG and FMHG regions are low. Hence the percentages as revealed by the results are small. Compared to Flora Macdonald Highland Games that generate total direct spending of $106,076. The local residents spent $43,111. Grandfather Mountain Highland Games generate a total direct spending of $1,853,948 ($1.8 million). The local residents incur $534,562 and this is excluded from the economic impact.

Looking at the economic contribution (money generated in the region) of GMHG and FMHG on their respective regions, the results reveal that the Grandfather Mountain Highland Games only contribute .04% to its region and the Flora Macdonald Highland Games contribute .001% to the total economy of its region. Tourism expenditures of the Grandfather Mountain Highland Games are spread over ten counties. The promoters of these Games should try to reduce the number of counties involved in hosting their event besides the Avery County (where the Games are held). This event can make a very significant contribution if more rooms are provided in Avery County and consistent room rates are offered across a few closely involved counties. A concentrated impact is certainly better from the host region perspective. It would increase local involvement, create more jobs and generate more personal income. Tax revenue from the GMHG can be used to promote and develop the other area attractions.

However, while looking at the benefits for the entire state, a policy maker might argue that having a larger economic impact area is beneficial. It will distribute personal income and provide an opportunity for counties enroute to the GMHG to benefit from the event. This is an incentive to market the location of counties that are not frequently visited. They can develop their attractions, lodging and eating & drinking establishments encouraging the visitors to spend the night to and from the GMHG.

Moreover, as the results reveal, the Highland Games involve high-intensity activity and since they are repetitive in nature, the economic impact occurs every year. This provides a continuity effect for the GMHG event. Besides, approximately 50% of the visitors at GMHG and FMHG were repeat visitors. The benefits of repeat visitation are numerous and include:

1. a reduction in the risk of event financial failure;

2. a likely increase in organizational efficiency (improved quality of visitor experience) for subsequent events;

3. reduced uncertainty and risk of future trip decisions;

4. and finally less risk and better time period in which to secure returns from an investment (Adelaide Grand Prix, 1986).

From the out-of-state visitor point of view, a visit to a once only event in an 'unknown' destination is a high risk travel decision, whereas in the case of an ongoing event happening every year where the initial staging has been successful, the uncertainty and risk is considerably reduced. The increasing visitations to the GMHG and FMHG show that they have become credible destinations for visitor attendance in future years.

References

Adelaide Grand Prix, (1986), The Centre for South Australian Economic Studies, *Report* Hyde Park Press Private Ltd, Adelaide, Australia.

Alward, G. E. (1995),"Opportunities for Analysing the Economic Impacts of Recreation and Tourism Expenditures," *Using IMPLAN In: Proceedings of the Annual Meeting of the Southern Regional Science Association*, Philadelphia, Pa.

Ammons, T. (2000), *"Interview,"* Flora Macdonald Highland Games, Red Springs.

Archer, B. (1977a), Bangor Occasional Papers in Economics, 10, Bangor, University of Wales Press.

Aruna, P. B., Cubbage, F., & Hamilton, R. (1998), "Economic Impacts of Forestry on North Carolina" *Report*, Department of Forestry, College of Natural Resources, North Carolina State University.

Bitta, A., Loudon, D., Booth, G., & Weeks, R. (1978), "Estimating the Economic Impact if a Short-Term Tourist Event," *Journal of Travel Research*, pp. 11-15.

Blarcom, B. V. (1997), "The Magnitude of Procedural Errors in Assessing the Economic Impacts of a Short-term Recreation Event in a Small Community, A Case Study," *Travel and Tourism Research Association Annual Conference Proceedings, June*, Lexington, Kansas.

Briassoulis, H. (1991), "Methodological Issues. Tourism Input-Output Analysis," *Annals of Tourism Research*, 18, pp. 485-495.

Brokensha, P. & Tinks, A., (1984), "Adelaide Festival of Arts," *Interim Report on Economic Impact, South Australian Department for the Arts, Graduate Studies Centre*. Elton Mayo School of Management, S. A., Institute of Technology.

Burgan, B & Mules, T. (1992), "Economic Impact of Sporting Events," *Annals of Tourism Research*, 19, pp. 700-710.

Burns, J. P. A., Hatch, J. H., & Mules, T. J. (1986), "*The Adelaide Grand Prix: the Impact of a Special Event*," The Centre for South Australian Economic Studies, Adelaide.

Crompton, J. L., (2000), "*Measuring the Economic Impact of visitors to Sports Tournaments and Special Events*," VA: Division of Professional Services. National Recreation and Park Association.

Davidson, L., & Schafer, W. (1980), "A Discussion of Methods Employed in Analysing the Impact of Short-Term Entertainment Events." *Journal of Travel Research*. Winter 18, pp. 12-16.

Della, A. J., Loudon, D. L., Booth, G.G. & Weeks, R.R. (1997), "Estimating the Economic Impact of a Short Term Tourist Event," *Journal of Travel Research* 16 (3), 10-15.

Donaldson, E. (1986), "*The Scottish Highland Games in America*," Pelican Publishing Company, Gretna.

Faulkner, B. (1998), "*Evaluating the Tourism Impacts of Hallmark Events*" Bureau of Tourism Research, Australia.

Fletcher, A. (1989), "Input-Output Analysis and Tourism Impact Studies," *Annals of Tourism Research*, 23 (2), 514-529.

Frechtling, D. C. and Horvath, E. (1999), "Estimating the Multiplier Effects of Tourism Expenditures on a Local Economy through a Regional Input-Output Model," *Journal of Travel Research*, 37 (4), 324-332.

FMHG Brochure, (2000), *Flora Macdonald Highland Games*, Red Springs, NC.

FMHG Office, (2000), "*Information*," Flora Macdonald Highland Games, Red Springs.

Gartner, W. C & Holecek, D. F. (1983), "Economic Impact of an Annual Tourism Industry Exposition," *Annals of Tourism Research*, 10, pp.199-212.

GMHG magazine, (1997), *Grandfather Mountain Highland Games and Gathering of Scottish Clans*, Forty-second Annual Games, Linville, NC.

GMHG office, (1999) "*Information*," Grandfather Mountain Highland Games Inc., Linville.

Grado, S. C., Lord, B. E. (1998), "Economic Impacts of Conferences and Conventions, *Journal of Convention and Exhibition Management*," 1 (1).

Heng, T. M., & Low, L. (1990), "Impact of Tourism in Singapore," *Annals of Tourism Research*, 17, pp. 408-418.

Johnson, R. L. & Moore, E. (1993), "Tourism Impact estimation," *Annals of Tourism Research*, 20.

Kim, C. W., Scott, D., Thigpen, J. F., & Kim, S. (1998), "Economic Impact of a Birding Festival," *Festival Management and Event Tourism*, 5, pp. 51-58.

Kottke, M. (1988), "Estimating Economic Impacts of Tourism," *Annals of Tourism Research*.

Lickorish, L. L. & Jenkins, C. L., (1997), *An Introduction to Tourism*, Butterworth Heineman, Oxford, UK.

Long, P., & Perdue, R. (1990), "The Economic Impact of Rural Festivals and Special Events: Assessing the spatial distribution of expenditures." *Journal of Travel Research*, Summer, 28.

MIG, (1999), "*Implan Professional Version 2.0 Social Accounting & Impact Analysis Software*," Minnesota IMPLAN Group, Inc.

Mohr T., Fletcher, R. T., & Clabough, T. (1993), "A Comparison of Socio-economic characteristics, Regional Expenditures and Economic Impact of Visitors to Historical Sites with other Recreational Visitors," *Journal of Travel Research*, Summer, pp. 30-35.

Pigram, J. J., & Cooper, M. J. (1989), "*Economic Impact Analysis in Tourism Planning & Development*," New Zealand man & biosphere Report.

Pleeter, S. (1980), "Economic Impact Analysis: Methodology and Applications," Boston: Martinus Nijhoff.

Pyatt, G. & Round, J. (1985), "*Social Accounting Matrices: A Basis for Planning*," Washington DC: The World Bank Press.

Ray, C. (1998) "*Scottish-American Heritage Community and celebrations in North Carolina*," Ph.D. Dissertation. Chapel Hill, North Carolina.

Ryan, C. (1996), "*A Survey of Seven Events and Economic Impacts in Palmerston North. Report*," Massey University.

Ryan, C. (1998), "Economic impacts of small events: estimates and determinants – a New Zealand example," *Tourism Economics*, 4 (4), 339-352.

Taylor, D. T., Fletcher, R. R., & Clabough, T. (1993), "A Comparison of Characteristics, Regional Expenditures and Economics. Impact of Visitors to Historical Sites with other Recreational Visitors," *Journal of Travel Research*, 32 (5), 30-35.

Thorbecke, E. (1985), "The Social Accounting Matrix on Consistency Type Planning Models," *Social Accounting Matrices: A Basis for Planning*, Pyatt, G. and Round, J. (eds), 207-256, Washington DC: The World Bank.

Tyrell, T. J. and Johnston, R. J. (1994), "A Framework for Assessing Direct Economic Impacts of Tourist Events: Distinguishing Origins, Destinations, and Causes of Expenditures," *Journal of Travel Research*, 40, pp. 94-100.

Uysal, M & Gitelson, R. (1994), "Assessment of Economic Impacts: Festivals and Special Events," *Festival Management & Event Tourism*, 2, pp. 3-9.

Var, T. & Quayson, J. (1985), "The Multiplier Impact of Tourism in the Okanagan," *Annals of Tourism Research*, pp. 497-513.

Wagner, J. E. (1997), "Estimating the Economic Impacts of Tourism," *Annals of Tourism Research*.

Festival Tourism in the Caribbean: an economic impact assessment[1]

Keith Nurse

University of the West Indies, Trinidad & Tobago

Introduction

Tourism is the mainstay of most Caribbean economies having surpassed the traditional agro-based and natural resource-based export economy in terms of foreign exchange earnings and employment. Relative to other regions in the world the Caribbean has the highest level of dependence on the industry when tourism receipts are compared with services and merchandise exports. In the ten-year period from 1989 to 1998, the region enjoyed a growth in surplus (i.e. receipts – expenditures) from US$6.5 to $11.3 billion. This was achieved through an annual average growth rate in tourist arrivals of 4.5% and 8% in tourist receipts, which is comparable with international tourism growth. Over the period, tourist arrivals in the Caribbean as a share of total arrivals in the Americas have stabilised at 12.5%. Receipts, on the other hand, have declined from 13.3% to 12.3% (WTO 1999).

The region's continued success is not assured given emerging trends. A large share of the growth in Caribbean tourism is attributed to the significant increase in cruise ship arrivals and the rapid spread of "all-inclusive" resorts. Both tourism products provide for higher levels of quality control within a framework of vertical integration. The downside is that they allow for increased external control, foreign exchange leakages and lower levels of local value-added (Patullo 1996). In addition, the growth in Caribbean tourism in the 1990s is directly related to rapid expansion in Cuba and the Dominica Republic. In comparison, growth in arrivals has been much slower in the Commonwealth Caribbean and the Dutch and French West Indies (CTO 2000).

Caribbean countries are considered relatively high priced destinations. The profitability of most hotels and tourism-related firms are affected by high operation costs due to the large import bill in the industry. These observations signal that the regional tourism industry is losing its competitiveness from a financial perspective. It is also recognized that tourists today are looking for more than just "sun, sand, sea and sex" and thus even the image of Caribbean tourism is under competitive pressure. This is exemplified in the shift away from high-impact mass tourism towards more environment-friendly and community-oriented travel options such as eco-tourism, adventure-tourism as well as cultural and festival tourism.

An analysis of the international experience with cultural and festival tourism suggests that there is much scope for growth. Changes in the tastes and demographics of international travellers are such that there is greater demand for authenticity in the tourism experience and consequently a shift

[1] The findings in this paper are from a study entitled "Festival Tourism in the Caribbean" sponsored by the Inter-American Development Bank.

away from mass tourism (EIU 1993; McCarthy 1992). It also appears to be an effective means by which a country can differentiate its tourism product in the increasingly competitive world of global tourism. This approach calls for a strategy of market segmentation and niche marketing. It also calls for increased investment in the arts and cultural industries to differentiate the local experience and to establish an identifiable "brand".

Festivals are public themed celebrations that exhibit the history, worldview, and social and cultural identity of a community (Getz 1997: 7-8). Festivals are as old as human civilisation and play an integral role in the development of world society. A critical aspect of festivals is the way in which they facilitate creative expression, allow for social catharsis and bolster the cultural identity and confidence of a people. From this standpoint festivals can be an important ally in promoting authenticity in the tourism industry as well as fostering a positive socio-cultural impact (Bushell & Jafari 1996). This is manifest in strong word-of-mouth promotion and the general "good-feel" that they generate. A sustainable festival tourism strategy is therefore reliant on creating a significant psycho-cultural impact.

Festivals have emerged to be an important contributor to the tourism industry throughout the Caribbean. In many territories the peak in tourist arrivals coincides with some event, particularly a musical or carnival festival. This is the case in Trinidad and Tobago, St. Lucia, Barbados, Jamaica, St. Kitts and the Dominican Republic. Festivals throughout the region contribute in a significant way to boost tourism arrivals, visitor expenditures and hotel occupancy rates. Festivals have also made an important contribution because they perpetuate and transplant Caribbean culture and values and influence global culture, media and public opinion. In spite of this contribution to the diversification and the competitiveness of the tourism industry there is little or no published data, with a few exceptions, by the various national and regional tourism authorities.

The synergy between tourism and the arts, entertainment or cultural industries is largely under-researched in the Caribbean. This state of affairs can be explained by the fact that the cultural industries have traditionally been viewed as leisure and recreational activities and not as a commercially viable sector. For example, there are few studies of the business and economic aspects of the music and audio-visual sectors. Another problem is that the demand-pull of the cultural industries tends to be excluded if not minimized in analyses of the tourism industry. This is in relation to both the role of the performing arts in providing entertainment in the hospitality sector (i.e. live performances in the tourism zone: hotels, resorts and restaurants) as well as the contribution of festivals and other events in enhancing the image of a destination.

The economics of festival tourism

Festival tourism can be viewed as a sub-component of the larger phenomenon of cultural tourism. The term cultural tourism is subject to much confusion and varied interpretation. For example, cultural tourism is often viewed as synonymous with heritage tourism, historical tourism, arts tourism or ethnic tourism. There is an element of truth in each term in that cultural tourism can be viewed as including activities such as touring historical, heritage and archaeological sites; visiting art galleries, museums and craft exhibitions; and attending arts performances, live entertainment and festivals. A useful definition is that offered by McCarthy (1992: 2):

> "Cultural tourism describes the phenomenon of people travelling for the sake of experiencing either another culture ("the concepts, habits, skills, arts, instruments, institutions, etc., of a given people in a given period; civilization") or the cultural attractions of particular place (its museums, festivals, galleries, artists, musicians, theatre, architecture, etc.)."

A review of the literature on cultural tourism suggests that a large proportion of the studies focus on heritage sites (e.g. monuments) and the "high" arts (e.g. art galleries and opera). An area that is often neglected is that of live entertainment and popular culture (Hughes 1996). This observation is of particular significance to the countries of the Caribbean in that many of the heritage monuments are institutions of oppression, for example, colonial forts, plantation houses and sugar mills. The heritage of the mass of the population is rendered invisible in historic buildings and monuments. This is so because the heritage and legacy of the masses is celebrated in the popular arts, which embody social protest, affirm social identity and recall psychic memory. The popular cultures of the region embody both celebration and resistance and are sites for the public display, negotiation and contestation of the varied social tensions and struggles of the society against class, race and gender oppression as well as representations of nation and empire. These sentiments are embodied in the following quote from Rex Nettleford (1990: 9):

> "Great Houses standing firm on hillocks overlooking lands where slave villages with houses made of the most perishable materials, may be part of the heritage. But such edifices stand to be used as evidence of the "lack of history" among the vast majority who some would say created nothing. Yet in the absence of such stone-and-mortar structures are other structures carved in the imagination and intellect of the mass of the population. So songs, stories, music, dance, religious expressions and rituals of the people handed down from generation to generation become central to the heritage."

An important feature of popular culture is that it is a major contributor to global culture through the commodification in the cultural industries. Commodification has facilitated globalisation. This has been applicable to several popular culture art forms from the Caribbean. This is evident in the export success of musical genres like reggae, zouk, calypso, meringue, salsa, dancehall and soca (Nurse 1997). It is also the case with the large number of overseas Caribbean carnivals (Nurse 1999). It can be argued that Caribbean popular culture, more than any other feature of Caribbean society, has had the greatest influence in advancing the region's position and stature in the global cultural political economy and consequently, the region's popular culture should be central to the cultural and festival tourism initiative.

> "Perhaps, the best example of people identification with the tourism product by way of heritage promotion is the development of Sunsplash, the reggae festival which attracts certain visitors to Jamaica for that reason and none other, to share in the heritage of popular music which is the creation of the people of Jamaica and now deemed as natural to it as are the sun, the sand and the sea (Nettleford 1990: 9)."

Cultural tourism has emerged to be an important innovation and a new source for competitive advantage in the global tourism industry. The World Tourism Organisation estimated that 37% of all trips have a cultural element (EIU 1993). Increasingly, it is being appreciated that the relationship between the tourism and cultural industries is such that cultural industries generate demand for tourism while tourism generates additional markets and income for the cultural sector (Myerscough 1988).

In instances where the cultural industries create a tourism demand it can be viewed as the "culturalisation" of tourism. Alternatively, where tourism determines the growth of cultural industry then it can be termed the "touristification" of culture (Carlsen & Jafari 1996). The latter generally raises some concern about issues of authenticity in that the tourism enterprise has a long tradition of portraying indigenous cultures in an exotic and imperialist manner. The former is generally viewed in a more positive light in that the cultural tourist of this inclination tends to have a lot of knowledge and experience of the particular art form and thus invests in authenticity. It is this form of cultural tourism that this study explores.

Appreciation of the relationship between tourism and the cultural industries has grown with increased attention to the economic importance of the arts. For example, a British study notes that "the benefits to tourism are the expansion of special interest groups, a new potential clientele, and finally an expanded season as the arts are not dependent on the weather" (Myerscough 1988: 91). The contribution of the arts to the tourism economy was estimated to be 41 % of overseas tourist spending. It is also suggested that arts-related tourists stay 75 per cent longer and spend 64 per cent more per trip (Myerscough 1988: 85-86). The study concludes that arts tourism has a promising future because:

- The trade is a new and expanding market.

- It has an up-market profile.

- Levels of satisfaction are high.

- Willingness to repeat the holiday or take a short break was high.

The benefits to tourism of the cultural industries have gained in recognition on the other side of the Atlantic. In New York, it was estimated that approximately 40 percent of overseas visitors are cultural tourists, in what is measured to be a $2.5 billion industry (Alliance for the Arts, 1997; McKinsey & Company 1997). As in the case of the UK cultural tourists who visit New York tend to stay longer, spend more and have a keen interest in the arts, live performances and festivals. Another example is the case of Ontario, Canada. The Ontario tourism industry strategy projects that:

> "The single greatest emerging motivator for travel in the 1990s is 'understanding culture'; 'cultural, historical or archeological treasures' are also important considerations for people planning a trip. As a result, Ontario's strong arts, culture and heritage environment provides unique opportunities for growth. By building on existing events and festivals, Ontario will be able to capitalize on this growing trend in world tourism (ACTS, 1994: 35)."

There are some very good economic reasons for embracing the concept of festival tourism. The experience with festivals and other cultural events is that they tend to create a tourism demand that is resilient and less susceptible to economic downturns. Festivals have several key economic and social roles:

- As attractions capable of spreading tourism geographically and seasonally, especially to destinations lacking alternative appeal.

- As animators of sites and other attractions.

- As catalysts for infrastructure development, including urban renewal and heritage conservation.

- As creators or enhancers of destination images.

- As alternatives to built attractions and high-impact tourism (Getz 1997: 51-55).

The economic impact of festivals is also quite significant. One of the better-documented festivals is the Edinburgh Festival in Scotland. The festival, which has multiple events, operated on a budget of £5.0 million and generated income of £44 million in festival related activities (e.g. tickets, programmes, merchandise, refreshments at the venues) and £9 million in accommodation, travel and food (Casey et al 1996: 100). A 1992 study in the UK estimated the total annual income of arts festivals to be £40.6 million of which box office receipts accounted for 43.3%, business sponsorship 16.7% and arts funding bodies 17.2% (Rolfe 1992: 70).

Caribbean festivals and tourism

Throughout the Caribbean festival tourism is gaining prominence in the tourism calendar. In many respects this growth is built on the success of a few festivals:

- *Reggae Sunspiash* in Jamaica, which started in the late 1970s and was succeeded by *Reggae Sumfest* in the early 1990s, can be viewed as the pioneer in terms of festival tourism in the Caribbean in the way in which the internationalization of reggae music became a magnet for tourism.

- *Trinidad Carnival*, which is a model to many regional and overseas Caribbean carnivals, has evolved into a festival tourism product and an entertainment industry not from strategic intervention but through an organic process of community development, aesthetic innovation and diasporic relations.

- *Santo Domingo's Festival de Merengue* is an outdoor week-long celebration which was originally sparked by Puerto Rican visitors in the late 1960s and has been fuelled by summer travel by the large diasporic Dominican population.

- The *St. Lucia Jazz Festival* from inception was geared towards creating a demand-pull in a trough period in the tourism calendar. The festival has had strong media appeal and attracts an up-market audience of international and intra-regional tourists.

- The *Barbados Cropover* festival, originally a sugar cane harvest festival, was revived by the national tourism agency in 1974 to fill the void in the tourism off-season. The festival attracts mainly overseas nationals and intra-regional visitors.

- The *St. Kitts Music Festival,* which features multiple genres of music, was started in 1996 to act as a demand-pull for visitors in the low tourist season and to generate media exposure for the tourist destination. Returning nationals and intra-regional visitors are the major patrons.

Each of these festivals is observed to have a significant impact on visitor arrivals, airlifts and hotel occupancy rates with spillover effects on media industries, local transport (e.g. car rentals) and the food, beverage and restaurant sectors. Actual data on the economic impact of these festivals is largely un-documented, however. Where there is data the impact has been considerable.

Economic impact: the case studies

Of the six festivals studied only three festivals (Trinidad Carnival, St. Lucia Jazz and Barbados Cropover) have done exit surveys, which provide quality data on visitor arrivals and expenditures. The following table provides an overview of the economic impact of the festivals.

Table 1   *Summary of economic impact of festival tourism in the Caribbean (1998)*

	Trinidad Carnival	St. Lucia Jazz	Barbados Cropover
Budget US$mn	2.0	1.55	1.021
Visitor arrivals	32,071	9,929	4,428
Share of annual visitor arrivals	9.2	3.9	0.86
Visitor expenditures US$mn	14.08	14.15	2.42
Share of annual visitor expenditures	7.6	4.9	0.34
Cost-benefit ratio: visitor exp./budget	04	913	237
Hotel occupancy rate (%)	95	74.5	53.3
Entertainment expenditures US$mn	3.1	n.d.	0.240
Departure taxes US$mn	0.517	0.099	0.055

The main finding of the study is that festivals create a strong demand-pull for visitors. The best case is that of Trinidad carnival which accounted for 9.2% of arrivals and 7.6% of visitor expenditures for the year 1998. The festival with the next best performance was that of St. Lucia Jazz, which contributed 3.9% of visitors and 4.9% of visitor expenditures. In the case of Barbados the Cropover festival accounted for 0.86% of annual tourist arrivals. The respective share of annual tourist expenditures was 0.34%.

Most festivals impact positively on hotel occupancy levels. The best example of how festivals impact on an off-season is that of St. Lucia where the month of May was converted from one of the worst tourist months to a position where it now enjoys above average occupancy levels (74.5%). A comparable example is the case of Reggae Sunsplash in Montego, Jamaica. When compared with a peak week (first week in February) in the winter tourist season hotel occupancy levels in the week of Sunsplash averaged fourteen percentage points higher for eleven years, 1981 and 1983 to 1992.

The case of the Dominican Republic is also instructive. Arrivals and hotel occupancy levels in Santo Domingo jump in the month of July when the Merengue festival occurs. Over the period 1995 to 1999 the month of July averaged an occupancy rate of 71.7%, which puts it as the third highest month.

In the case of Trinidad Carnival the festival is able to generate occupancy rates above 90%. This is achieved because of the large influx of visitors relative to the small hotel plant in Trinidad.

The festivals make a measurable impact on government taxes. The most illustrative case is that of the Trinidad Carnival. The festival has a large number of visitors and generates departure taxes of US$0.5 million, one-quarter of the budget of the festival. There are other tax benefits. When value-added taxes (15%) are applied to visitor expenditures of US$14.08 government earns US$2.1 million in indirect taxes. The combined effect is that taxes generated by the festival exceed government's initial investment of US$2.0 million by approximately $600,000.

Festivals are not known for generating a large number of jobs or year-round employment, at least not directly. In this study it is notable that:

- The carnival type festivals (Trinidad Carnival and Barbados Cropover) have spawned entertainment industries that generate employment for artists and cultural entrepreneurs during the season and year round.

- During the 1998 Trinidad Carnival the sale of carnival related goods and services amounted to US$3.1 million. In Barbados the entertainment related expenditures for 1998 were $240,000.

- Year round employment is generated in the local and regional hospitality sector in addition to overseas performances in Caribbean carnivals and other festivals throughout the region and in North America, Europe and Japan.

- The indigenous music festivals (the Merengue Festival and Reggae Sunsplash and Sumfest) have also impacted positively on their respective music industries, which are estimated to earn over US$50 million in the export of goods and services.

Media value is one of the key benefits that these festivals provide to the host economy. The St. Lucia Tourist Board estimates that the media value of the Jazz festival is in excess of the budget of the festival. The tourist-inspired festivals have attracted stronger media value than the other festivals. The foreign music genres facilitate easier access to international media and broadcast networks. The carnivals and the indigenous music festivals have found it far more difficult to gain such media value because of the limited exposure the art forms and the genres of music currently attract.

The benefit-to-cost analysis indicates that most festivals have a healthy yield or return on investment. The festival with the highest estimated benefit-to-cost ratio is that of the St. Lucia Jazz festival with 9.1:1. Trinidad Carnival is ranked second with a ratio of 7:1. Barbados Cropover generated a ratio of 2.4:1. These ratios, especially of St. Lucia and Trinidad, appear to be very competitive when compared with top international festivals like the Edinburgh Arts Festival, which generated a benefit-to-cost ratio of 11:1.

General findings

The Caribbean festivals studied have made a significant impact on the tourism sector in terms of creating a new tourism season and/or filling the void in the tourism calendar by boosting airlifts and improving hotel occupancy levels.

Caribbean festivals have done much to generate new tourism demand from the short break travel market, as well as from diasporic and intra-regional tourist, groupings that are largely omitted in tourist marketing plans of most Caribbean tourism organisations.

The spending of festival tourists, which is considered "new" or incremental and counts as an export industry, has been very significant as a share of total visitor expenditure, where the data on visitor arrivals has been documented by exit surveys. Festival tourists are observed to be quite knowledgeable about the art forms and the region's culture and history. Their spending habits are such that they tend to stay longer and spend more on local goods and services than the conventional tourist. They also tend to be repeat visitors and good word-of-mouth spoke-persons. High calibre (e.g. jazz and indigenous music festivals) and unique Caribbean festivals (e.g. carnivals) have an up-market appeal, attract international media and have proved to be a cost effective means to gain media exposure (e.g. publicity) and enhance the image and attractiveness of a tourist destination.

Caribbean festivals have been pivotal, especially carnivals and indigenous music festivals, in the development of an entertainment sector with export capabilities. Festivals give a fillip to the entertainment sector through creating new clients, markets and media exposure. It also stimulates infrastructure development, heritage conservation and investment into the arts.

Festival tourism in the Caribbean makes an important contribution to the wider economy in that it increases government tax receipts, generates employment and sectoral linkages, attracts business sponsorship & cross promotions and has a spillover effect on ancillary sectors like the media and advertising industries, auto rentals and restaurants. Successful festivals build the society's cultural confidence and image of self-worth and identity. In this way it creates a synergistic relationship between the tourism industry and community development.

Governments throughout the region have begun to incorporate festivals in a tourism development strategy. However, policy formulation and related research (e.g. economic impact assessments) have lagged behind and limited efforts have been made to invest in the development and infrastructure in the arts and cultural industries.

Issues and recommendations

The festival context in the Caribbean is such that there are an increasing number of festivals, particularly music festivals. Countries like Barbados and St. Lucia have developed what can be described as a festival tourism strategy. One of the emerging problems associated with this development is the increase in regional competition. This is particularly evident in the proliferation of jazz festivals. The increased competition in festival tourism is also occurring with the carnivals. Countries like St. Lucia, Jamaica, Barbados, St. Vincent and the Grenadines and Antigua have been aggressively promoting their carnivals in the last few years. A problem of product differentiation has begun to arise as most of the carnivals source many of the same artists.

Marketing is one of the critical areas for upgrading among festival organisers. Most of the festivals lack marketing plans with clearly defined target markets and visitor profiles, as well as advertising and promotions strategies. One of the critical issues facing the various festivals is the problem of a shortage of trained personnel in the area of festival management. There is a dependence on foreign expertise in external marketing, artist procurement and stage management. Technical skills such as sound, lighting and stage are competitively procured from within the region.

Financial management and reporting is one of the weakest areas for festival organizers. For example, most of the festivals are not able to communicate effectively the yield and benefits of the festival relative to the costs. Business sponsorship is another weak area of festival management. This is so because the corporate community has had limited experience with festival and arts sponsorship and many festival organizers don't have skills in writing business and sponsorship proposals.

A key recommendation is the creation of a regional association of festival organisations. There is much scope for joint marketing, cross promotions, the pooling of resources and the joint procurement of technical services. The success of Caribbean festivals has been built on the calibre of the artists and the quality of the experience. Most new festivals need a gestation period of three to five years before they show some positive yield and benefit. Festivals require a sizable investment upfront to establish the brand and reputation.

Good festival management and planning requires proper measurement. Government participation or assistance in festivals should involve research and evaluation mechanisms. A key recommendation is that festival organizers need to continuously document and measure the economic impact of the festivals.

References

ACTS (1994), *Ontario's Tourism Industry: Opportunity, Progress, Innovation.* (Advisory Committee on a Tourism Strategy) Toronto, Ministry of Culture, Tourism and Recreation.

Alliance for the Arts (1997), *The Economic Impact of the Arts on New York City and New York State.* (City of New York, Arts Research Center).

Archer, B. (1996), "Economic Impact Analysis" *Annals of Tourism Research* 23 (3), 704-707.

Bushell, R. & Jafari, J. (1996), Developing Cultural Tourism Opportunities. *Annals of Tourism Research* 23 (4), 954-955.

Carisen, J. & Jafari, J. (1996), Culture and International Tourism. *Annals of Tourism Research* 23 (4), 955-958.

Casey, B. *et al* (1996), *Culture as Commodity? The Economics of the Arts and Built Heritage in the UK.* (London, Policy Studies Institute).

OTO (2000), *Main Statistical Report 1999.* Bridgetown, Caribbean Tourism Organisation.

EIU (1993), *The Market for Cultural Tourism in Europe.* London, EIU Travel and Tourism Analyst No. 6.

Fletcher, J. (1989), "Input-Output Analysis and Tourism Impact Studies" *Annals of Tourism Research.* 16, 514-529.

Getz, D. (1997), *Event Management and Event Tourism.* New York: Cognizant Communication Corp.

Hughes, H. (1996), Redefining Cultural Tourism. *Annals of Tourism Research.* 23 (3) 707-709.

Lea, J. (1988), *Tourism and Development in the Third World.* London, Routledge.

McCarthy, B. (1992), *Cultural Tourism: How the arts can help market tourism product; How tourism can help promote markets for the Arts.* Oregon.

McKinsey & Company (1997), *You Gotta have ART!: Profile of a Great Investment for New York State.* (New York, McKinsey & Company).

Myerscough, J. (1988), *The Economic Importance of the Arts in Britain* (London: Policy Studies Institute).

Nettleford, R. (1990), "Heritage Tourism and the Myth of Paradise." *Caribbean Review* 16 (3&4), 8-9.

Nurse, K. (1997), The Trinidad and Tobago Entertainment Industry: Structure and Export Capabilities. *Caribbean Dialogue*, 3 (3), 13-38.

Nurse, K. (1999), The Globalisation of Trinidad Carnival: Diaspora, Hybridity and Identity in Global Culture. *Cultural Studies*, 13 (4).

Patullo, P. (1996), Last Resorts: *The Cost of Tourism in the Caribbean*. Kingston: Ian Rnadle.

Pearse, D. (1981), *Tourist Development*. Harlow: Longman.

Rolfe, H. (1992), *Arts Festivals in the UK*. London: Policy Studies Institute.

WTO (1999), *Tourism Market Trends Americas, 1989-1998*. Madrid: WTO Commission for the Americas.

The Dubai Shopping Festival as a catalyst for tourist development and urban transformation[1]

Hisham S. Gabr

Cairo University, Egypt

Introduction

Research and professional interest in festivals is growing rapidly following the considerable increase in tourism development over the past few decades. This chapter examines one of the most important and "successful" of all festivals, the annual Dubai Shopping Festival (DSF), and focuses on its impact on tourism development and urban transformation in the city. It thereby explores the relationship between festivals and tourism and the way in which these bring about the physical transformation of cities. The aim of this study is to develop a theoretical understanding of the mechanism of the festival-tourism relationship and the potential impact of such a relationship on the tourism industry, on the fabric of the city, and on the urban community at large.

Festivals and special events have occurred since the dawn of civilisation. Special ceremonial events can be traced as far back as the Ancient Egyptian civilisation, when the inaugurations of Pharaohs, as well as other mythical or religious events, were celebrated. Subsequently, similar types of events and festivals have taken place throughout history, but it is only in the last few decades that festivals and events have grown into an independent industry worldwide. With the expansion in the tourism industry and the increasing diversification of tourist behaviour, festivals and events have recently prospered worldwide.

Shopping festivals in particular have developed as a result of the evolution of shopping needs and consumer behaviour. Moreover, they fit in perfectly with the tourism and socio-economic objectives of a country or city. The festive framework within which the shopping activity is set aims at creating an overall ambiance that will induce people to visit a place. Visitors will consequently be tempted to shop and spend their money while having a pleasant experience.

The Dubai Shopping Festival (DSF) has been chosen as a case study to illustrate the role of festivals and events in the development of tourism and to discuss the relationship between festivals and architectural development, urban transformation, and variations in urban life. Dubai City is the capital and main city of the Emirate of Dubai, one of the seven emirates that make up the federation of the United Arab Emirates. This paper describes the Dubai Shopping Festival (DSF) and analyses some of the factors leading to its success. The intention is to emphasise the role of the city's structure and discuss the impact of the festival on tourism development and on the physical and urban transformation of the city.

---

[1] This paper was prepared during the author's secondment to the United Arab Emirates University.

Dubai's shopping festival and special events

Following the industry's accepted standard definitions of events (Richie, 1984 and Getz, 1997, cited in Allen *et al,* 2002), the DSF can be regarded as a recurring hallmark event, whose size and scale transform it into an event that is intertwined with the image and culture of the city of Dubai. Currently, Dubai's name is increasingly associated with the annual shopping festival. The city has built up a reputation as a shopping paradise in the Gulf region. Dubai and its shopping festival have become inseparable.

The festival started as a shopping attraction. However, after several successful years, the festival has grown into a citywide festival, combining shopping with entertainment, cultural and recreational events. This hallmark event actually contains within it several major events, each of which attracts a large number of affluent visitors and which could stand as a festival in its own right. Examples include sporting events, such as the Dubai Desert Classic golf tournament and the Dubai World Cup horse race, cultural events, such as the Global Village, and entertainment events, such as the weekend street parades and the daily fireworks.

The festival is the culmination of joint efforts between the government and the private sector. Several official organisations are involved, including the Department of Tourism and Commercial Marketing, the Department of Economic Development, the Department of Civil Aviation, the Dubai Ports Authority and Jebel Ali Free Zone, Dubai Police, the Nationalisation and Residency Administration, and the Dubai Municipality. The overall efforts are managed by a single committee called the DSF Supreme Committee chaired by the President of the Department of Civil Aviation and Chairman of Emirates Airlines and comprising representatives of major companies and municipal departments.

A unique marketing feature of the festival is its thematic approach. Each year the festival takes on a special theme, which is used as a marketing tool similar to that chosen for a planned thematic conference. Common to all the themes so far is the emphasis on family values. The result is arguably the world's largest family festival. Behind this choice of the family as the festival's underlying theme is the strategic decision to create an image that highlights the festival's suitability for the entire family. As such, this theme echoes the cultural values and traditions of Dubai and the region. The result is a festival that attracts various family members with diverse lifestyles.

The DSF was launched in the winter of 1996 and has attracted millions from around the world every year since. Slogans such as "the world's best brands at the world's best prices," combined with world-class entertainment and sporting events, and record-breaking daily raffles, have put the festival on the international tourist itinerary. The yearly festival, its theme, and its highlight events have been described thus by the organisers:

> "The first Dubai Shopping Festival was held in 1996, from February 15 to March 28. The theme was, "The Most Amazing Festival Ever for Families." The raffle winnings were huge, with 43 Lexus GS300 cars plus 43 kilos of gold.

> The second Dubai shopping Festival was held from March 27 to April 26 in 1997. The theme was, "The Most Spectacular Family Festival on Earth." Again the winnings were enormous with 41 Lexus GS300's and 31 kilos of gold given away over 31 days. Entertainment included international performers, nightly Aqua Fantasia and fireworks shows, and more. Dubai had a citywide carnival atmosphere. Shopping was great with sales and bargains from over 2,000 participating outlets.

In 1998 from March 19 to April 18, the third Dubai Shopping Festival was another hit. The theme was, "Children of the World Meet in Dubai." Prizes included 31 Nissan Patrol Super Safari cars, 109 Lexus GS300s, 46 kilos of gold, and lots more. Entertainment included a nightly Aqua Fantasia Show, the World's Biggest Children's Birthday Party, and Sesame Street Shows. The usual street entertainment and spectacular nightly fireworks over the Dubai Creek were sensational. Vanessa Mae performed at the opening ceremony and the International Children's Orchestra played at the closing ceremony.

From March 18 to April14, 1999, "The Family Get Together of the Millennium," theme attracted many. A Nissan Patrol Super Safari was raffled off every day and 38 kilos of gold were given away over 28 days. In keeping with the theme, events concentrated on family ties, caring, and integrity. Children enjoyed Popeye the Sailor shows, Dolphin shows, Magic Circus, and a nightly Aqua Fantasia show. There were also seminars, workshops and plays for families.

In the year 2000 from March 1 to March 31, the theme, "To Mother with Love," was another Dubai Shopping Festival success. Winnings included 31 Rolls Royce cars, 31 Nissan Patrol 4x4's, and 57 kilos of gold. The Guinness Book of World Records declared it as the largest ever shipment of Rolls Royce cars. Other world record breakers included the world's largest cradle, sofa, mattress, greeting card, crown, and more. Ideal Arab Mother and Ideal Arab Family competitions were held. Disney on Ice, The Smurfs show, Magic Circus, and over 200 street performers entertained the whole city. Dubai Shopping Festival attracted over 2.5 million people that year.

In 2001, from March 1 to March 31 Dubai Shopping Festival ran with the theme, "One World, One Family, One Festival." Raffle prizes were 31 Lexus GS-300 cars, 31 Lexus LX 470 4-wheel drives, 56 kilos of gold, and lots more. One prominent event was the Dubai Desert Classic with the best golfer in the world, Tiger Woods. Performers, like Adnan Sami, Asha Bhonsle, Fairouz, Googoosh, and Julia Boutros entertained crowds. The International Circus, Planet Pepsi, the Family Fun Fair, Dolphin and Crocodile shows, and Monster Trucks entertained children. The event attracted over 2.5 million visitors.

In 2002 for the month of March, Dubai Shopping Festival used the same theme as the previous year, "One World, One Family, One Festival." Entertainment included Shaggy and Artful Dodger, the Gipsy Kings, Layali Dubai concerts, and Caracalla's theatrical play, 2001 Nights. The Dubai World Cup, PGA Golf, and PTA Tennis were some spectacular sporting events that entertained hoards of visitors. Winnings from Lexus totaled 80 Lexus cars and 4x4's plus Dhs 8 million. Other contributions were 35 Nissan Patrol Super Safaris, 40 kilos of gold, and over Dhs. 100,000 from Visa." (Official Website for the DSF, http://www.mydsf.com; retrieved September 2002).

As described in this account, world-renowned golf, tennis, and equestrian events have been held, and internationally or regionally renowned entertainers have joined in the festivities. Furthermore, celebratory events for children, youngsters and adults, for parents and singles, have added a special social dimension to the festival. The give-away raffle surprises exploit the human lure for money. Although the shopping component may seem to be a mere backdrop to the entertainment and other events, it does in fact remain the basis of the festival.

For without the available shopping opportunities in the city, the festival may have not achieved its continuing success.

Both traditional souks and contemporary malls are shopping venues. Shops apply to take part in the festival. The special discounts they offer are usually monitored by city officials to prevent fraud. Dubai offers myriad shopping options. A wide variety of products from all over the world are available and bargaining is allowed. The intermixing of the souks and the malls makes the city truly unique in its shopping opportunities. Newer ultra-modern malls have not replaced the traditional souks, but instead are constructed for a wider shopping audience with diverse lifestyles and needs. The prospects for the potential shopper are great. In support of these shopping venues are the open minimal tax import-export business policies. Jebel Ali Free Zone, the largest in the region and home of many international corporations, acts as one of the main entry points for merchandise and products through its world-renowned port. Products that are unavailable locally can be easily brought to the customer from anywhere in the world at a competitive price.

The motives of festival visitors are multiple. Crompton and McKay (1997) have empirically tested several socio-psychological motivational domains. They found that visitors desire novel experiences, cultural exploration and the acquisition of knowledge, social interaction, and mental and physical refreshment or escape. They also wish to socialise with known groups, to socialise or interact with groups unfamiliar to them, to enhance kinship relationships and family togetherness, and to engage in behaviour reminiscent of that of an adolescent or child. More importantly, their study found significant differences in the relative importance of the motives to different types of events. At the same time, they concluded that some similarities in motives exist across several types of events, hence the importance of multiple motives. Diversity of motives across events and the importance of event specific motives were corroborated by other research (Nickelson & Pearce, 2001), but not enough evidence found to support the existence of similarities in motives across events. Visitor motivation is an intricate area of study, but is extremely relevant to the DSF. Considering the complexity of the DSF and its events, one can expect visitors' motivations to vary in their relative importance but can expect them to fall within the major categories mentioned above.

Not all festival visitors are shoppers, and not all shoppers are festival goers. The recreational tourist is an equally important festival visitor as the shopper. One of the strengths of the festival is that it offers opportunities for multiple activities that go beyond mere shopping. No wonder slogans such as "shopping with an experience" are increasingly used as marketing tools.

The shopping experience and the festival experience

The notion of shopping and its development globally and locally over the past few decades has a lot to do with the proliferation of shopping festivals. If we follow the historical development of shopping, we notice how the local store made way for the suburban shopping centre with its supermarket, which in turn led to the inner city mall with its department stores, and to the ongoing development of the super mall (Thorns, 2002). The transformation in the shopping environment reflects and influences the transformation in shopping needs and consequent behaviour. In essence, shopping has changed from a necessary activity for the satisfaction of basic needs to more of a pleasure and recreational activity that can satisfy higher order human needs. In addition to the typical shopping activities of buying and eating, newer activities include meeting people, watching others and being watched by others and spending leisure time.

The shopping experience has shifted from the classic to the innovative, from the predictable to the unpredictable. Dubai has many types of shopping experiences. The city has the local street, the traditional souk, and the contemporary mall. What is interesting is the shift in the environmental features of these shopping venues during the festival period, as will be discussed below.

A discussion of shopping trends is closely related to the broader conceptualisation of consumption and commodification. Parallel to the development in shopping has been the launch of diverse consumption opportunities that have created a shift in people's lifestyle trends and way of life. The swing from a production oriented society to a consumption oriented one has radically altered the way people spend their time and money (Thorns, 2002).

Newcomers have entered the shopping business and have greatly shaped our shopping experience. The entrepreneurs and big business companies who develop and own or lease the shops in the mall have set the standards and expectations for shoppers. Competition has increased among malls. Advertising has escalated and new ways of attracting shoppers and persuading them to buy have been developed.

The shopping environment has a lot to do with the shopping experience. The streets of the Al Seef, Al Rigga, and Al Muraqqabat areas of the Deira district of Dubai are located close to each other and have developed into busy shopping venues during the festival. Art, sports, and fun activities are held in these three streets. Street decorations are installed. Temporary street shopping kiosks are erected during the festival. These temporary installations have proved to be a crowd-puller. The old gold souk and the historical market, both in the Deira district, are another magnet for specialised shoppers. The malls scattered all over the city are huge crowd-pullers for both dedicated and casual visitors. When attempting to observe the spatial structure and location of these souks and malls within the city's urban fabric, one finds rather interesting juxtapositions but clear territorial boundaries (Figure 1). The distribution of shopping settings in the city suggests the existence of distinct shopping districts that have their own specific character leading to different experiences for the visitor. The study of shopping settings should therefore occur at various levels of the city, similar to what Pearce (2001) has suggested for studying tourist settings in the city. In addition to common research at the city level such as in the geography and spatial structure of cities, a closer look at local levels is needed in order to define individual experiences. The study of shopping at the city level is one thing, but shopping districts occupy another spatial domain that requires specific research attention, as experiences might differ from one district to the other. Even shopping sites on a micro-scale are also deservedly in need of research attention for the same reason.

The festivity of the DSF event is what transforms a mundane shopping experience into a joyful and glamorous one. The events of the festival have attracted more visitors. The business of festivals has boomed worldwide with astounding effects on the economic and cultural life of cities and their citizens. Historically, cultures across the globe have always celebrated special events, whether mystical, religious, or cultural. People have celebrated private events and have shared celebration in public events. Reasons for people to participate in festivals or celebrative events vary. They include rejoicing and celebration, commemoration and remembrance, or the search for enjoyment and gratification. Festival business is considered by many to be a sub-branch of tourism while others consider it a growing industry in itself, justified by the economic and community benefits it brings. Expert professionals, specialised schools, scholarly journals, and dedicated international organisations have quickly evolved to assist in and gain from the opportunities that festivals and special events present.

The International Festivals and Events Association (IFEA) based in the USA with affiliations in Europe, Asia, and Australia is one such professional network. The international journal *Event Management* is an example of a specialised journal in this field.

Figure 1

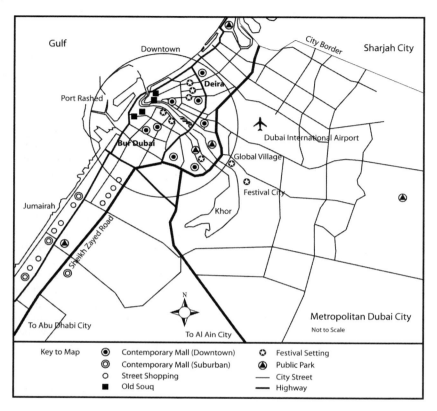

Shopping and festival experiences are a kind of tourism experience. Research suggests that tourism experiences are a function of meaningful and affective comparison between expectations and the actual experience, where the individual differences between tourists are of particular significance (Vitterso *et al*, 2000). Experiences are related to tourists' desires and motivations. In Dubai, the DSF festival reflects people's desire for social interaction, for leisure and entertainment, and for engaging in commodity use.

Regardless of whether shopping is subservient to the festival or *vice versa*, the marriage between the two represents an intelligent marketing vision. Nowadays, the festival is still called the shopping festival, with shopping being considered the backdrop activity. However, one cannot claim that it is an attraction for shoppers alone or for festival goers alone, but rather a harmonious mixture of both. As such, the shopping festival has transformed a shopping experience into a joyful affair. It has led to an expansion in the choices available to attract tourists, and has thereby influenced tourism development in the city.

The festival and urban tourism development

Festival-related tourism is a development tool which the authorities are using as a means to achieve widespread economic growth and cultural rewards. The festival is designed to attract more tourists and increase the benefits of tourism. Consequently, business sales are expected to flourish and the economy prosper. Attention to the potential benefits of tourism is a successful strategy for getting away from relying solely on oil as the major source of income in Dubai. Economic diversification efforts have recently become a national priority for the Gulf States. Dubai was the pioneer of such efforts in the region and has been fairly successful ever since. Perhaps Dubai was driven by the fact that it does not produce significant amounts of oil, but rather relies upon its alliance with the Emirate of Abu Dhabi, the largest producer of oil in the country.

The benefits of the shopping festival for the tourism industry are widespread and considerable, and the socio-economic impact of mega-events has been recognised (Roche, 1992). A discussion of tourism development per se is far-reaching and goes beyond the scope of this chapter. The tourist industry has established itself as a solid professional business and research field and more thorough discussion can be found abundantly elsewhere in numerous books and journals such as *Annals of Tourism Research* and *Journal of Travel Research*. However, relevant to our discussion is the impact of festivals on urban transformation through the mediating role of tourism. Hence, a rudimentary understanding of tourism is central to understanding the need of a city to change.

Adopting the classic push-pull motivational framework for understanding why tourists travel and which destinations they choose (Dann, 1977), Dubai can be viewed as a destination that possesses the pull factor (attraction of destination) and the potential visitor can be seen to possess the push factor (reasons to leave home). Further research suggested that the push and pull factors work simultaneously in the travel decision-making process (Dann 1981; Uysal & Jurowski, 1994), indicating the importance of developing Dubai as an attraction to fulfil its role as the pull side of the equation. It is within this framework of push and pull factors that a discussion of Dubai's attractiveness as a tourist destination is embedded. In its goal to achieve maximum attraction, the city requires sensitive urban transformation.

Therefore, urban transformation partly serves the city's efforts to develop the necessary pull attributes that will, hopefully in the eyes of city developers, give the potential tourist the urge to visit the city, assuming that the push factors are already present. Relevant to this case is the growing discipline of urban tourism since the 1990s, in which tourism and urban studies converge, for an understanding of notions such as city attractiveness, city tourist districts, urban transformations and urban processes (Pearce, 2001; Judd & Fainstein, 1999). Also relevant is the specialised area of study called urban aesthetics, where architects and urban designers collaborate with social scientists to study the attributes that makes a city more beautiful and attractive (Nasar, 1992).

A more recent study adopted a means-end theory to further our understanding of the push-pull theory by emphasising the role of meaning. The study suggested that people make purchase and consumption decisions after evaluating the meanings associated with products such as goods, services, destinations, and ideas (Klenosky, 2002; Gutman, 1982). The means refers to the pull attributes of the destination, and the ends refer to the push forces important to the traveller. The importance of meanings of destinations or of the built environment in general has been emphasised elsewhere in the fields of architecture and environment-behaviour studies (Rapoport, 1990). People interact with environments and the resulting satisfaction with their experience is largely correlated with their positive evaluation or reaction to meanings associated with the place. Meanings at a manifest level reflect the physical observable properties of the destination, while those at a more latent level result from the traveller's experience of the destination (Klenosky, 2002; Rapoport, 1990). Klenosky (2002) concluded from his empirical study on spring break destination choices that a hierarchical relationship exists between the manifest and latent meanings of pull attributes. The physical attributes of the city, such as beaches, specific locations, atmosphere or cultural attractions ultimately led to a higher-level sense of excitement, accomplishment, self esteem, fun and enjoyment, through a medium-level series of motivations such as the desire for novel experiences or the desire to enjoy nature, to learn more and to meet people. This conclusion suggests the need to identify Dubai's pull attributes at various levels;

knowledge that can have significant urban development, marketing, and management implications for the city's future.

With respect to Dubai's pull attributes and their associated meanings, little if any empirical research to date is available. Earlier theoretical propositions have suggested that attributes such as novelty, urban complexity, streetscape qualities, and urban maintenance have attractive qualities for visitors to Dubai (Gabr, 1999). The historical and cultural component represents another potentially attractive attribute of the city (Gabr, 2000). Beyond Dubai, Klenosky (2002) summarised the tourism and travel literature on empirical studies that examine the push and pull factors. According to his review, major pull items were hospitality and service, historical, cultural, and sport activities, safety and security, culture, education, novelty, and cosmopolitan environment and facilities. Interestingly, these items are all claimed by marketing and development to be part of the image of Dubai. These pull attributes have arguably considerable appeal to potential visitors. The relative significance of these pull attributes can differ among visitors. Only future empirical research can test the validity of these propositions in the case of Dubai.

Another important theoretical contribution to this discussion is the concept of sustainable tourism. The fundamental premise of sustainable tourism is that transformation should serve the present needs of tourists, tourism businesses and host destinations while protecting destination resources, and maintaining cultural integrity and ecological systems for the future (Middleton, 1998). One can argue that rejuvenating cities through the use of festivals can contribute to sustainable tourism if depletion of resources is prevented.

This can be difficult to achieve and easy to overlook. Although not explicitly mentioned, Dubai's tourism marketing efforts implicitly pay attention to sustainable values. The importance of heritage is implied by the preservation of historical buildings and the promotion of traditional culture and morals is supported by the family values theme of the festival. The city adapts to the festival events in a cycle of sustainable development that maintains its vibrancy and vitality. The city, in response to tourist development strategies, adapts by changing its fabric and transforming its urban pattern, thus affecting the life of its citizens and visitors.

Festivals and urban transformation

The study of urban culture and urban form illustrates the concept of urban transformation and the dynamic nature of cities. Urban transformation does not only serve tourist development. Cities have developed to serve common functions and common purposes, to encompass human activities and encourage human associations, to further human participation in cultural processes and to represent human culture (Mumford, 1989). Cities have transformed in response to changing functions and purposes such as building needs, social factors, and political ideologies to name a few. In successful cases, the fabric of the city moulds itself to accommodate changing activities. In cases of failure, the fabric of the city is detached from human meaning and behaviour. Dynamic socio-economic and cultural factors in our modern age have speeded up the rate of urban transformation and taken it to levels and forms never experienced before.

Visitors to the Dubai Shopping Festival are a mixture of local residents of the city and foreign tourists. Tourists include international visitors, regional tourists from Arab and Gulf States, some of whom may even drive to Dubai, and local tourists from within the country. The marketing strategy of the DSF organisers has gone beyond the local market by targeting global markets in order to attract the affluent and enthusiastic shopper from around the world. Advertisements for the city and its festival have appeared in many media, including global television and satellite channels such as CNN and others. The city has sought to create an image that supports its economic objectives and that matches the shopping festival's goals. The predominant image of the city has been profoundly intertwined with the marketing scheme for the festival. The image of Dubai as the commercial city of the Gulf is one such predominant image that is growing in popularity. Although other reasons exist, this commercial image is thought to be crucial for attracting visitors to the festival. To create the desired image, the city has had to transform and evolve in support of the elements making up the image. The Al-Maktoum family, the ruling family of Dubai Emirate, has long been trying to transform the city into an international cosmopolitan business centre, with all the necessary amenities but without some of the problems associated with city life such as crime and theft. Their perceptive vision has been vital for the rapid, smooth, and farsighted transformation of the city. This city endorses the image of a safe haven for dwellers and families seeking a decent way of life. The relatively limited size and population of Dubai compared to larger metropolitan cities has helped in achieving the desired image. The demographic characteristics of city dwellers have contributed to the achievement of the image. The majority of the city dwellers are expatriates who have moved to Dubai to seek a better place to live and work. They are psychologically geared to supporting the government's efforts for building a safe and financially viable city. The UAE nationals are the minority but embody a culture of friendship, tolerance and kindness. The city's mix of cultures is remarkable, as is the way in which the different sectors of the population have rallied around a common purpose, that of raising the standard of living for all its inhabitants, whoever they may be. Another remarkable feat of the city's transformation is the very short time it took the city to develop.

Forty years ago, the city was a tiny town amidst the desert. Eighty years ago, the city was a cluster of primitive dwellings scattered in the desert.

Image, as a psychological construct, is a crucial element in understanding the relationship between the festival and tourism on the one hand, and the city's form on the other. It forms the link between the desire for pull attributes and actual urban transformation of the city. The study of the images associated with places, together with image formation, structure, application and influence, has been a popular theme in psychology, marketing, architecture, and environment behaviour studies. Classic theories of the image of cities have pointed to the importance of legibility components such as landmarks, districts, and nodes in comprehending the spatial and cognitive structure of the city (Lynch, 1960). The cognitive image one has of a city is influenced by the image one has of the physical structure of the city. A legible city is assumed to positively affect users. Several key buildings that have recently been built have become landmarks of this kind. The twin Emirates Towers downtown and the Burj El Arab Hotel along the coast are two of the better known ones. They have had a notable impact on people's structural image of the city. In fact, the silhouette of Burg Al Arab has been chosen by the Dubai Transportation Department as the city's logo on all new vehicle license plates. These two buildings in particular have transformed the image of the city from one of youth and modernism to one of maturity and postmodernism. Many other modern buildings have assisted in creating such a transformation, including banks, hotels, office buildings, residential towers, and, particularly relevant to the festival, a large number of shopping malls. The city prides itself on its urban development and exhibits it through the media. Media advertisements select some of the most prominent examples of architecture and urban development as images to attract viewers. Image formation, which can be close to or far from reality, has often raised questions of authenticity, particularly in tourism (Hughes, 1995). However, previous tourism research has supported the use of these elements as significant predictors of image perception (MacKay & Fesenmaier, 1997).

Kevin Lynch's seminal work has not only been important in urban design but has also been conceptually and methodologically linked to tourism studies (Pearce & Fagence, 1996). Particular linkages useful to festival research include the study of cognitive mapping, visitor orientation, consumer behaviour, market research assessment, aesthetics for tourism, destination image and choice, marketing and promotion of places, and heritage management. With respect to destination image in tourism research, Pike (2002) reviewed 142 papers that analysed destination images from

1973 to 2000. Only 26 of those papers (18%) studied the city as a destination. Most of the remaining papers conducted research on a wider scale, at the level of provinces, states or countries, while 23 papers focused on a narrow scale, at the resort area level. Apparent from this review is the centrality of the destination's image for the traveller's decision making, and hence the importance for destination marketers to develop favourable images. Common and central to image studies in tourism, urban design, and environment behaviour studies, and as indicated earlier, is the comparison made by the traveller between his or her expectation of the destination, and the actual perceived experience of the destination. Satisfaction with the destination experience should result from a positive congruence between the traveller's expectation and the real experience. On the other hand, dissatisfaction might result from a mismatch between expectation and reality.

The physical characteristics of a city's transformations and the meanings attached to them, from which marketers develop favourable images, can additionally be understood using Rapoport's (1990) classification of fixed feature, semi-fixed feature, and non-fixed feature elements. City malls, hotels and restaurants are examples of fixed elements.

Streetscape decorations, public space beautification and landscape embellishment are examples of semi-fixed or movable elements. They can be removed at the end of the festival. Parades, public gatherings and outdoor activities are examples of non-fixed elements. The transformation of the city involves a combination of all three types of features. The built environment is composed of the buildings, the furniture and the behaviour of people. People attach meaning to all three types of features, but particularly salient are the meanings derived from the semi-fixed and non-fixed features. Once streets are decorated prior to the festival for example, the entire city's image is transformed. Expectations rise. Local visitors to the city immediately have high expectations of their festival experience. Comparisons with previous years are made. Plans are made to visit the festival. The hosts, particularly the shop owners, start to get ready both psychologically and commercially. Watching parades, street performers, artistic displays on sidewalks or fireworks, for example, may convey to people feelings of joy and celebration, social interaction and togetherness.

The city has had to transform itself to provide the necessary means for the festival and related tourist activity. Conversely, the festival has transformed the city to accommodate its events and visitor requirements. The relationship between festivals and urban transformation is a reciprocal and mutual relationship. For a shopping festival to work requires the harmonious interplay and fine tuning of several key elements in the city. Infrastructure is one vital element. The city's world renowned new airport, the well planned city streets and highways, the highest quality telecommunication network, are all relatively recent elements of the city's infrastructure and they are continually being transformed and improved. Newer highways and streets are being built, the airport is expanding, and telecommunications are continually updated. A business oriented culture and friendly hosts are other vital elements. The human element combines with the physical element to achieve a harmonious blend.

Therefore at a planning level, the city's structure and fabric are being transformed in accordance with the rulers' vision. However, the city continues to be transformed in a different way, specifically for and during the DSF. It is amazing how the city of Dubai beautifies itself in preparation for the festival, by allocating most of its architectural and urban resources to the festival and its visitors. The visitor who comes to Dubai during the festival period will undoubtedly observe numerous additions and changes to the normal streetscape and urban settings of the city. Glamorous streetscape features and advertisement boards glisten at night. Already attractive flower displays are enhanced with the addition of newer colourful plants. The use of the city's public spaces during and before and after the festival illustrates their importance for accommodating changing activities. The Khor's shorefront with its promenades, public parks, and waterway receives huge numbers of people enjoying festival rides, watching fireworks and parades, or strolling about in the evening. The Khor, which has few shopping venues per se, plays its role in the festival events. It acts spatially and symbolically as a central organising element to the festival events, just as it is central to the city's urban pattern.

Plans are underway for building the Dubai Festival City, a large urban mega project that provides additional specific amenities and building resources for festival events. The programme includes provision for several huge theme parks and hotels. A key site along the Khor has been designated for the project, which is planned to be completed in phases. In recent years, the Global Village, one of the most important festival venues, which draws thousands of visitors and creates crowded streets, has been held in a tent-like structure temporarily put up for this purpose. The site was along the Khor at the edge of a public park. This transformation is of a temporary kind; however, the venue has proved to a huge attraction for families from all walks of life.

Interestingly, the preserved historical sites in Dubai are rarely used in the festival, in contrast to common practice (Janiskee, 1996). The Dubai Museum and the house of the "father" of the city, the late Sheikh Rashed Bin Maktoum, are regular destinations for visitors. Efforts are underway to study the utility of historical sites during the festival while preserving their fragile fabric and sense of historical dignity.

The architecture and the urban and landscape environments of the city therefore play an important role as the setting for the festival's events. They are the stage upon which urban life takes place. They are responsible in shaping the character of the human activities. Congruency between the setting and human behaviour is essential for successful human-environmental interaction, which is an important ingredient of city life. Elements other than those related to the physical environment are just as important, and these include urban management (cf. Chakrabarty, 2001), event management, and marketing (cf. Allen *et al*, 2002). This raises the subject of how to identify the overall factors for festival success and evaluate their relative importance. This paper by no means underestimates the importance of non-environmental factors. It simply draws attention to the role of the physical environment in city tourist development.

Conclusions

As discussed in the previous section, the urban resources of the city are important for the success of the festival in that they shape our shopping and celebratory experiences. These urban resources are transformed to serve the requirements of the festival and the visitors' needs. Urban transformation is subservient to tourist development goals. In addition to the supporting factors, a major reason for a festival's success has to do with the variety and diversity of the opportunities it offers, and their receptiveness to user needs. The opportunity to do something is a precursor for actually doing it. Therefore, the urban landscape and the opportunities that it provides for shopping and festive activities form the setting in which events can occur. The city's change has been argued to be an issue of image formation, which is one major element for attracting or "pulling" potential visitors. How Dubai transforms its image, how visitors perceive this image and how they actually experience their visit to the city remain open-ended questions for future research.

Needless to say, the discussion does not imply that urban transformation only results from tourist development; it merely considers its potentially large impact on the city. City developers and tourist developers should work together to establish urban development strategies and architectural and physical plans that account for shopping festival activities. In particular, they should give careful consideration to urban spaces that act as stages for many of the semi-fixed features that are prominent in the festival. Hotels, resorts, and other fixed feature elements are just as important. However, by having spaces and structures that house temporary events, marketers and developers have the luxury to design dynamic events as per different occasions and markets. Moreover, the city becomes increasingly responsive to the changing needs and wants of ever-changing visitor profiles. A city without opportunities for the semi-fixed and non-fixed elements would fail to cater for events of a dynamic nature such as the shopping festival. The streets, the sidewalks, the public parks, and urban plazas are examples of city elements that can house the changing events. In essence, attention to and provision of public space as opposed to private space is vital for an energetic city. People's right to access city spaces, the Khor and the beaches is essential for the success of the shopping festival experience.

However, successful shopping festivals cannot succeed in isolation. Several factors need to be present to support and complement the festival's success. Thinking more broadly, the success of the Dubai Shopping Festival cannot be disentangled from the forces shaping global economic development that restructure known definitions of consumption and commodification. The reshaping of the consumption versus production equation with the introduction of a range of consumption experiences and opportunities in urban life has fuelled the business of commodification. As Thorns (2002) has pointed out, the shift in economic activities from large-scale rigid production to small-scale flexible runs, from a smaller selection of commodities to a larger and more varied selection, from similarities among commodities to differences, from standardised items to specialised ranges, and from mass markets to niche markets have virtually created the political and economic framework within which wider shopping experiences are possible. One can therefore argue that when certain factors exist to a sufficient degree, festivals of all kinds can be useful vehicles for rejuvenating and revitalising urban tourism serving local and foreign visitors as well as the hosts.

Compared with the Dubai Shopping Festival, few festivals and hallmark events seem to have such a huge impact on one city, particularly a cosmopolitan one. Because of its success, a less popular summer festival has been put in place. This latter caters to the local tourist market and attempts to revitalise an economically sluggish summer season. The urban transformations of the city offer opportunities for social interaction, congregation, for being outdoors and being with one's family.

It is hoped that this chapter will encourage future research in the area of urban transformations resulting from festivals and tourist development. Much research is required to understand the mechanisms of festival success and their effects on the city. Another area of research could be the motivations of visitors to Dubai. While it is suggested that urban tourism reconfigures urban areas, the process by which destinations emerge or develop needs in-depth research efforts. Pearce (2001) and others have summed up the interest and need for urban tourism research and have proposed a theoretical framework that accounts for the various levels of urban impact, from that of the tourist site at one extreme, up to the tourist district level and the city level, and finally up to the regional, national and international level. Recent conferences have also called for research into urban tourism and its role in reconfiguring urban areas (Buhalis, *et al*, 1999). Research is also required specifically in Dubai to identify the city's pull factors, their importance and influence on tourists. Integrating research from various disciplines is to be encouraged. Instead of reinventing the wheel, much can be learnt from relevant theories and applications from other disciplines, and these can in turn be developed further.

This chapter has drawn attention to the impact of shopping festivals upon urban structures and transformations. Cities do change all the time. Dubai's path of change has turned it into a cosmopolitan city for the 21st century that is trying to balance progress with culture, modernity with tradition, and business with pleasure. Whether the development efforts of the city will continue to achieve something or not remains to be seen in the future. Nevertheless, the urban and social ills afflicting most big cities are just around the corner unless the necessary precautions are taken in time. The first signs of this, such as congested streets, suburban sprawl, environmental degradation, promiscuous activities, employment difficulties and social imbalances are already in evidence, but fortunately in a primitive form. Only the vitality and support of the government, city dwellers and visitors, combined with diligent planning, appropriate policies, and visionary strategies, can maintain the city of Dubai as an attractive liveable settlement capable of prosperous transformations.

References

Allen, J., O'Toole, W., McDonnell, I., & Harris, R. (2002), *Festival and Special Event Management*. Milton, Australia, John Wiley.

Buhalis, D., Maitland, R., Viveiros, L. (2000), Urban tourism. *Annals of Tourism Research*, 27 (1), 229-231.

Chakrabarty, B. K. (2001), Urban management: Concepts, principles, techniques, and education. *Cities*, 18 (5), 331-345.

Crompton, J. L. & McKay, S. L. (1997), Motives of visitors attending festival events. *Annals of Tourism Research*, 24 (2), 425-439.

Dann, G. M. S. (1977), Anomie, ego-enhancement and tourism. *Annals of Tourism Research*, 4, 184-194.

Dann, G. M. S. (1981), Tourism motivation: An appraisal. *Annals of Tourism Research*, 8, 187-219.

Gabr, H. (1999), Qualities and strategies of urban aesthetics in UAE cities. *Proceedings of Planning & Urban Development in GCC Conference*. University of Qatar, Qatar, pp.29-42.

Gabr, H. (2000), Heritage and Architectural Preservation for Tourist Development: Reflections on Historic Bastakia District in Dubai, UAE. In Mike Robinson (Ed.) *Tourism and Heritage Relationships: Global, National and Local Perspectives*. Reflections on International Tourism Conference. University of Northumbria at Newcastle & Sheffield Hallam University, Sheffield, pp.197-210.

Getz, D. (1997), *Event Management and Event Tourism*. New York, Cognizant Communication Corporation.

Gutman, J. (1982), A means-end chain model based on consumer categorisation processes. *Journal of Marketing*, 46, 60-72.

Hughes, G. (1995), Authenticity in tourism. *Annals of Tourism Research*, 22 (4), 781-803.

Janiskee, R. L. (1996), Historic houses and special events. *Annals of Tourism Research*, 23 (2), 398-414.

Judd, D. R., Fainstein, S. S. Eds. (1999), *The Tourist City*. New Haven, Yale University Press.

Klenosky, D. B. (2002), The "pull" of tourism destinations: A means-end investigation. *Journal of Travel Research*, 40, 385-395.

Lynch, K. (1960), *Image of the City*. Cambridge, MIT Press.

MacKay, K. J., Fesenmaier, D. R. (1997), Pictorial element of destination in image formation. *Annals of Tourism Research*, 24 (3), 537-565.

Middleton, V. T. C. (1998), *Sustainable Tourism: A Marketing Perspective*. Oxford: Butterworth-Heinemann.

Mumford, L. (1989), *The City in History: Its Origins, its Transformations, and its Prospects*. San Diego, Harcourt.

Nasar, J., Ed. (1992), *Environmental Aesthetics: Theory, Research and Application*. Cambridge, Cambridge University Press.

Nicholson, R. E. & Pearce, D. G. (2001), Why do people attend events: A comparative analysis of visitor motivations at four South Island events. *Journal of Travel Research*, 39, 449-460.

Official Website for the Dubai Shopping Festival
http://www.mydsf.com/about_dsf/dsf_home_tpl.asp?mode=DSF retrieved September 2002.

Pearce D. G. (2001), An integrative framework for urban tourism research. *Annals of Tourism Research*, 28 (4), 926-946.

Pearce, P. L., Fagence, M. (1996), The legacy of Kevin Lynch: Research implications. *Annals of Tourism Research*, 23 (3), 576-598.

Pike, S. (2002), Destination image analysis-a review of 142 papers from 1973 to 2000. *Tourism Management*, 23, 541-549.

Rapoport, A. (1990), *The Meaning of the Built Environment: A Non-verbal Communication Approach*. Tucson, AZ, Arizona University Press.

Richie, B. J. R. (1984), Assessing the impact of hallmark events: Conceptual and research issues. *Journal of Travel Research*, 23 (1), 2-11.

Roche, M. (1992), Mega-events and micro-modernisation: On the sociology of the new urban tourism. *British Journal of Sociology*, 43 (4), 563-600.

Thorns, D. C. (2002), *The Transformation of Cities: Urban Theory and Urban Life*. New York, NY, Palgrave Macmillan.

Uysal, M., Jurowski, C. (1994), Testing the push and pull factors. *Annals of Tourism Research*, 21 (4), 844-846.

Vitterso, J., Vorkinn, M., Vistad, O.I., Vaagland, J. (2000), Tourist experiences and attractions. *Annals of Tourism Research*, 27 (2), 432-450.

Porto 2001, European Capital of Culture: re-contextualising the event in a global competitive environment

Paula Alexandra Malta
Aveiro University, Portugal

Maria Inês Pinho
Porto Polytechnic Institute, Portugal

José Escaleira
Viana do Castelo Polytechnic Institute, Portugal

Introduction

Cities and culture are referred to in reflections concerning contemporary social changes as two centralities in reconfigurations of territories, societies and ways of life (Fortuna, 1997; Fortuna *et al*, 1999, Santos & Abreu, 2000). A broad, if not universal shift from rural to urban society has long been acknowledged in the international arena. Most recently, the World Bank (2000) emphasised that within a generation the developing world will be predominantly urban and the number of urban residents in developing countries will double, making the scale of this urbanisation unprecedented. In the European Union, about 80% of the population lives in cities and towns. And yet, the implications of urbanisation are not limited to demographic considerations alone. These developments are just one of the dimensions of the ongoing round of global restructuring which involves enormous changes regarding urban areas and puts them in the front line of development processes. Cities and towns not only are growing in size and number, they are also gaining new influence and power.

Cities' centrality – a territorial centrality – results from the fact that, within today's world the established political and economic networks and systems privilege cities as nodes that are interconnected as 'centres of the world' (Santos e Abreu, 2000). Some conceptions of globalisation processes downplay the concept of 'nation' and make cities pre-eminent players in the global world economy.

The global restructuring of social, political, and economic relations implies changes in the way cities are governed (Harvey, 1989) and consequently shaped. Literature in social sciences speaks about a shift from government to governance, a reconfigured conceptualisation resulting from three broad trends and developments.

First it is suggested that a process of 're-scaling' is taking place, with nation-states typically devolving control from the national level to municipal and regional tiers. Here, new 'partnership' institutions of urban governance have taken on greater authority and autonomy in policy-making for urban areas, such as in economic development, social services, the provision of infrastructure, and spatial planning. Second, policy emphasis has typically shifted from demand-oriented redistribution toward supply-oriented competition. This had been associated with cities seeking to define, develop and display claims of 'competitive advantage' in their media image, for tourism and inward investment in the global 'marketplace'. A third and associated development has been the outsourcing and transferring of public sector powers, resources and functions to non-state and quasi-state bodies. Here it is argued that greater efficiencies can be achieved through the adoption of private sector management models and practices.(Purcell, 2000):

Improving cities' competitiveness places big demands on urban governance and management. In this context the urban agenda is also deepening to encompass further elements such as the integration of culture. In fact, some dimensions of the global restructuring processes described above are focused both on the consolidation of the production system and mass consumption and on the development of a leisure culture with two major dimensions – cultural industries and cultural tourism. Among other factors, changing demographics, increasing wealth and emerging technologies have raised access and demand for both material and immaterial forms of cultural consumption such as arts, music, performing arts and museums, as well as with festivals (Haselbach, 2002). This has brought about important changes for cities, namely the affirmation of cultural leisure as an object of mass consumption, with providing and enabling such consumption seen as another function that the urban system has to incorporate in its planning and management strategies.

The recent addition of "World Heritage Cities" to the United Nations Educational Scientific and Cultural Organisation (UNESCO) International Convention for the Protection of the World Cultural and Natural Heritage has encouraged the recognition of cityscapes as another key link between cities and culture. As stated in the UNESCO Recommendation of 1976, the safeguarding of historic areas and "their integration into the life of contemporary society is a basic factor in town planning and land development".

Santos & Abreu (2000) consider that culture's centrality crosses both material and immaterial components and is engraved within the idea of increasing dematerialization of economies and societies, progressively marked by communication and information processes. Richards (2001b:2) uses the expression "culturalisation of society" referring to the fact that "everyday life is increasingly characterised by a de-differentiation of previously distinct social and cultural spheres, with the emergence of an economy of signs, the convergence of 'high' and 'low' culture, 'art' and 'life'. Objects and people have become increasingly mobile, and boundaries between previously distinct cultures are increasingly being eliminated".

These ideas resonate, for instance, in the establishment of the UNESCO World Decade for Cultural Development (1988-97), a programme emphasising the importance of conserving cultural heritage through both the promotion of identity and cultural diversity and the stimulation of economic development.

Another example of the explicit recognition of the increasing centrality of culture in a European context is its inclusion since 1991 in the Maastricht Treaty on European Union. Here it is recorded that an aim of the European Union (EU) is to contribute to "the flowering of the cultures of the Member States" (Article 3 of the Treaty on European Union). Maastricht gave a specific basis for a legal action on culture. In 1997, through the inclusion of a new article in the Amsterdam Treaty, which states that "the Community shall take cultural aspects into account in its action under other provisions of this Treaty", the foundations upon which EU involvement in culture is undertaken are strengthened. Measures in the sphere of culture belong now to the list of the Community activities foreseen in support of the EU's overall objectives. Thus, culture is now seen to be one of the Union's major objectives and the EU must take cultural aspects into account in all of its activities.

Although there was no specific cultural policy, since the early 1980s the EU has brought about several measures actively and specifically targeted at the field of culture. The European City of Culture community action is just an example amongst the various cultural actions undertaken. And yet, the EU action on culture, besides the direct measures affecting the sector, also proceeds from non-specific measures. Indirect support has come through mechanisms and measures resulting from articulation with the key principles and institutions of Community integration (e.g. subsidiarity, sustainable development and European citizenship) and indirect actions resulting from the application of other EU policies (e.g. regional policy, research and development, education and vocational training). In fact, in accordance with the subsidiarity principle, the European added value of EU cultural interventions lie in the actions that cannot be sufficiently undertaken at Member State level and therefore, by reason of scale and/or impacts, are better implemented by the Community. As a result of an acknowledgment of culture's contribution to job creation, to the strengthening of regional cohesion and to increasing the effectiveness of regional distinctiveness, important financial aid is earmarked for cultural development through the structural funds, particularly the European Regional Development Fund (ERDF), in the context of the regional policy. Roseta (1998) outlines that "the Union can influence member's national cultural policy, through recommendations adopted by the European Council, which although not binding, can have legal effect and can be useful instruments for guiding national cultural legislation". Nevertheless, these measures don't require the harmonization of Member States' cultural policies.

This recent high priority afforded to culture at the EU is reflected in the implementation of several community actions specifically aimed at assisting aspects of culture. These include 'Kaleidoscope' in support of artistic and cultural activities (1996-98), 'Raphael' on cultural heritage (1997-2000), 'European Cultural Month event', and the 'Culture 2000' research and development programme. The Culture 2000 programme represented one of the most significant and specific measures launched by the EU following its definition of the first European Community Framework in support of culture (2000-04). The Culture 2000 programme objective is to contribute to the promotion of a cultural area common to the European citizens. It considers culture to be "both an economic factor and a factor of social integration and citizenship; for that reason, it has an important role to play in meeting the new challenges facing the Community, such as globalization, the information society, social cohesion and the creation of employment".

Indicators of supply and demand for cultural tourism in Europe

For many there is little doubt that cultural tourism (if often broadly and somewhat vaguely defined) is one of the largest and fastest growing segments of global tourism. The World Tourism Organisation (WTO) identifies cultural tourism as one of the most significant demand trends in the tourism market, with a growing number of special interest travellers who identify and rank the arts, heritage and/or other cultural activities in their top five reasons for travelling.

Looking at some of the available data regarding cultural supply, many examples underline the growing importance of culture and cultural attractions in modern societies. In the museum area "over €600 million were invested in new attractions in the UK in the year 2000. In Spain, the number of museums has doubled during the post-Franco era" (Richards, 2001:3). A comparable pattern appears when analyzing Portuguese figures. The number of museums open to the public rose from 229 in 1985 to 303 in 1995 (INE, 1985, 1995). Santos (2001) stresses that, in Portugal, the increasing social awareness of the value concerning cultural heritage is accompanied by a reinforcement of the financial support allocated to the national heritage. From 1985 to 1995, Portuguese expenditure on national heritage rose by 144.7%. Cultural production is also reinforced by the rapid increase in festivals and cultural events. In 1993, the EIU (1993: 37) stressed that "cultural destinations which do not offer events tend to lose out to those which offer a specific reason for an immediate visit" and suggested that the failure of Italian art cities to develop international event tourism was certainly influencing the stagnation of tourism results in Italy. Janiskee (1994) points out that there has been an annual increase of 4.6% in the number of festivals and events staged in the US since 1930 with almost a 40% increase just in the decade of the 1980s. More recently, Getz's (2000) work on festival and event based tourism also bears out the high intrinsic level of interest in cultural events.

Going hand-in-hand with the increase in provision, a similar pattern can be drawn about the growth in cultural attendances. In the early 1990s, the WTO asserted that 37% of all trips had cultural motivations and estimated an annual growth rate of 15% till the end of the century (EUI, 1993). EUCLID (2001) states that Europe has rich and varied heritages to meet the growing demand for cultural practices, goods and services and suggests that "30% of tourist destinations are chosen by virtue of the presence of heritage sites which can be visited, and this number increases to 45-50% if the wider cultural sector such as festivals or important cultural events, is included". Cultural attractions such as museums and monuments constitute the largest sector of the European attractions market. The figures presented by the European Heritage Group show that attendance at museums, historical monuments and archaeological sites has doubled between 1977 and 1997. Analysing museums' attendance evolution in Portugal, between 1980 and 2000, empirical evidence reveals an average global increase of 252% throughout this time period, representing an annual growth rate of 17.6%: while in 1980 museums accounted for 2.1 million visitors, in 2000 those flows reached 7.4 million (INE, 1980, 2000). To sum up, MacCannell (1976) notes that "the construction, exchange and movement of attractions is a perfect index of modernisation".

These trends have not, however, passed without critical comment. Richards (2001a: 8) questions whether there really is a real growth in interest in culture using several arguments. First, stimulated by the expansion of culture's conceptual definition that promoted the incorporation of additional meanings and functions (e.g. from high to popular culture), the apparent growth of cultural consumption can be partly explained by the increasing range of phenomena classified as 'cultural'.

Richards (1995, 1996, 2001a, 2001b) also argues that evidence suggests that the growth in cultural tourism is at least partly supply led and that cultural tourism provision is outstripping the growth in demand. In Europe, "the supply of cultural attractions has in fact been growing faster than the number of cultural visits over the past decade, and this trend is accentuated by the growing number of localities anxious to market their unique culture to tourists" (2001b: 6). Richards also finds limited empirical support for the growing interest in culture. The author suggests that the growing attendance at cultural attractions does not constitute in itself evidence that people are becoming more interested in culture, rather it is in part a reflection of more tourism and leisure visits in total. Furthermore, recent data suggests that cultural attractions are not gaining a larger share of the attraction market and some surveys on the degree of cultural motivation among tourists also offer little support.

Nevertheless, even if it is exaggerated, culture is a centrality in modern societies and the rationale for this increasing visibility, namely on the EU political agenda, is essentially driven and informed by the paradigm, prevalent since the 1980s throughout Western Europe, that constructs culture as an economic tool (Bianchini & Parkinson, 1993); a means of economic diversification, job creation and urban regeneration. In fact, the foundations upon which recent EU involvement in culture is undertaken highlight that "cultural industries in recent years have experienced a major growth with increasing relevance to European economy and employment".

Cities, competition and event-led strategies

The emergence of culture as a driving force of the restructuring economies of Europe is strongly associated with the growing importance attributed to 'it' in the urban planning and management context that stresses the cultural and leisure 'industries'. Analysis of local and urban policies show that the last decade of the 20th century was characterised local particularities deemed to be cultural being considered as a resource and a competitive advantage (Peixoto, 2000). Thus, the cultural policies themselves have shifted their emphasis from 'social welfare' to economic purposes and city-image enhancement programmes.

While in the 1970s, policies to address the erosion of the economic base of many cities in northern Europe and for regenerating cities' centres were based on retail and office expansion, by the late 1980s the expanding functions became culture, leisure and tourism and the regenerative joint effects of their marriage. Moreover, it was commonly asserted that globalisation entails a growing competition between cities, which, in turn, puts their modernisation strategies under pressure. It is thus argued that culture helps cities to position themselves against competitors through product differentiation and inclusion on the international stage through the unique qualities of their cultural resources (Fortuna, 1998; Richards & Bonink, 1995). The *genius loci* of cities therefore is used to confront decaying or obsolete industrial economies. Many of Europe's cities boast new, enlarged or renovated museums, theatres, concert halls and performing arts centres; festival market places, a calendar of events, famous new landmarks and rejuvenated quarters (Cockerell, 1997: 45). A survey launched by the Port Authority of New York – New Jersey suggests that 56% of people who had moved to New York City declared the variety of cultural attractions as a major motivation (Hughes, 2000: 169).

In this sense, cities' and urban systems' development results from both concentration and polarisation processes, not only within the political, economic and administrative fields, but also amongst cultural and symbolic ones. We should point out the relevance of heritage and cultural events in the re-configuration of urban economies, namely through externalities generated by tourism dynamics, within symbolic and internal identity reconstitution processes and the creation and projection of a cities' image. In this context, Santos & Abreu (2000) state that large city-capitals accumulate political, economic and cultural centralities (London, New York, Paris or Tokyo), while other cities get constituted as knots of cultural and artistic international circuits, specialising without direct equivalent in the economic or political fields (e.g. Cannes – cinema). As we see it, other cities become visible due to their heritage's relevance, namely those historical cities designated as World Heritage Cities, appearing as a brand-image of places seeking to compete. Large-scale cultural events, such as capitals of culture are also exploited for competitive advantage even if they are one-off initiatives.

Because of the prestige attached to the World Heritage List, the number of applications to World Heritage City status has risen over the last years from 71, in 1989, to 198 in 2002. Moreover, while in 1989, 45% of the cities listed belonged to European countries, in 2002 that figure exceeded 59% (117 cities), and this imbalance in the representation of the List continues to grow. This data shows that World Heritage City status has became a target of those cities where the major cultural tourism destinations are located (Peixoto, 2000). Many authors have been warning that inclusion on the World Heritage List has become an aim in and of itself namely because of the economic returns that are expected linked to its tourism market value: "added prestige, heightened visibility, are deemed to ensure guaranteed revenues from tourism" (Zouain, 2002: 2). Several studies conducted on the World Heritage certifications suggest a very strong correlation between the growth of nominations and that of tourists and revenue flows (Peixoto, 2000; Zouain, 2002).

Comparable to the emphasis on heritage in the World Heritage List is the stress given to the staging of large international events, such as universal expositions or the cultural capital event. Furthermore, events are also being increasingly placed at the centre of urban development policies and in particular tourism expansion strategies as a response to the need of continuously reinventing and improving cities' attractiveness in order to maintain their share in the competitive tourism market.

The approach to urban transformation that has been pursued by many cities in Europe and North America throughout the 20th century[1] has largely revolved around the celebration of several cultural urban mega-events but also other types of fairs, congresses, religious and sporting events, in a proliferation process intensified by inter-city competition. Universal Expositions, Olympic Games, World Football Championships[2], European Cultural Capital events seem to be good examples from which to argue for the noticeable changes induced by modernisation and growing inter-city competition.

The year 2000 was a major reference point in the organisation of a wide range of large events involving strong impacts on the mobility of people, money, capital, information, images. The WTO (2001) suggest that spurred on by a strong global economy and the special events held to commemorate the new millennium, international tourism reached, in 2000, levels never seen before, with growth over 1999 by an estimated rate of 7.4%, its highest value in nearly a decade. Although the WTO considered that Europe was the star performer of world tourism in 2000, with tourists attracted to Italy for the Vatican Jubilee and to Germany for Expo 2000 held in Hanover, this event's proliferation, both in number and diversity, intensified by inter-city competition, determined the failure of some initiatives.

For example, Expo 2000, with an audience of 18 million visitors didn't reach the forecast of 40 million and wasn't able to effectively compete against the numerous other mega-events. Partially due to the competition of Seville Universal Exposition and the Barcelona Olympics, a similar clash happened to Madrid in 1992, the year the city held the European Cultural Capital title. If it is true that the new context holds increased opportunities for cities' international visibility, this market acceleration generates increased competition: cultural audiences raise their expectations and demand even larger and more elaborate events.

Examples of urban strategies based on events are, in fact, numerous. Except for Denmark and the countries of Central and Eastern Europe, nearly all the European countries have hosted large events at least once. Within a globalised and highly competitive context, European cities are struggling to locate events of guaranteed success and to use them as strategies for urban redevelopment and city-image modernisation. Some researchers termed these processes as the "festivalisation" or "eventisation" of urban development policies. Harvey speaks about the "mobilisation of the spectacle" (1989 in Both & Boyle, 1993). Investing in an event-led strategy anchored in the appointment as European Capital of Culture (ECC) in 1990, Glasgow, a declining manufacturing city, left the era of industrial economy and is now the third most visited city in Britain, behind London and Edinburgh. The above perspectives are also specifically true in the Portuguese case where the last two decades witnessed an upsurge in the staging of large cultural manifestations – such as XVII European Exposition of Arts, Science and Culture in 1983, the

---

[1] Although large events are ancient manifestations (e.g. Olympic Games).

[2] Assigned to one country, not to a specific city but involving several urban centres.

Europália in 1991, "Lisbon European City of Culture 1994", "Expo'98 – Lisbon World Exposition" and "Porto 2001 – European Capital of Culture"[3] – with all of these profoundly shaping the Portuguese urban landscapes. Expo'98 left not only some major tourist attractions such as the biggest oceanarium in Europe, but managed to redevelop a semi-derelict area by the Tagus river, now spanned by the Vasco da Gama bridge, Europe's longest.

The essence of such manifestations results from their critical mass due to the unique combination of a relatively large number of artists and performances, together in one place over a short period of time (Hughes, 2000: 90). But what is a large event? Carreras (1995) considers that the definition of a large event presupposes a wide variety of manifestations, which require significant investments, the targeting of the international market and the extensive participation of the mass media all over the world.

However, for many there is some confusion about the criteria imposed to define the boundaries of 'large' events. Some invoke economic impact as the main criterion: "simply organising a large manifestation is not sufficient; it must also have a positive impact on tourist consumerism and it must contribute to the increasing demand in the transport sector, in commerce and other productive activities" (Montanari, 2002). Once large events are perceived as occasions to re-launch or reinstate a city in the international arena, it is not surprising that recent debate about mega-event's conceptualisation has centred on international exposure parameters. For Montanari (2002) "an event can be defined as 'mega' not only due to its dimensions or the number of visitors it succeeds in attracting but rather due to its ample international diffusion via press, radio, television or internet" and subsequently an "event has more positive impacts the more it succeeds in guaranteeing positive repercussions on the image of the location and thus extending over time the profitable effects".

The contribution of cultural events to urban restructuring and redevelopment processes is well documented (Hall, 1992; Bianchini & Parkinson, 1993; Richards, 1996; Getz, 1997; MacDonnell, 1999). Having explored the undercurrents informing the eventisation of contemporary urban policy-making, they tend to focus on the significance of events in regeneration and diversification of the urban economy; the mobilisation of internal potential; helping communities to identify with their own city and to develop civic pride; improving the community's access to culture; tourism expansion; destination image enhancement and place marketing; and, impacts of flagship and mega-events as catalysts for urban redevelopment.

The European Capital of Culture Event – a versatile tool for urban redevelopment

The issue of synergies between economic activities grouped together under the rubric of cultural industries has been raised in the evolution of urban policies, where event-led strategies based on cultural initiatives take place. Regarding the expected benefits of such events for the urban economies, the "event formula" is appreciated as a strategic investment. Festivals may therefore be designed for the achievement of several long-term goals from artistic development and cultural heritage conservation to urban renewal processes and place promotion and marketing. Here lies one of the reasons for the shift from social concerns in cultural policies to an emphasis on economic development and urban boosterism.

---

[3] Or, events such as the 2004 UEFA European Football Championship, the biggest international sporting event ever staged in Portugal, with its associated programme of cultural events.

As noticed elsewhere, events are playing an increasingly important role in shaping urban landscapes and becoming essential policies and strategies in the competitive context for European cities. In such an environment, cities can no longer concentrate on the national arena, but must be active on the European stage. Hughes (2000: 91) notes that although many cities now host annual festivals of varying degrees of significance, some of the most significant have been one-off festivals such as the designation as European City of Culture.

The European Commission (2002) states that since its creation "the (European City of Culture, or Cultural Capital – ECC) initiative has been more and more successful amongst European citizens and has a growing cultural and socio-economic impact in the numerous visitors it has attracted". The 17% increase in visitor numbers to Dublin, in 1991, when the city hosted the European Cultural Capital event, while the numbers to Ireland as a whole felt by 2%, illustrates the high profile of this initiative. About "Lisbon European City of Culture 1994", Myerscough (1994:196) outlines that during that year, the city was successful in attracting tourists, as well as the attention and awareness of the city as a tourism destination, once it is claimed by ICEP, that Lisbon'94 led to Portugal's biggest exposure in the international press since the revolution of 1974. Following these steps, in 1997, the Organisation of American States proposed a similar programme termed American Capital of Culture.

Overlapping the tendencies registered in the number of World Heritage Cities applications, the "number of candidates for the nomination (as European Cultural Capital) has substantially increased, as cities vie to attract an event which is now viewed as a tool for economic regeneration rather than a purely cultural manifestation" (Richards, 1996: 28). In response to the widespread interest in staging the ECC event, the programme includes the possibility of involving, in a given year, more than one city in a collaborative partnership organization, twinned as was the case in 2000, when no fewer than nine cities announced their interest. Due to the intense lobbying of several cities vying for the designation for 2000 and to the absence of agreement on a single one, the EU Ministers of Culture decided to mark this symbolic date by giving the title to all nine contenders[4]. Furthermore, as more and more cities from both inside and outside the EU, are seeking to be ECC, in 1990, the "European Cultural Month" was created. The scheme is similar to the ECC concept but is concentrated in a shorter period and is intended mainly for cities located in Central and Eastern European countries[5]. The strong competition to be designated as UK nomination for the ECC 2008, eventually won by Liverpool, is another illustration.

The idea of designating a different city each year as "cultural capital" goes back to 1983 and was launched by the Greek Ministry of Culture. The European Community adopted this proposal in 1985 and Athens became the first ECC[6]. When the ECC programme was born, it was anticipated as an opportunity for a renewed focus by cities on their own cultural heritage and their distinctive cultural identity and vitality and a way to help bring the citizens of the member states closer together. The aims were basically twofold: to make culture of the cities accessible to a European audience; and to create a picture of European culture as a whole. Inevitably, as the event developed it has been used in different ways by the cities, either to support, extend or challenge the original

---

[4] However, poor evaluations of the more recent ECC initiatives stress that these partnerships jeopardise the initial conception and rather then reinforce positive impacts, tend to dilute them by a spreading process.

[5] The first city selected to host the European Cultural Month was Krakow. After it ten others were chosen: Graz (1993); Budapest (1994); Nicosia (1995); St. Petersburg (1996); Ljubljana (1997); Linz (1998); Valetta (1998); Plovdiv (1999); Basel (2001) and Riga (2001).

[6] The others were: Florence (1986), Amsterdam (1987), Berlin (1988), Paris (1989), Glasgow (1990), Dublin (1991), Madrid (1992), Antwerp (1993), Lisbon (1994), Luxembourg (1995), Copenhagen (1996), Thessaloniki (1997), Stockholm (1998), Weimar (1999), Avignon, Bergen, Bologna, Bruxelles, Helsinki, Krakow, Reykjavik, Prague and Santiago de Compostela (2000), Porto and Rotterdam (2001), Bruges and Salamanca (2002), Graz (2003), Genoa and Lille (2004), and Cork (2005).

ECC concept. In the beginning, the ECC programme didn't configure the outcome of a carefully developed and structured plan to solve specific urban problems. The ECC has gone beyond its original configuration: changes on approaches, procedures, organisational models, networks, rules, financial allocations and festival programmes or artistic conceptions varied massively. Even its own designation changed in 1999, when the "European City of Culture" was renamed "European Capital of Culture". Although the ECC initiative was always supposed to be viewed more than an arts-festival staging a year-long programme of cultural events, those changes underwent further and deeper extending and encompassing new objectives. Characterised by a double content related to the consolidation of the existing urban fabric and the articulation of new territories but also the promotion of economic development, clearly focused to encourage degrees of urban internationalisation and globalisation (so that a marketing opportunity is given to cities to project their images on the international arena), the programme has evolved over the years from simply the establishment of cultural networks to a versatile development tool capable of achieving multiple objectives such as urban redevelopment (Roseta, 1998; Cogliandro, 2001). Here, the ECC concept faces one of its major challenges to overcome its ephemerality and become an effective tool in urban redevelopment processes.

In this connection, there is a general recognition that the turning point came with the designation of Glasgow in 1990. The ECC award redefined the city but Glasgow also contributed to the redefinition of the ECC concept itself. Unlike its predecessors, Glasgow was not a capital city or one of the established cultural destinations of Europe such as Athens, Florence or Paris. Glasgow won the nomination largely on the basis of planning to use the event to stimulate urban regeneration and boost the image of Glasgow as a cultural city. The Year certainly didn't solve all Glasgow's urban problems. It did though deliver a tremendous boost to the city and left long-lasting benefits. Hoping to repeat Glasgow's success, cities have been using the European title as a lever not only to enhance international cultural exposure but also to launch urban redevelopment processes. This potential to achieve long-lasting benefits encompassing cultural experiences, employment opportunities, new growth and regeneration was the emphasis of all of the bidding British towns and cities that entered the competition to hold the title of ECC 2008, with Liverpool succeeding in its bid to a large extent on the basis of the support and involvement of the local community. Speaking about the Portuguese case, in 1994, Lisbon also recognised the power of the event as an engine for regeneration. According to Roseta's evaluation (1998) of the impacts linked to the ECC 1994 program, the city is "on a higher development path than would have been if the event had not happened".

How can cities use the ECC event to promote urban redevelopment? To over-generalise is a major temptation. The ECC event is repeated annually in different cities and diversity is the key feature. Differences in size, ambitions and needs draw the event in infinite directions. In fact, the inscription of the ECC in different historical, social and territorial urban contexts, in other words, the urban context, is the determinant factor of the approaches and interventions undertaken. And, it's precisely here, in the use of the "indigenous model, i.e. one that is flexible and allows freedom of interpretation to reflect specific needs and aspirations of different kinds of cities" (Cogliandro, 2001: 13), that the ECC programme can be judged.

Porto 2001, European Capital of Culture: an event-in-context

Porto, together with Rotterdam, was European Capital of Culture during 2001. After the special programme of 2000, which involved nine cities, 2001 featured two Cultural Capitals. Porto received the accolade one year after Santiago de Compostela (Spain) and one year before Salamanca (Spain), thus augmenting the visibility and cultural leadership of the northwest part of the Iberian Peninsula. Like other cities which had formerly held the Capital of Culture title Porto is neither a capital city nor an established cultural destination. Taking account of the perceived success of previous host cities, this opportunity was viewed as a means for urban redevelopment through cultural regeneration and was shaped in a wider context moulded by the following key forces:

(i) Porto is a double periphery

Being a double periphery – of the city in the country (Oporto is the second city of Portugal and always stood in the shadow of the capital Lisbon) and of the country in the EU – the city vies, through the use of the ECC program, for a place on the European cultural map which should allow, at least during 2001, for the city to achieve a 'place on the map'.

(ii) Culture and tourism at the core of the urban development strategy in Porto

Since the 1990s and as part of the general urban policy framework, in order to enhance the quality of the living environment in Porto city and its metropolitan area, the city authorities have been implementing a cultural policy with two main purposes: (i) diversification, qualification and consolidation of different cultural and artistic expressions; (ii) and, tourism destination development. With this strategy, two objectives were aimed at simultaneously, to raise the attractiveness of Porto to its own citizens and for visitors. Major investments were made in: encouraging the growth and qualification of the cultural creation conditions by financing local cultural production and creativity, restoring cultural attractions, creating new cultural infrastructure and promoting the city's place in cultural European networks. On the other hand, the efforts and strategies formulated to promote Porto's city cultural development recognized and gave due attention to the potential of tourism, leading to the adoption of a proactive tourism strategy, in which the framing and organisation of major national and international events is a vital element.

This approach was fundamental and instrumental in Oporto's designation as European Capital of Culture for 2001. Moreover, this success marked the progress achieved in the cultural and tourism fields and demonstrated the extent to which "the organisation of large events is a consequence of the cities' competitiveness" (Montanari, 2002).

(iii) The internationalisation of Porto

Cultural attractions are often seen as iconic of global culture and this idea is enshrined in the designation of the European Capital of Culture each year or in the designation of World Heritage Sites. The joint effect of these two certification processes provided, in recent times, the entrance of Porto to the challenges of internationalisation.

In 1996, the Unesco World Heritage Committee designated Porto's historic centre as a World Heritage City, considering "that the site is of outstanding universal value as the urban fabric and its many historic buildings bear remarkable testimony to the development over the past thousand years of a European city that looks outward to the west for its cultural and commercial links". The classification also extends to the left bank of the Douro River taking in the Oporto wine lodges that line the riverbank in Gaia. According to its own conceptualisation, the World Heritage City category enables a focus on cityscapes and therefore encourages the preservation of each historic area as a coherent whole, encompassing not only its physical elements but also the human activities it engenders. The goal is to preserve the city's human face, thereby connecting contemporary life with the past, and contributing to group identity and civic pride. Fortuna (1998: 12), speaking about Évora, another Portuguese city also certificated as a World Heritage City, but whose findings can be compared with Porto, notes that the inscription process in the Unesco World

Heritage List makes places to go beyond their boundaries and become part of the global picture as "in a cultural sense, only that which is unique and locally valuable can become global". In 2002, the international visibility of Porto was reinforced with the inclusion of the landscape of the Douro Valley, the site of the production of port wine, in the Unesco World Heritage List, giving yet more international prominence to Porto's urban and urban fringe landscapes.

The nomination of Porto as European Capital of Culture 2001 placed the city amongst the network of European cities that may be seen as worth visiting, given the assertion that the classification as a World Heritage Site is a long-term asset that goes beyond the designated year. However, a few remarks are required. First only the development of a regular event programme may allow for the long-term tourism prospects for the city. The idea was that around Porto 2001 new flows of visitors should be organised since the event constituted a cultural and tourist attraction which contributed to an increase in the economic dynamics of the historical part of the city, by encouraging more visitors to spend more time there. These visitors were supposed to stay longer not only because of the city's historical patrimony but also because of the uniqueness of the cultural events, which re-animated the urban landscape. Furthermore, if the Capital of Culture was a major opportunity, exceptional non-regular events are not enough to project a city at an international level, where competition is very sophisticated and aggressive.

Porto 2001, European Capital of Culture: objectives, priorities, organisational approach and programme implementation

Being a city with less accumulated capital than others the challenge of the European Capital of Culture for Porto consisted of the development of a long-term strategy, in other words, to launch initiatives that should continue to emerge and develop after the formal closing. This assumption is well expressed in the idea "building bridges to the future", incorporated in the Porto 2001 logo and slogan. In fact, being more concerned with long-term economic and social benefits rather than a short-term cultural focus, the event was incorporated into the overall framework of urban policy-making. The adopted approach emphasised that such an initiative should leave a legacy whose positive effects should last way beyond its closure at the end of 2001. Long-term markers should be left behind through a more dynamic cultural life, renovated spaces, improvements in streets, squares and gardens, new cultural equipment and structures, and improvements in the image of the city. The overall objectives were: (i) broadening local participation in cultural life; (ii) consolidate recent cultural dynamics and generate new ones; (iii) enhance the lives of those living and/or working in Porto city and region; (iv) place the city among the network of European cities that are worth visiting for their cultural programming; (v) act as a catalyst for the development of new permanent facilities and regular events; (vi) facilitate access to different forms of culture; (vii) and, further the internationalisation of the city.

The implemented urban redevelopment strategy possessed two sides: renovation but also the creation of new urban territories. The consumption of culture is increasingly used as a means of economic regeneration and the creation of cultural facilities is an important weapon in the competitive struggle to attract inward investment to cities. On the other hand, comparatively few cities rely solely on their heritage. New attractions need to be developed – museums, galleries, exhibitions – which will renew interest and prompt repeat visits and generate new visitors.

The image of many cities fluctuates between two poles – modernist images and heritage images – forming a hybrid configuration which emerges as simultaneously an awareness of the past, an investment in the present and a perspective on the future (Mons, 1992; Sciorra, 1996, Fortuna, 1998), the development of new cultural attractions – material and immaterial/events – was a challenge and an effort in promoting a balance between two poles: (i) "too much past" – centred on the local and regional identities and symbols; and, "too much future" – an emphasis placed on a cultural policy of cloning the models of international culture.

Following the organisational model adopted since 1991 of creating an independent company to run the ECC year, an organisation was created to manage Porto 2001 ECC – The PORTO 2001, S.A. This professional, centralized structure had a global financial budget of €230 million supported by the Portuguese government (91%), private patrons (7%) and Porto City Council (2%). This is a good example of the management of urban destinations through partnerships and collaborative arrangements between public and private sectors. However, the balance in the funding contributions of the partners should be noted.

The financial allocation of €230 million covered 4 programmatic areas (Figure 1): urban renewal; restoration and construction of cultural spaces and equipment; cultural programming; and, other projects. Considering the global budget's composition strong inequalities emerged: a range of extremely diverse types of projects was supported, but the bulk had been used for material initiatives.

Urban Renewal was the major investment area with approximately 39% of all commitments. The urban renewal process undertaken aimed to solve some of the problems related to the presence of a very old urban structure, in particular the renovation of Porto's downtown which is the heart of the city's historic district, classified as a World Heritage Site. The processes of change in Porto's downtown are linked to the ideas of recuperation and valorisation of public space: repaving streets, remodelling gardens and squares, improving urban mobility. Another major change is a focal area of the city was the Atlantic avenue – Porto's seaside city park, which is a project of the Catalonian, architect Manuel Solà-Morales. Although many of these repairs are still running, the city will gain an undeniable advantage in terms of improvements in the urban "décor" and general pleasure in the urban environment.

Figure 1 *Porto 2001 global financial budget: segmentation by programmatic areas (in million €)*

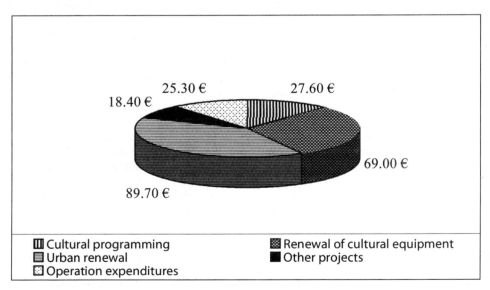

Source: The PORTO 2001, S.A.

The renewal of cultural equipment, being responsible for 30% of total investment, was the second largest earner. Large amounts were earmarked for the construction of new cultural spaces and facilities such as the Music Hall and the Almeida Garrett Library. Others were allocated to the renewal of facilities: Soares dos Reis National Museum – once a royal palace, this museum occupies a building from the early 1700s; Cadeia da Relação – a former prison, houses Porto's Centre of Photography; Carlos Alberto National Auditorium; Coliseu – in order to stage major international musical productions; S. Bento da Vitória Monastery – the transformation of the cloisters for a performance space for the National Orchestra of Porto.

While these two areas accounted for more than 69% of the global budget, more reduced sums went to Cultural Programming and Other Projects Areas. 12% of the investment was done under the Cultural Programming Area; Other Projects Area received €18.4 million, which was the lowest percentage allocation (8%).

Figure 2   *Financial composition of the Cultural Programming Area (in €)*

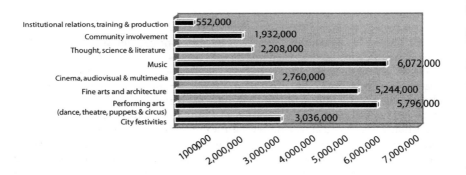

Source: The PORTO 2001, S.A.

The Cultural Programming Area was structured in seven categories, along a budget related to institutional relations, training and production investment needs (Figure 2). The analysis of the financial support specifically allocated to each category highlights one key feature: no marked contrasts in terms of polarization of the investment emerge. Although this means that no specific areas were target, music received the most substantial financial aid available (22%). In second place dance, theatre, puppets and circus was the category that most polarized the financial aid provided (21%), followed by fine arts and architecture (19%), which was the third major recipient of the financial support allocated to cultural projects.

Although data available is referenced to October 2001, which makes difficult an accurate assessment about provision and demand by category, the elements gathered enable us to point out some major characterisation features:

- Fine Arts, Architecture and City – Events included in this framework were under a double coordination responsibility (Porto 2001 S.A. and Serralves Foundation) with distinct strategies. While Porto 2001 S.A. worked with young and unknown artists and emphasised Porto's architectural fabric as cultural symbols of the city. Serralves through photography, video, cinema and contemporaneous, modern and classical arts exhibitions, made possible the intersection of Portuguese and international culture.

Serralves was also responsible for the management of the Photography Portuguese Centre and the National Museum Soares dos Reis programmes. A price policy discount of 50% for students and third age people was implemented on paid events.

- City Festivities – This programming area had two objectives: the first one was to provide opportunities for locals to attend arts events; the second one was to establish a framework co-operation between Porto and foreign performers. Another striking feature was the strong rotation observed in terms of places used as material supports to those events. Festivities like "2001 Summer Nights", "Bridges of Dreams", "Electro Parade" and "Frestas – Street Festivals" involved large attendances: their numbers were, respectively, 10,000, 70,000, 30,000 and between 10,000 and 20,000 individuals. The price policy strategy considered events with free admission.

- Thought, Literature, Science – Under this category, a total of 96 conferences were organised: 40 on scientific themes, 23 related to literature and 33 on other themes. To expand conference audiences, well known Portuguese and foreign personalities were invited. Attendance rates varied between 16 and 100%, strong amplitudes that didn't depend on entrance prices, as the majority was free, but mostly on the lecturers and themes presented.

- Dance, Theatre, Puppets and Circus – The dance programming brought to Porto single shows presented by international famous companies, performing in two cultural spaces: Rivoli Municipal Theatre and S. João National Theatre. With the theatre programming area, Porto 2001 looked to encourage growth and qualification of the cultural creation conditions, which were incorporated in different strategies: cultural spaces and facilities acquisition, insertion in European networks, creation of a theatre production nucleus and financing several theatre festivals. Puppet events were under special supporting measures since it's a performing art with a long tradition in the city (e.g., International Puppets Festival and the Porto Puppets Theatre). Finally, the circus area has refreshed itself: nowadays, dance, theatre and fine arts are being developed. Workshops, debates, informal meetings with artists and companies and a specific programme with one of the residential companies were the strategies followed. About audiences, the major contrasts were not between the 4 performing categories but between shows. In general terms, dance or theatre shows did not have bigger audiences then puppets or circus. Policy prices followed the pattern already identified. Once more, price was not the relevant explanatory variable in participation rates, while publicity and organisation can be assumed as key explanatory factors. Theatre festivals such as Fazer a Festa, Fitei and Ponti presented the large audiences, respectively, 80%, 60% and 75%.

- Community involvement – The overall aim of developing audiences by encouraging and strengthening participation in order to produce and accept culture was one priority of Porto 2001. This was, in fact, the main motive behind the individualisation of this area, reinforcing a series of initiatives implemented with considerable impact before 2001. These audiences totalled 225,974 individuals.

- Music – A major component was represented by the symbolic production of Porto 2001: The Music Hall, whose repairs are far away from being concluded. Churches, museums, auditoriums, and theatres were stages of numerous musical activities. Co-productions and networks between institutions, festivals and contests were also launched. Evidence shows that music was the programming cultural area that registered the largest audiences (most of the events reached 100% audiences) in spite of the generally higher prices.

- Cinema – Was anchored to another ambitious event, "Odyssey in Images", a big multimedia, television and cinema festival for all publics. Fantasporto and Pessoa Virtual Museum are some illustrations. Networks with other international cinema festivals such as Rotterdam (Netherlands) or S. Paulo (Brazil) were established and the attendance rates were high.

An effort in evaluating the Porto 2001 year noted the following key elements:

(i) Growth in the number of events staged and attendances – between January and October 2001, 363 events were staged; attendances reached 1,037,627 individuals at organised events, representing an average attendance rate of 75%. These figures gave a tremendous boost to the entire cultural sector of Porto and one result was an apparent increase in the interest in cultural events.

(ii) Museums were important crowd pullers.

(iii) In terms of tourist audiences, although important financial resources were allocated for marketing strategies in foreign markets, Porto 2001 the Cultural Capital year was judged not to have been successful in generating visits from foreign tourists. Porto airport, the major entry gate for foreign visitor, excluding for Spanish visitors, registered a decrease of 3%; the number of tourists in Porto city decreased by 10% compared with the preceding year.

Internal and external causes can be advanced. Internal explanations lie in the absence of a strong marketing policy (in the foreign markets, very few knew that Porto was European Capital of Culture in 2001). This contradicts the assertion that a large event necessarily presupposes an increase in media coverage of the host city. Data, which supports these findings, is found in Richards et al. survey (2002: 57), which conclusions state that Porto didn't seem "to have benefited from the Cultural Capital year in terms of its image outside the city". Others emphasised that the massive repairs and works in the city gave the idea of an uncomfortable city: the first impact were the works at the airport; then because of the repairs it was difficult to draw a tourist itinerary, even accessibility to hotels was difficult. However, some remarks must be made. First, in terms of cultural audiences, tourists weren't the only, or most important target. Second, comparing with former initiatives, the European Capital of Culture year had a mixed effect on visitor numbers. Some cities have experienced significant increases in overnight visitors, but there were cases where the number of visitors actually declined. In fact, the ECC event itself does not therefore necessarily lead to an increase in staying visitors and may rather result in growth in day visitor numbers.

Nonetheless, the main explanation for the disappointing figures may be found in the global tourism dynamics registered in 2001. In 2001, international arrivals declined by 0.6 per cent, the first year of negative growth for international tourism since 1982. The events of September 11th, which determined the results of international tourism in 2001 as well as the way in which certain destinations and sectors were affected, were only one factor, although the most important, for the decline in tourism statistics. Even before, during the first eight months of the year, there was a cooling in growth of outbound travel from countries like Germany, Japan and the United States. One the other hand, 2000 was an exceptional year for tourism, with special millennium events boosting international arrivals by 7% and, in some cases, causing travellers to advance trips that would have been taken in 2001 (WTO, 2002).

(iv)   Strong presence of local audiences and correlative under-representation of foreign visitors at arts performances – foreign visitors tended to be concentrated at monuments and museums, where the language barrier was less of an issue. In theatre productions the language barrier is stronger for foreign tourists though less so for musicals or music concerts, opera and ballet. If tourists were the target audiences, then a generalised, globalised cultural product needed to be offered, which would have made few concessions to the cultural needs of the local population.

(v)   Local and regional audiences were over-represented, reflecting that Porto 2001 seemed to attract the participation of citizens of the city and the region.

(vi)   Events based on contemporary cultural productions attracted younger audiences with higher levels of cultural capital like university students who were in general over-represented. These findings are again in line with those of Richards et al. survey (2002: 61), which indicate that respondents "were predominantly young. Over half were aged under 30, and students accounted for a high proportion of visitors".

Conclusions: Porto and the dream of a global city

Porto is undergoing a process of recomposition and change of its urban environment – resources, agents, strategies – largely due to the city's inclusion in the international agenda induced by two major cultural regeneration processes used and converted into promotional tools, namely the Unesco permanent designation of Porto as World Heritage City and the successful nomination for European Capital of Culture 2001, which although being a one-off event had the potential to provide longer term benefits. In 2004 the internationalisation processes went further following the city playing host to part of the UEFA European Football Championship. These processes project the city beyond its own boundaries and into global arenas.

The internationalisation process is a symbol, as well a resource and a challenge. It is in this context that the 2001 Capital of Culture event needs to be evaluated.

Although the expected positive impacts will continue over time and therefore can not be evaluated over the short-term following the conclusion of the event, Porto 2001 does seem to have managed to: boost the urban renewal process; extend the capacity of the cultural sector by the renovation and creation of new cultural facilities; promote an increasing supply and demand for cultural events; and, bring culture nearer to the population.

What does the future hold for Porto as a cultural tourism destination? What cultural strategies must be followed? The answers must be found in the need to redefine the "critical success factors" as an initial step in the process of outlining long-term goals and implementing an effective management model where aspects related to the length and timing of festivals, flexible responses to changing contexts, internationalisation, financing, fees and patronage, events reputation and innovation are important elements.

Some proposals are already on the table. After Porto 2001 a programme of market development needs to be implemented in order to build on the opportunity created by the event and to address the areas of latent demand. A large-scale once-only event not always makes a fundamental contribution to urban regeneration, namely in terms of tourism demand, unless it fits to a long-term strategy, which also provides for re-evaluations. Smaller annually repeated festivals and a series of events anchored in Porto's urban system are necessary in order to convince visitors that there is "always something happening" in this city.

Stressing Montanari's idea (2002) that competition, especially on a European scale, should be balanced with co-operation between cities, strategic alliances on the basis of shared interests should be activated, namely built upon the stimulation of cultural networks. In fact, should cities be partners or rivals? Time and physical proximity between Santiago de Compostela, Porto and Salamanca suggest an opportunity to create a network of cultural relations that last beyond the Capital of Culture years based on institutionalised common projects. Three major co-operation areas are already identified: World Heritage Cities, UniverCities and culture and landscapes of frontier. By such means Porto can go on being a symbolic and actual global city.

References

Bianchini, F., Parkinson, M. (1993), (Eds) *Cultural Policy and Urban Regeneration: The West European Experience*, Manchester, Manchester University Press.

Booth, P. and Boyle, R. (1993), "See Glasgow, see culture" in Bianchini, F. and Parkinson, M. (1993) *Cultural Policy and Urban Regeneration: The West European Experience*, Manchester, Manchester University Press.

Cogliandro, G. (2001), *European Cities of Culture for the year 2000. A wealth of urban cultures for celebrating the turn of the century*, European Commission in http://europa.eu.int/comm/culture/index_en.html.

Domingues, A. (1996), "Política urbana e competitividade", *Sociedade e Território*, 23.

EUCLID (2001), "Tourism, the EU and Culture", *Eureka Briefing. European and international information, news & analysis*, 5.

European Commission (2002), in http://europa.eu.int/comm/culture_en.html.

Featherstone, M. (1994), *Consumer Culture and Postmodernism*, London, Sage Publications.

Ferreira, C. (2000), "Intermediação cultural e grandes eventos. Notas para um programa de investigação sobre a difusão das culturas urbanas", *Oficina do Centro de Estudos Sociais da Faculdade de Economia da Universidade de Coimbra*, 167.

Fortuna, C. (1998), "Detraditionalization and tourism: old memories, new functions and the reconstruction of city images", *Oficina do Centro de Estudos Sociais da Faculdade de Economia da Universidade de Coimbra*, 127.

Fortuna, C. (Org.) (1997) *Cidade, Cultura e Globalização: Ensaios de Sociologia*, Oeiras, Celta.

Getz, D. (2000), "Festivals and special events: life cycle and saturation issues" in Gartner & Lime (Eds) *Trends in outdoor recreation, leisure and tourism*, Cabi, Wallingford.

Hall, C., (1992), *Hallmark Tourist Events: Impacts, Management, and Planning*, London, Belhaven Press.

Harvey, D. (1989), "From managerialism to entrepreneurialism: the transformation of urban governance in late capitalism", *Geografiska Annaler* 71B: 3-17.

Harvey, D. (1989), *The urban experience*, Baltimore, The Johns Hopkins University Press.

Haselbach, D. (2002), "Cultural management in a 'throw-away-society' – short lived arts accelerate cultural developments", *Proceedings from the IFEA Conference*, Bonn.

Hughes, H. (2000), *Arts, entertainment and tourism*, Butterworth-Heinemann Ltd, Oxford.

Instituto Nacional de Estatística (INE) (1979, 1996, 2001), *Estatísticas da cultura, desporto e recreio 1980,1995, 2000.* (Culture, Sports, and Leisure Statistics), Lisbon, National Statistics Institute.

Janiskee, R. (1994), "Some macroscale growth trends in America's community festival industry", *Festival Management and International Journal* 2 (1), 10-14.

MacCannell, D. (1976), *The tourist: a new theory of the leisure class*, Macmillan, London.

Montanari, A. (2002), "Tourism and mega-events. The restructuring of urban areas and the dream of the global city", Presentation in the *International Conference "The tourist historic city"*, Bruges.

Peixoto, P. (1997a), *Imagens e usos do património urbano no contexto da globalização*, Dissertação de Mestrado em Sociologia, Faculdade de Economia da Universidade de Coimbra.

Peixoto, P. (1997b), "L'économie symbolique du patrimoine: le cas d'Évora", Oficina do Centro de Estudos Sociais da Faculdade de Economia da Universidade de Coimbra, 100.

Peixoto, P. (2000), "O Património Mundial como fundamento de uma comunidade humana e como recurso das indústrias culturais urbanas", Oficina do Centro de Estudos Sociais da Faculdade de Economia da Universidade de Coimbra, 155.

Porto 2001 (2001), Porto 2001- Capital Europeia da Cultura, Programação Cultural 13 de Janeiro a 30 de Setembro, Porto.

Porto 2001 S. A. (2001), Porto 2001– Capital Europeia da Cultura. Balanço dos primeiros seis meses de actividade, Porto.

Purcell, M. (2000), "Globalisation, urban enfranchisement, and the right to the city: towards an urban politics of the inhabitant" in http://faculty.washington.edu/mpurcell/cv.htm.

Ribeiro, M. (1998), *Lisboa 94 no mapa das Capitais Europeias da Cultura: eventos culturais e desenvolvimento local.* Dissertação de Mestrado em Geografia, Faculdade de Letras da Universidade de Lisboa.

Richards, G.; Bonink, C. (1995), "Marketing cultural tourism in Europe", *Journal of Vacation Marketing*, 1, 2, pp. 173-180.

Richards, G. (1996), (Eds.) *Cultural Tourism in Europe.* CAB International, Wallingford.

Richards, G. (2001), "Cultural tourists or a culture of tourism? The European cultural tourism market" in J. Butcher Eds, *Innovations in cultural tourism.* ATLAS, Tilburg.

Richards, G. (2001), (Eds.) *Cultural attractions and European tourism.* CABI Publishing, Wallingford.

Richards, G. (2002,) *Rotterdam and Porto, Cultural Capital 2001: visitor research*, ATLAS, Tilburg.

Roseta, I. (1998), *Cultural policy and hallmark events as tools for urban regeneration: the case of Lisbon European City of Culture 1994.* MSc in Regional and Urban Planning Studies, London School of Economics and Political Science.

Santos, H., Abreu, P. (2000), "Cultura e cidades: espaços, dinâmicas, públicos. Algumas pistas de análise", *Oficina do Centro de Estudos Sociais da Faculdade de Economia da Universidade de Coimbra*, 152.

Santos, M. (2001), "Portugal. National report" in *Council of Europe/ERICarts Cultural policies in Europe: a compendium of basic facts and trends*, 2001.

World Bank (2000), Cities in Transition: World Bank Urban and Local Government Strategy in http://econ.worldbank.org/

WTO (2002), Tourism highlights 2001. World Tourism Organisation, Madrid.

Zouain, G. (2002), "Heritage, art and economics", Presentation in the *International Conference "The tourist historic city"*, Bruges.

The Impacts of Mega-events: the case of EXPO'98 - Lisbon

Jonathan Edwards, Miguel Moital and Roger Vaughan

Bournemouth University, UK

Introduction

The ever increasing level of competitiveness between tourist destinations has led tourism authorities to cooperate with other national agencies in a search for development strategies that can differentiate the destination from its competitors and strengthen its appeal in potential or actual markets. Among the possible strategies, the hosting of mega-events to achieve these goals has become popular in the past four decades particularly for major urban centres. Many different cities and states compete every year, and at many different levels, to organise these large-scale events (Verdaguer, 1995). Mega-events have the ability to substantially stimulate both the supply-side (through improvement of infrastructure, tourist equipment and organisational skills) and the demand-side (due to the promotional effects caused by international media exposure) of a tourist destination. Governments have recognised the potential of mega-events to re-shape tourist destinations and a number have endeavoured to host them. This is not to say that the only purpose of hosting a mega-event is tourism as many other aspects of the community in which events are hosted may benefit from their organisation. But tourism is undoubtedly one of the industries that can benefit from the staging of mega-events, particularly in the longer term.

According to Ritchie (1984) World Fairs represent one of the first forms of events specifically developed to focus attention on a particular urban destination. The responsibility of organising the last exposition of the 20th century was given to Lisbon and EXPO'98 was the 59th chapter (BIE, 2002) of a long and rich story of World Fairs, which started in London in 1851. EXPO'98 was officially sanctioned as a World Exposition by the Bureau of International Expositions (BIE). It ran from May 22nd until 30th September 1998 and was a specialised exposition exploring the theme "The Oceans: A Heritage for the Future". There were 160 official participants, with 146 countries and 14 international organisations represented. The number and nature of participants resulted in EXPO'98 being the most international of all expositions ever held (Parque das Nações, 2002). Following the successful management of EXPO'98 the site was transferred to the management of the Parque de Nações (or Nations Park) who are overseeing the continuing development of the site for residential, leisure/tourism and commercial use.

Staging mega-events inevitably demands the allocation of a large amount of resources, which are most often provided by the public sector. The argument for the assignment of considerable amounts of capital to the organisation of mega-events is that the investment will have major impacts on the region and ultimately the benefits will exceed the costs. The need to assess the extent to which the predicted impacts actually happened has led to the development of methodologies to assess these impacts. These have in many cases focussed on the economic impacts although some researchers have studied impacts in other areas, such as planning, environment and the attitudes of residents.

One of the fields that has been neglected is the impacts that are perceived by those working in the tourism industry. This chapter provides not only an overview of EXPO'98 but it also offers a preliminary review of the impacts that major players in the management of Lisbon's tourism industry perceive to have arisen from EXPO'98, upon tourism in Lisbon, the capital of Portugal.

Both secondary and primary sources have been drawn upon in preparing this material. Secondary data was gathered from general academic and professional literature as well as data made publicly available by the Lisbon Tourism Bureau (Associação Turismo de Lisboa), the Portuguese National Tourism Board (Direcção Geral do Turismo – DGT), Parque EXPO'98 and the Nations Park (Parque das Nações – PN). Primary data collection focused on the impacts of EXPO'98 on Lisbon's tourism as perceived by the key players in Lisbon Tourism Industry. Therefore, in-depth semi-structured interviews were carried out with the Presidents of ATL (Lisbon Tourism Association), APAVT (Portuguese Travel Agents Association) and AHP (Portuguese Hotels Association).

Dimensions of mega events

Events can be classified according to two underlying motivations – leisure and business. More specifically, leisure events may be sport or culturally oriented and business events may be meetings (e.g. summits) and conferences. Mega events are usually leisure type events, although it has been argued that large business events, such as conferences, may also be considered as mega-events. This is argued to be the case if they are held in medium-sized cities that do not frequently host such large events, where the host community is highly involved in the organisation process, the effects are spread throughout the city and if it brings national/international prestige (Hiller, 1995). Although the definition of mega-events will always remain subjective (Getz, 1997), there has been a debate about what makes an event 'mega' or 'hallmark'. Mega events have been defined as short-term events with long term consequences for the host city (Mossberg, 1997; Roche, 1994). This short definition puts the emphasis on two attributes – the limited duration and lasting effects after the events. Getz (1999) also links the definition of mega-events to time and effects, but identifies, from a tourism point of view, the type of effects (or 'impacts' in his words) that a mega event may have. According to Getz, a mega event is a 'planned occurrence of a limited duration which has an extraordinary impact on the host area in terms of one or more of the following: tourist volumes; visitor expenditures; publicity, leading to heightened awareness and a more positive image; related infra-structural and organisational developments which substantially increase the destination's capacity and attractiveness' (Getz, 1999: 5). Hall (1992: 2) gives a similar view by pointing out that they are 'major one-time or recurring events of limited duration, developed primarily to enhance the awareness, appeal and profitability of a tourism destination in the short and/or long term'. In light of these definitions, EXPO'98 may be considered a mega-event in that tourist volumes rose significantly, it had a high international visibility, it induced changes in the tourism organisational structure and it resulted in a large development of infrastructure and tourist equipment. In fact, virtually all authors (e.g. Mules, 1998; Bramwell, 1997; Getz, 1997; Roche, 1994; Hall, 1992) refer to World Fairs (together with the Olympics) when illustrating examples of mega-events.

The task of assessing whether changes occurred and most importantly, if those changes are the result of the event is a challenging one. Ritchie (1984) proposed a framework for the assessment of the impacts of mega-events. He suggests that six types of impacts can be identified:

- Economic, tourism/commercial, physical/environmental, social/cultural, psychological and political/administrative.

Economic impact studies have received the greatest attention from researchers (Ritchie, 1984; Roche, 1994) and this may be explained because events are usually seen as an essentially economic initiative (Hiller, 1998). Since the first economic impact studies (e.g. Vaughan, 1977), many reseachers have proposed methodologies to assess the economic impact of events. The economic evaluation of events has tended to use one of three forms of economic evaluation – tourism multipliers, input-output analysis and cost-benefit analysis and each has his own advantages and drawbacks (Hall, 1992). More recently, other methodologies were proposed, such as those based in time series models (Holmes and Shamsuddin, 1997).

Tourism impacts are related to the changes in perception and awareness about the destination (Ritchie, 1984). Although it has been pointed out by many researchers that impacts upon the image are one of the most important effects of mega-events (Roche, 1994; Hall, 1992), and destination image studies are a common topic in tourism literature, there is limited research relating to the impacts of mega events upon the image of a destination. Carlsen and Williams (1999) suggested that destination image resulting from event image is affected not simply by the event period itself but by six separate aspects: the initial bid, event planning and policy, event programming, event promotion, event theming and on-going event advertising. Mossberg (1999) applied the framework developed by Echtner and Ritchie (1993), which uses both structured and unstructured statements, to the evaluation of destination image in a mega-event context – The World Athletics Championships held in Gotemborg. She found no evidence of changes in perceptions of the destination's image after the event. It may be that the indoor nature of the event, coupled with its short duration, limited the nature and extent of the images conveyed and therefore they were not sufficient to change the perceptions of the destination. Ritchie and Smith's (1991) study is probably the most comprehensive to date in evaluating the image impacts of a mega-event. They assessed the extent to which the 1988 Calgary Olympic Games impacted upon the international levels of awareness and the image (perceptions) of the host city. Their four-year study examined the changes at different points in time prior to, and following, the event, with primary data being collected in eight European countries and ten American states. They found the event to have dramatically increased levels of awareness and substantially modified the image of the City of Calgary, although it was also apparent that a significant rate of awareness and image decay should be anticipated.

Two main reasons may be behind the shortage of research on image impacts of mega-events. The first is the difficulty in bringing together the necessary resources required (mainly financial, human and logistic). The second is the lack of tradition in longitudinal surveys in tourism research. Image impact assessment requires measurement, at least, in two different points in time, before and after the event.

Physical and environmental impacts are a consequence of changes in environment and landscape/cityscape associated with and often required for the hosting of a mega-event. In some cases there is an opportunity to restore polluted and derelict sites in terms of their physical, chemical, biological and visual character. These changes are usually accompanied by the installation of infrastructures - roads, water, waste disposal - together with the construction of new facilities. EXPO'98 was no exception as part of the site was reclaimed from run down, abandoned refinery sites and involved the installation of sophisticated infrastructure. The developers of EXPO'98 also took the opportunity to use the redevelopment as a flagship in respect of best practice with regard to environmental standards.

The *Socio-cultural impacts* of mega-events have also been the focus on research. Jeong (1999) identified the positive and negative aspects of the Seoul Olympic Games on host community development from a tourism perspective. He opted for a micro-level (community wide) instead of the macro-level (city or region) perspective because he wanted to specifically assess the perspective of those who were likely to have suffered more disruption of pre-existing patterns of activity and lifestyle. He concluded that residents did not perceive any noticeable socio-cultural impacts and that they supported future hosting of large-scale events. One of the few longitudinal studies on residents perceptions of a mega-event was conducted by Mihalik and Simonetta (1999). Although they found that resident support to the hosting of the Olympics remained strong over time, they also found perceptions of negative impacts to increase as the games got closer, mainly those related with disruption of daily life.

Psychological impacts are among the most difficult to measure and may be rather simplistically summarised in terms of how both the residents and the business and commercial sectors feel about their location and prospects before, during and after the hosting of a mega event. Ritchie (1984) operationalised these impacts in two factors – prestige and hospitality. In assessing the impacts of mega-events, many studies have attempted to assess the extent to which they had psychological effects from the resident's point of view. For example, the aforementioned studies of Mihalik and Simmoneta (1999) and Jeong (1999) and the study by Cegielsky and Mules (2002) all included questions about prestige (recognition effects). Jeong (1999) further assessed the perceived impacts on spirit of hospitality. All these studies give support to the assumption that events have strong psychological impacts on the host community.

Political/administrative impacts may be observable at many levels but in major urban areas they may be most apparent in terms of city, regional and possibly national processes and structures. As Ritchie (1984) argues, political goals can be the primary driving force behind efforts to attract or establish events such as World Fairs. The political goals may be, for example, the strengthening of dominant ideologies or the promotion of individual interests (Hall, 1992; Ritchie, 1984).

Studies on world expositions

Bearing in mind the long history of Expos, and the fact that they are one of the main mega-events in the world, one might expect an extensive body of literature. However, this is not the case as research had tended to focus more on sport-based events, notably the Olympic Games, and studies of the tourism impacts of Expos are few. Maybe the reason behind this has been the apparent failure of some expositions to realise their anticipated impacts, not only in the short-term but also in the long term. Of the studies available, that by Mules (1998) of EXPO'88 in Brisbane, Australia, showed how the event was the catalyst for the establishment of the Queensland Events Corporation and to changes in urban form and urban lifestyles. He argued that EXPO'98 was used as a 'big bang' to convert the whole area into modern urban living and recreational space. Robertson and Guerrier (1998) compared the trilogy of events which took place in Spain in 1992. They argue that large hallmark events are one way that cities can create an image internationally and attract investment with the aim of promoting long-term growth. In terms of sustainability, the Seville Expo has not been a success as it has failed to exploit the success of the exposition. According to these authors Seville's image has suffered because of the speculative rather than the strategic approach taken to the Expo. Holmes and Shamsuddin's (1997) study is one of the few empirical studies to evaluate both the short and long term impacts of an Expo. Using economic models, they studied the economic effects of World Exposition 1986 held in Vancouver, Canada on US demand for British Columbia. Not only did they assess the impacts during the exposition, but they also partially calculated the impacts during a longer period of time (1987-1993). They found the long-term effects of EXPO'86 to be very large, probably larger in total than the short-term economic benefits. Their justification for the highly positive long-term impacts was the increase in attractiveness that resulted from the world-wide exposure of the Vancouver area by the fair.

One of the earliest studies of EXPO'98 was conducted by Carrière and Demazière (2002) about the urban planning process. They argue that EXPO'98 was not only an event, but a catalyst for urban restructuring. They further concluded that the EXPO'98 approach to planning is 'part of a current trend in urban development to make use of large international events in order to create a distinctive urban neighbourhood, whose primary purpose is to change the image of the City' (p. 72). The second study of EXPO'98 (Baleiras *et al*, 2002) was an economic impact study that focussed on assessing the impacts of the EXPO'98 global project on public sector revenues. The authors found the additional total public revenues to be 4435 million Euros. Their analysis was divided by nine types of sources of revenues, with tourism being one of them. According to their study, tourism was responsible for 7,8% of the additional revenues, or 344 million Euros. At the time of writing the full study has not been released by Parque das Nações SA, the company that commissioned the study, and therefore the methodology employed has not been made public yet.

The case of EXPO'98 in Lisbon

The analysis is divided in four sections. The first section explains the *context* in which the idea of organising a World Fair emerged and developed, the second will review the *process* adopted and implemented, then thirdly the resulting *outputs* will be presented and finally the *outcomes* will be discussed.

Context

As the literature shows (Hiller, 1998; Roche, 1994) events research should focus not only on effects, but also on causes. Therefore, in order to understand the rationale to engage in such a large project it is necessary to review the prevailing context.

In the second half of the 1980s two factors, in particular, were influencing events in Portugal. One event was the achievement of political stability in 1987, when a single party gained an absolute majority in the Parliament which lasted until 1995. The other event was the admission of Portugal as a full member of the European Union (EU) in 1986. This provided an opportunity for Portugal to make up for lost time, by making major structural changes with financial support from EU development programs. As a relatively under-developed country Portugal was anxious to make progress toward the standards of well being and prosperity of developed European countries. Due both to its geographical location and the positions it occupied in the most important economic and social indicators Portugal may be regarded as a peripheral country in the wider European context. The relatively poor infrastructure of many parts of the capital Lisbon and the uneconomic nature of poorly located industry were clear handicaps to the development of a thriving urban economy capable of offering a good quality of life to its citizens.

According to the EXPO'98 Plan (Parque EXPO'98, 1994), the demographic evolution of Lisbon in the 1970s and 1980s was characterised by younger middle class individuals leaving the City to live in the surrounding boroughs. Lisbon has lost over one third of its population since 1970 due to sub-urbanisation (Carrière and Demazière, 2002). In economic terms, the decline of the industrial structure led to the abandonment and degradation of many parts of the City (mainly in the east). The emerging service sector concentrated heavily in the city centre and the consequence was a desertion of many old neighbourhoods. In respect to urban development, there was a clear imbalance with the isolation and social segregation of the eastern side of the City. In terms of the transport system, the lack of major investment was leading to severe traffic congestion. Furthermore, the relationship of the City with the river was gradually being eroded and green areas were becoming spatially unbalanced as public spaces were sacrificed to give priority to circulation and parking (Parque EXPO'98, 1994).

Consequently opportunities and strategies for urban regeneration were actively sought and the hosting of a major event of global significance was one of the strategies proposed, and taken forward as what we now know as EXPO'98. In order to win international support and approval a defensible theme for the Exposition had to be proposed and justified. Previous Expos have been used as an opportunity to commemorate historical events. Brisbane 1988 International Exposition was included in the commemorations of the bicentennial celebration of the European Colonisation of Australia; Seville 1992 Universal Exposition the arrival of Colombo in America. The proposers of the Lisbon exposition also chose a historical rationale. In the late 15th century, the Portuguese engaged in an odyssey to 'discover' and link peoples on Earth. These events reached a climax in 1498, with the arrival of Vasco da Gama in India, and in 1500, with the arrival of Pedro Álvares Cabral in Brazil. At that time, Portugal performed a unique role in the economic, scientific and technological development of the world. Five hundred years later the Portuguese government saw, in the organisation of a major event, an opportunity to appropriately commemorate these maritime achievements of the late 15th century.

In the 1980s, Portugal's economy was changing, as traditional sectors were in crisis and with tourism emerging as an important economic activity. Until the 1980s, tourism development had been based on a single product – sun and sea – mainly in the Algarve and in the Estoril/Cascais coast west of Lisbon. The over development of many Portuguese sun destinations, increasing competition from emerging Mediterranean (European and African) and long-haul destinations, and the inability to respond to emerging new tourist motivations all contributed to Portuguese tourism confronting market based problems.

In order to confront the changes associated with tourist demand, the Portuguese tourism authorities re-oriented tourism policy, by pursuing a multi-product strategy. Portugal, they argued, should be seen not only as a sun country with hospitable people, but also as a country with a rich culture, beautiful nature, modern congress and conference facilities and high level organisational skills. At this time Lisbon's tourism was restricted. There was some business tourism, mainly businessmen who came to Lisbon to deal with local entrepreneurs, and incentive travel. Lisbon was also a point of call for cruise ships. However, overall, Lisbon was losing competitiveness to other Iberian cities like Barcelona, Seville and to a lesser extent Madrid, all of which had gone through a modernisation process in preparation for the Olympic Games, EXPO'92 and the 1992 European Cultural Capital respectively.

EXPO'98 – an event for tourism?

Mega-events usually have a large impact on the tourism industry, but tourism may or may not be the rationale for hosting a mega-event. As Getz (1999, p. 5) points out, 'achieving tourism-related goals is generally one of the most important reasons stated for bidding on a large event, although other economic, social, political and environmental goals are also important'. In light of the context explained above it is not surprising that EXPO'98 was a multi-goal project. According to Expo Global Plan (Parque EXPO'98, 1994), the exposition had six main objectives: (1) reassertion of a national vocation, (2) repositioning of the country in the new European context (3), urban regeneration (4) celebration of the discoveries; (5) tourism promotion and (6) economic stimulus. This suggests that although tourism was thought to be one of the industries that could benefit from the Exposition, the Exposition was not hosted primarily for tourism. However, it is worth pointing out that tourism is the only industry specifically addressed in the goals of the Exposition.

As far as tourism was concerned, the expectation was that 'as an international event, the Exposition will be broadcast by the media and will draw attention to Portugal. Many tourists will visit Portugal, either because of the Exposition or for the Exposition, and the long-lasting impact on tourism demand should not be ignored' (Parque EXPO'98, 1994: 14).

Process

Organising a world exposition is both costly, time consuming and complex. This section deals with the organisation and hosting of the Exposition and with post exhibition site management. Five hundred years after the maritime achievements of the Fifteenth century the Portuguese Government created a commission to organise festivities and events that would honour these achievements – the CNCDP (National Commission for the Celebration of Portuguese Discoveries). Following an initial maturation of the idea of hosting a world exposition, a working group was specifically created to conduct the preparation of the candidature. The sequence of main events and acts that led to the granting of the exposition to Lisbon by the BIE is shown in Table 1.

Table 1   *Sequence of events leading to the granting of the Exposition*

Date	Event
October 1989	The Working Group gives to the government a memorandum in which the candidature of Lisbon is suggested.
November 1989	The candidature of Lisbon is presented to BIE.
1990	Studies were conducted in order to find the best place to locate the Exposition and to identify infrastructure requirements. The working group suggests two locations, one in the West of Lisbon and the other in East Lisbon, both on the riverside.
February 1991	The government selects the eastern location, and creates the Commission for Promoting the 1998 International Exposition in Lisbon.
October 1991	The Commission finishes the plan for promoting the Lisbon candidature and the government hands it over to BIE.
December 1991	BIE General Assembly accepts Lisbon candidature.
June 1992	BIE General Assembly chooses Lisbon to host the 1998 World Exposition.

Source: Adapted from Parque EXPO'98 (1994)

The Expo project required the regeneration of 340ha of urban space, 70ha of which was identified as the main Expo site. The choice of the eastern location was based both on the availability of sufficient land and the urgent need for regeneration of this part of the City. As a non-residential area housing displacement problems were minimal and land costs reasonable. Regeneration was urgent due to the existence of severe urban and social degradation since the area was previously occupied by highly polluting petrochemical industries. Having such a large area, just four kilometres away from Lisbon's historical centre and on the waterfront of the Tagus river, was incompatible with the goal of making Lisbon a 'world city'. Hosting a World Exposition in this area represented an opportunity to improve the environment and quality of life in Lisbon, to balance the eastern and western sides of the City and more importantly, to set the standards for future urban development. As Carrière and Demazière (2002) state, the ambition was to make the Nations' Park (actual name of the whole regeneration site) the focal point of the development of the whole metropolitan area.

In order to organise the Exposition, the Government created, in March 1993, a Development Agency – Parque EXPO'98 S.A.. The government granted to this Agency autonomy in terms of site planning, so that bureaucratic and legal difficulties posed by the existing legal framework could be overcome. In effect, Parque EXPO'98 saw its role as that of an urban planning body, whose activities, far from being limited to just the preparation of a one-off short-term event, were involved in long urban restructuring (Carrière and Demazière, 2002).

Of particular importance in the organisational framework was Parque EXPO'98 responsibilities for the international tourism promotion of the event. This decision was highly controversial and the tourism industry frequently pointed out that the promotion of EXPO'98 was inappropriate. The reason critics gave for their analysis was not only the lack of experience and preparation of the agency to work on tourism promotion, but also the irrelevance of this task in comparison with other more important priorities of the company, such as having the site ready for the Exposition.

As a result of the widely reported post-Expo uncertainty of Seville'92 in Spain, one of the requirements for EXPO'98 was to think both in the short-term (i.e. hosting Expo) and in the long-term (the day after Expo). Such huge investment required by a World Exposition could only be maximised in the long term and not simply within the four months of the event. Thus, one premise present in every planning decision was to think of a use for each square meter of built space in the future. It was considered a "global project" in that it 'comprised two objectives: the Lisbon World Exposition and the urban regeneration of 340 hectares in an excellent location in the eastern part of Lisbon on the bank of the River Tagus' (Parque EXPO'98, 1999: p. 22).

This long-term view of the project also required another important point of reference. Bearing in mind previous examples, the Expo organisers were committed to an integrated long term use of the site. That is, the site should fulfil business, retail, residential and leisure/tourism functions. The reasons for this multi-function perspective resulted not only from the failure of the previous single-use perspectives but also from a willingness to move forward from planning strategies that clearly differentiate areas in terms of separate functions. In the light of this long-term strategy, after Expo ended in September 1998 the site was closed to be adapted to the new use and opened one month after as The Nations Park.

From the outset of the Project it was stressed by the public authorities that the overall project would be based on a break even financial strategy. In fact, this feature of the Project has been regarded as innovative in terms of similar major redevelopment projects (Carrière and Demazière, 2002). The State granted the development company a guarantee in support of the company's contractual obligations, i.e., in relation to the loans contracted by it (Parque EXPO'98, 1999). The costs of the Exposition were nearly 1600 million Euros. Figure 1 shows the how this amount was spent by main area.

Revenues came from three main sources: the Exposition (tickets, renting and sponsoring), the after Expo sale of land and structures and contributions from the EU. According to Carrière and Demazière (2002), EU investment was estimated at around 8% of the overall budget of the operation. Given that, although the Exposition itself would lose money, this would be compensated by the profits from the sale of land and structures. The important point is that all together the revenues should be sufficient to pay the investment. Since the project is expected to end only by 2009, only at this time final calculations can be made in order to assess the achievement of the break-even goal.

Figure 1 *Major costs of EXPO'98*

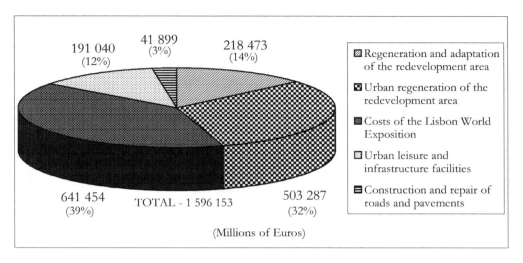

Source: Parque EXPO'98 (1999)

Outputs

As explicitly stated by the authorities interviewed for this study, EXPO'98 transformed the whole City. Ranging from tangible to more intangible, these changes are perceived to have given new competitive advantages for the tourism industry. This section aims to explain the legacy of the Exposition that is believed to have had this positive impact upon tourism and its influence on the competitiveness of Lisbon as a tourist destination.

An important output of Expo was the renewal and building of *infrastructures* in most parts of the City, mainly transportation facilities. The airport was modernised, roads were improved or built, thousands of parking places were created in the City, the underground network was developed, a new central train station was built, just to name the most important. In short, Expo was the motive to re-think and act on Lisbon's inner and outer accessibility. In terms of *city planning*, Expo aimed to reconcile the City with the river Tagus. Expo itself contributed directly to a new perspective in this field, as it added almost five kilometres of accessible riverside. But its contributions were far more important as stated by ATL's President, according to whom 'the authorities responsible for Lisbon Harbour, because of Expo and fearing competition from Expo, initiated a process that was demanded a long time ago – getting the City and the river close again – by reorganising spatially the harbour activities and liberating areas for leisure use'.

The Lisbon authorities wanted to avoid the existence of two cities – one new and highly modernised and one old and with some signs of degradation, and engaged in a process of *urban regeneration* of the most symbolic areas of old Lisbon. The City Administration intervened in this area mainly by promoting the urban regeneration of historical neighbourhoods. To facilitate the process and to bring together the necessary resources and will, the City Administration launched the 'integrated projects program' that focused not on isolated interventions but on a global intervention in the neighbourhood. The AHT President clearly outlined the effects of Expo in this field: 'the dynamic created in the City resulted in increased urban quality (more care, cleaner, putting things in the right place') adding that 'the urban impacts of Expo were spread all over the City'. Overall, the measures had a specific goal – to improve urban quality. By improving urban quality, the City is better able to meet the aspirations of residents and tourists as this factor is critical for tourist satisfaction. Another important output was the creation of new attractions and tourist equipment as well as the renewal of existing ones. The Nations Park is the symbol of the new Lisbon. This multi-function area widened the City of Lisbon to the east and provides a reference for other projects in terms of environment, quality of life and leisure activities.

As Table 2 shows, most of the attractions and structures built for Expo were maintained, and tourism is gaining from their existence. The most important ones are:

- Several attractions like the Oceanarium, which received between 1998 and 2001 more than 7 million visitors (Parque das Nações, 2002), and the Virtual Reality and Knowledge Pavilions.

- The Atlantic Pavilion, prepared to host thousands of people in such different events as congresses, sport championships, shows and concerts.

- The new Lisbon Expositions Centre, whose opening increased significantly the space for expositions and allowed the transformation of the old centre to a modern conference venue – the Lisbon Congress Centre.

Table 2   *Main attractions of EXPO'98: During Expo vs. after Expo*

Thematic inside offer	
During Expo	*After Expo*
Portuguese Pavilion	Retained with a non tourism/leisure function.
Knowledge of the Seas Pavilion	Retained as 'Knowledge pavilion – living science centre'.
Oceans Pavilion	Retained as Oceanarium.
Pavilion of the Future	Retained.
Utopia Pavilion	Retained as 'Atlantic Pavilion'.
Territory Pavilion	BIL – Lisbon International Bowling Centre.
Virtual Reality Pavilion	Retained.
Thematic outside offer	
During Expo	*After Expo*
Nautical Exhibition	Ended.
Water Gardens	Retained.
Garcia de Orta Garden	Retained.

Furthermore, the main services provided during Expo for visitors have been retained, giving the site its own life (Table 3). At the end of the Exposition a shopping mall was added to the list of services available on the site.

Table 3   *Main services provided at the EXPO'98 site: During Expo vs. after Expo*

Services	
During Expo	*After Expo*
Wide range of restaurants, from luxury to fast-food	Most of them retained
2 police stations	1 retained
Information Centres	1 retained
Child care centre	Ended
Sanitation facilities	Retained
Banks	Retained
Mail and communication	Retained
Press Centre	Ended
Health Centre	Replaced by new hospital

When the right to host a mega-event is granted to a city, one of the issues that the organisation has to provide for is the *accommodation* of millions of visitors. The easier solution (but short-term) is to build new or extend existing hotels in order to make available enough hotel rooms for the demand. This will pose a problem because after the Exposition the hotels will remain and the hotel industry is likely to face market problems since the motivation for the exceptional demand vanishes. Seville clearly opted for this solution, with the number of hotel rooms increasing two-fold, from 12,000 to 24,000 (Law, 2002), but faced the aforementioned problems after the Exposition. Knoxville 82, on the other hand, opted for a more creative solution. The number of new rooms increased but still facing a shortage of accommodation, the organisation opted for the creation of a housing bureau to subcontract and market rooms in homes, apartments and condominiums around the city (Evans, 1982).

Although there is an evident increase in hotel capacity in 1997 and 1998 in Lisbon (Table 4), the rate of growth is much more sustainable that its counterpart of Seville. In fact, this increase was outlined by the respondents as very important for the competitiveness of Lisbon. 'This increase is important. A destination must have a *critical mass*, dimension' said the ATL President. The increase in hotel capacity has been mainly achieved by the construction of 4 and 5 star hotels. About future growth, the ATL president says 'it is desirable to grow a little more, but the increases must be undertaken with care. There is not an unlimited capacity for growth'. The establishment of international hotel chains in Lisbon is also seen as desirable by ATL. He noted that the number of 'Hotéls de Charme' (small size, high quality hotels) has grown in Lisbon and considers it positive because it is more a qualitative than a quantitative increase.

Table 4   *Evolution in number of hotel rooms (2, 3, 4 and 5 star hotels) in the Borough of Lisbon*

Year	Rooms	Change (%)
1995	8237	-
1996	8215	-0,3
1997	8596	+4,6
1998	9436	+9,8
1999	9391	-0,5
2000	9102	-3,1
2001		

Source: Direcção Geral do Turismo (2002)

Outcomes

As a result of EXPO'98, five tourism-related outputs were identified: (1) Tourism administration of the City, (2) Hosting of tourism events, (3) Market segments in Lisbon, (4) Destination Image and (4) Tourism business levels. The remainder of this paper will analyse in detail how the Exposition contributed to these outputs.

Tourism administration of the City

A new relationship between players in the tourism industry was pointed out by the interviewees as one of the major changes resulting from EXPO. As ATL's President stated, 'just before the opening of EXPO'98 we started to think about how to take advantage of the experience of a radical change in the City and how to prevent the *hangover after the party* that is normal with Expos. This we felt could be better achieved by bringing together the public and private sectors in a common City tourism body'. In fact, the establishment of a public-private partnership for tourism organisation following a mega event is not new. This was also one of the outputs of the 1991 World Student Games in Sheffield, UK (Bramwell, 1997).

After a short maturation of the idea the City Administration and private entrepreneurs created ATL, a body that would be responsible for tourism in the City, equally shared by the private and public sector. In the planning stage two different cases were studied – Barcelona and Seville – and the first was used as benchmarking for the shape and scope of ATL. The example of Barcelona seems to have had a strong influence on Expo, not only in the re-organisation of the tourism administration of the City, but also in terms of urban redevelopment (Carrière and Demazière, 2002).

The City Administration transferred its responsibilities as well as its tourism budget to this Association and the private sector contributes an annual fee paid by each member/company. The Association has also developed a business group with companies servicing mainly tourist sector companies (consulting, training) in order to get additional funds to support activities related to its core roles (tourism promotion and information). The change in the City's Tourism Administration is recognised as having largely contributed to the good results after the exposition. The APAVT president stated that 'the success of tourism in the City is a direct result of the establishment of ATL and the partnership between public and private enterprises'. In his opinion, 'ATL brought the systematisation of the promotion, and higher professionalism'. The Hotelier's President, on the other end, highlighted the psychological effects of ATL. He stated that 'the respect that the association gathered induced in agents the need to improve service quality and that was reflected at all levels, including hotels'.

The consensual acknowledgement of ATL's role in the post-Expo success is further demonstrated by the dispute about who had the initiative to create the body. ATL president (who represented the City Administration in the planning process) stated that 'the City Administration challenged the private sector', while AHP counterpart stated that 'ATL was a result of pressure made by hoteliers and travel agents upon the City Administration'.

Hosting of events

The recognition of the highly positive effects of EXPO'98 has led the tourism industry to an unprecedented willingness to host other events. This willingness, together with the legacy of Expo in terms of an image of organisational capacity, infrastructures and equipment favoured the choice of Lisbon to host other events, mainly sports related. "If we did not have the Atlantic pavilion we would never have received a Tennis Masters", claims the APAVT president. Between 1999 and 2001, Lisbon was the stage for various world sport championships (Table 5).

Table 5   *Main events held in Lisbon between 1998 and 2001*

Year	Event
1999	World Junior Basketball Championship
2000	Bowling World Championship
2000	Masters Cup in Tennis
2001	Indoor Athletics World Championships
2001	Cycling World Championships
2001	Fencing World Championship

Although there is a consensus about the desire to host events, the study identified different approaches to the criteria to be used when bidding. Travel agents are the least selective – 'all events should be catered for' because 'a policy that continuously searches for new events will induce a continuous promotion policy' and will also 'keep expectations high'. APAVT also favours the existence of an event organisation policy. This policy, that would systematically search and bid for new events, 'should be comprehensive and ambitious'. To APAVT there should not be interruptions in the organisation of events.

ATL, on the other hand, is more selective when it comes to bidding for other events. Contrary to the APAVT position, ATL argues that there is a need to look at a cost-benefit analysis:

'Spending 5 million Euros for one event that lasts 3 days (the royalties paid to host the 2000 Tennis Masters)... Of course if you ask me if it is more important to bring a congress of 10,000 people where we only have to support the candidature expenses, the cost-benefit analysis is bigger. But we have those hundreds of TV hours, there are the visitors and it's a matter of image. But we always have to study the investment requirements. (...) It is desirable to hold events if they are self-funding'.

Hence, experience in the hosting of events seems to have given ATL a more critical approach to event bidding: 'There are other events that with much less investment – cycling and athletics championships – also offer a high exposure for the City'. The ATL President further argued that the role of the body should tend to give less financial support to the events and more to direct promotion, both nationally and internationally. Interestingly the AHP president summarised the importance of hosting smaller events – it "keeps the City alive and interesting in terms of tourism".

Market segments in Lisbon

The changes brought about by EXPO'98 resulted in an increased competitiveness of the City in international tourism markets, mainly due to the development of two main market segments – MICE and City Breaks – and two secondary – Golf and Cruises. The remainder of this section will explain how the Exposition contributed to Lisbon's competitiveness in these segments.

Lisbon already had a competitive positioning in the *MICE* segment, but EXPO'98, and the changes it induced, introduced the opportunity for the City to attract more and larger meetings, incentives and congresses. The ATL president gave a good example of how the City is now equipped to host larger events:

> 'For example, we had here in October [2000] and that was not the first time because we have done it before, a congress for 10,000 people, and the City remained the same, like the congress was not happening. When we hosted the ASTA congress in 1994, we had to take special measures, because it brought more than 5,000 people to Lisbon. We can now hold congresses for 10,000/12,000 and the City keeps running and living the same way. Today, there is no need to create exceptional circumstances to organise an event in Lisbon'.

The APAVT president reinforced the importance of the new facilities that allow Lisbon to host larger congresses and meeting. In his opinion, the City is now prepared for hosting events up to 17,000/18,000 participants. He further attributed this growth to the development in infrastructure, the enhancement of the organisational skills and the improvement of the quality of the destination.

EXPO'98 also induced major developments in the *City Breaks* segment. 'It was here that major changes happened', says the ATL president. Expo created the conditions for Lisbon to be promoted as a leisure city with a rich identity. According to ATL,

> "Lisbon was the last European Capital to be 'discovered' by Europeans for these short stays. I would say that there is a club of *citybreakers*, a group of people mainly from the most developed countries in Europe, that travel several times in a year for short stays and that repeat destinations. And there is a group of 20/25 cities in Europe which are city break cities. Lisbon was not in that club. Lisbon got into the club after the event."

He further outlines the importance of the strategy pursued, and the promotional efforts employed since then, in the success of this segment. 'Expo worked as a lever' and therefore it made the work of ATL easier. In this strategy, the creation of a calendar of regular events was seen as being of major importance: 'people go less because of what you have, the landscape, and more because of the stage, of what is happening'. Events were staged in the low seasons and the calendar of events promoted in Lisbon's priority markets.

Other measures adopted in this strategy by Lisbon's tourism helped the development of this market segment by improving the quality of the tourists' stay. Examples are the increase of tourist information centres, located near the main tourist attractions, and the launch of a card (Lisboacard) that facilitates mobility in the City, the entrance to attractions and gives discounts in stores and restaurants.

Although only one golf course exists in the Borough of Lisbon, there are 10 high quality courses within one hour, and ATL saw an opportunity to promote this product. The percentage of those visiting the City for golfing purposes rose three-fold between 2000 and 2001, from 0.2% to 0.6% (ATL, 2002). As to the Cruise market, in 2000 a total of 189,849 cruise passengers used Lisbon Port to disembark, embark or simply to visit the City for a few hours (Table 6). Although in 2001 this number dropped considerably (-21.6%), there was still a growth of 31.2% between 1997 and 2001.

As the ATL President noted, "In 1998 Lisbon surpassed Copenhagen and became the first Atlantic cruise port and it still keeps that position". According to him "the development of this segment was closely related to what happened with Expo". During the preparation works for Expo, important investments in Lisbon harbour resulted not only in improvements in existing infrastructure (notably level of comfort and security) but also an increase in the capacity to receive more and bigger cruises.

Table 6   *Evolution in cruise shipping passenger throughput in Lisbon Harbour*

Year	Rooms	Change (%)
1997	113476	-
1998	139850	23,2%
1999	161734	15,6%
2000	189849	17,4%
2001	148855	-21,6%

Source: Administração do Porto de Lisboa (2002)

Destination image

EXPO'98 was a highly visible event, both nationally and internationally. According to Parque das Nações (2002), 6312 journalists, from 88 countries, representing 2392 entities, requested accreditation to cover EXPO'98. Therefore, it is not surprising that one of the outcomes frequently outlined during the interviews was the ability of EXPO'98 to work as an image-maker for Lisbon's tourism. The international media coverage led to an unprecedented moment of international exposure. The ATL President believes that never before had the country or the City been presented so positively. To the APAVT president, publicity around Expo contributed to an improved perception of the City, an opinion reinforced by the AHT saying that 'EXPO'98 put Lisbon in the mouth of the world'. The 1.7 million foreigners who visited the Exposition will also have worked as tourism promoters in their countries of origin due to word-of-mouth effects. No major problems were reported during Expo (both ATL and AHP president outlined the lack of complaints to the tourism authorities) and thus they believed that the overall evaluation of the experience of visiting Lisbon was high.

Tourism business levels

All the interviewees agreed that the previous outputs and outcomes resulted in an unprecedented boost to the City's tourism industry. Not only were the results during Expo positive, but the Expo legacy has allowed the City to reach a higher level of competitiveness in international markets. This section starts by briefly evaluating the short-term results of the Exposition (i.e. during the Exposition). The long term perceived impacts (i.e. after the Exposition) will then be addressed in more detail.

A study conducted by DGT to evaluate the tourism results of EXPO'98 (Silva, 1999) will be used to evaluate the *short-term impacts* of the event. Table 7 compares the results of the study with the objectives of the Exposition.

Table 7   *Comparison between results and initial objectives of EXPO'98*

	Number of visits (thousand)			Number of visitors (thousand)			Rate of repeated visits	
	Real	Forecast	Deviation	Real	Forecast	Deviation	Real	Forecast
Portugal	7940,5	10349,7	-23,3%	3100	4600	-32,6%	2,56	2,24
Abroad	1873,7	4533,9	-58,7%	1700	2900	-41,4%	1,10	1,36
Spain	871,0	3521,9	-73,2%	750	N/A	N/A	1,16	N/A
Others	1002,7	1282,0	-21,8%	950	N/A	N/A	1,06	N/A
Emigrants	314,0	750,4	-58,2%	N/A	N/A	N/A	N/A	N/A
Total	10128,2	15634,0	-35,2%	N/A	N/A	N/A	N/A	N/A

Source: Silva (1999); N/A: not available

None of the objectives regarding number of visits and visitors were achieved with the single exception of the rate of repeated visits by Portuguese nationals. Overall, there was a negative difference of 35.2%, the poor performance of the Spanish market being mainly responsible for the shortfall. Of the 3.5 million expected only one quarter actually arrived. The main reason for this disastrous results may lie in the supposed 'uniqueness' of EXPO'98 in the eyes of the Spanish tourists. As Getz (1997) points out, uniqueness is a key point in making an event attractive to potential markets. Spain had held an Expo, six years before, exploring a similar theme, which is likely to have reduced the level of 'uniqueness' of the Lisbon event. The assumption that the event would be naturally attractive to the Spanish led to a misdirected marketing approach as well as to an overestimation of the attractiveness of the Exposition (and consequently to the number of visitors expected). Despite the negative performance of the Exposition in attracting the expected number of tourists, from the 1.7 million foreigners that visited the Exposition, 800,000 stated that visiting the EXPO'98 was the primary purpose of their visit to Portugal.

APAVT's president suggested that, 'The Expo project has a very strong infrastructure/urban component and less a tourist component. The tourist fruition of Expo has born when the Exposition ended'. Although this would suggest some frustration with the short-term Expo-related impacts, this was rapidly overcome by the *long-term impacts*.

One common method used to measure the performance of the tourism industry is to look at changes in the levels of business of tourism companies, notably hotels and other accommodation services. For the purposes of this paper, an analysis of the evolution of two variables – Hotel Occupancy Rates (OR) and Total Revenue per Room Available (TRRA) – was conducted. TRRA is calculated similarly to RevPAR, but instead of using price per room is based on the total revenue of the hotel, that is the total revenue of the hotel divided by the number of available rooms. The prices do not include VAT and have been adjusted for inflation. The results are shown in Figures 2 and 3. The base for the analysis is 1997 (the year before Expo) and the analysis runs until 2001.

A brief analysis of the two figures clearly shows that both OR and TRRA have increased between 1997 and 2001. In respect to OR, the highest increase was recorded by three star units, with an increase of 11.4 percentage points (from 71.8% to 83.2%).

The four star hotels occupancy rate grew 5.4 points and the five star by 3.7. The average growth for the three, four and five star hotels between 1997 and 2001 was 7.2 percentage points. An analysis by year shows a remarkable growth in 1998 for the three types of hotels (10.5 percentage points in average). In 1999 a slight decrease occurred, but the values are still noticeably higher than in 1997, the year before Expo (the average increase in 1999 when compared to 1997 was 7.1 points). 2000 was the best year ever for the tourism industry, with the 1998 results not only achieved, but exceeded (average of 2000 was 74.1%, one percentage point above the 1998 figure). In 2001 the occupancy rate decreased and an analysis of the behaviour by month indicated that the decrease could already be observed in February. Therefore, this decrease cannot be fully attributed to the cancellations and reduction of travel after the events of September 11th (although it seems evident that there were some impacts caused by this event, since September and October are peak months for tourism business in Lisbon). This decrease in OR may also be the consequence of the increase in number of rooms in 2001.

Figure 2   *Occupancy Rates: 1997/2001*

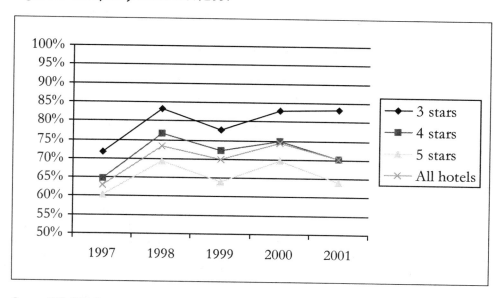

Source: ATL (2002)

As to Total Revenue per Room Available, there was a real increase between 1997 and 2001. It should be noted that these values are adjusted for inflation. Once again, the TTRA increased in an unprecedented way – the average growth in the period was nearly 25%. Following the slow down in 1999 (less 9.4%), in 2000 exactly the same TRRA as 1998 was recorded (76.6 Euros per room).

In 2001 the change, although positive, was almost irrelevant (0.1%). In the five-year period the highest increase was at the five star hotels (30.9%), followed by the four star units (14.5%). The TRRA of three star hotels grew 7.5% in this period.

It is noteworthy that while the five star hotels had the lowest increase in occupancy rate, they had the better performance in terms of total revenue per available room. Conversely, the three star hotels had the highest grow in occupancy rates but the lowest in TRRA. This suggests that hotels in different categories have followed different strategies.

While three star hotels seem to have endeavoured to maximise occupancy rates, five star hotel strategy was focused on maximising revenues. The four star hotels seem to have pursued a mixed strategy.

Figure 3 *Total revenue per available room: 1997/2001*

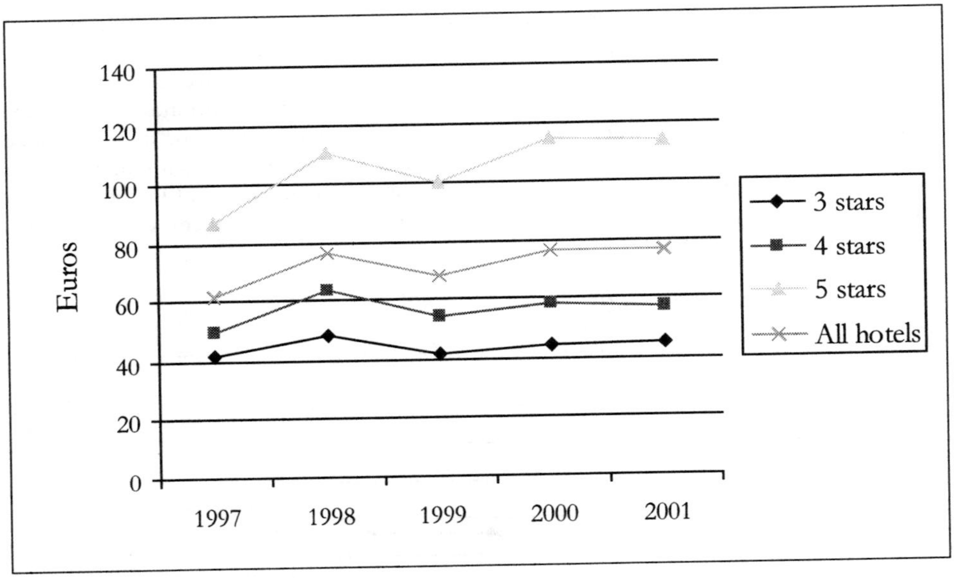

Source: ATL (2002)

Conclusions

Expos are one of the mega-events of the cultural world, not only because of their length but also because of the investments required and the number of national and international visitors attracted. In Portugal the tourism sector, particularly in the Lisbon area, responded positively to the opportunity offered by Expo and acted both internally and externally. In terms of its own responsibilities, the sector re-organised the tourism promotion of the City by creating a tourism association for Lisbon (ATL), which is thought to have led tourism businesses to embrace higher service quality standards and a higher efficiency in tourism promotion. In external terms, the sector involved both the City Administration and the National Government in the establishment of conditions that would enhance competitiveness of the City by supporting a defined strategy, mainly in terms of tourist equipment, planning and infrastructures. As a result, for example, the City is able to host large congresses, incentives and meetings and it may be argued that this MICE market is now in the mature stage of its life cycle in the Lisbon area. Additionally, Lisbon emerged as a player in the highly important European city break market, extending its portfolio of motivations for visiting the City.

EXPO'98 was the main mega event held in Lisbon (and Portugal) and this may explain why the perceived impacts are so high. Entrepreneurs tend to think that without Expo nothing would have been done and therefore all the positive results are attributed to Expo. Additionally EXPO'98 opened the debate about the need for an official policy in terms of bidding for future events which itself may be a reflection of a feeling of self confidence and a belief in the city/country's ability to develop and manage events of a global scale.

This increased self confidence is also reflected in the enhanced image of the City held by some of the major associations charged both with promoting Lisbon and in delivering a sophisticated tourism product.

Whilst it is probably too early to offer a final definitive analysis of the effects upon Portugal's and particularly Lisbon's tourism industry of EXPO'98, it can be argued at this stage, four years after Expo closed that the signs are good. Credit must therefore be given to those who were directly involved and who had the vision to see beyond the actual event and who were able not only to competently host an event receiving in excess of 10m visits, but who were able to hand on a prime development site with a range of major visitor attractions to a city which itself had a vastly improved tourism infrastructure.

References

Administração do Porto de Lisboa (2002), http://www.portodelisboa.com, (17-06-02).

ATL (2002), http://www.atl-turismolisboa.pt, (24-06-02).

Baleiras, R. N., Monteiro, R. S. and Reis, A. B., *Avaliação de Impactos do Projecto Global 'EXPO'98' nas Receitas do Sector Público Administrativo (Sumário Executivo)*, Lisboa: GANEC da Faculdade de Economia da Universidade Nova de Lisboa, May 2002.

BIE (2002), http://www.bie-paris.org/eng/index3.htm, (23-06-02).

Bramwell, B. (1997), "Strategic Planning before and after a mega-event", *Tourism Management*, 18 (3), 167-176.

Carlsen, J. and Williams, P. (1999), "Events tourism and destination image in Western Australia", *The impact of mega events*, Andersson, T., Persson, C., Sahlberg, B. and Strom, L. (eds.), ETOUR, Ostersund, pp. 69-80.

Carrière, J. and Demazière, C. (2002), "Urban Planning and Flagship Projects: Lessons from EXPO'98, Lisbon", *Planning Practice and Research*, 17 (1), 69-79.

Cegielski, M. and Mules, T. (2002), "Aspects of Residents' perceptions of the GMC 400 – Camberra's V8 Supercar race", *Current Issues in Tourism*, 5 (1), 54-70.

Direcção Geral do Turismo (2002), http://dgturismo.pt (24-06-02).

Echtner, C. and Ritchie, J. R. B. (1993), "The measurement of destination image: an empirical assessment", *Journal of Travel Research*, 32:Spring, pp. 3-13.

Evans, M., (1982), "Planning for the World's Fair: How to house 5 million guests", *Cornell Quarterly*, May, pp. 31-34.

Getz, D. (1997), *Event Management and Event Tourism*, Cognizant, New York.

Getz, D. (1999), "The impacts of mega events on tourism: strategies for destinations", *The impact of mega events*, Andersson, T., Persson, C., Sahlberg, B. and Strom, L. (eds.), ETOUR, Ostersund, pp. 5-32.

Hall, C. M. (1992), *Hallmark Tourist events: Impacts, Management and Planning*, Belhaven Press, London.

Hiller, H. H. (1998), "Assessing the impacts of mega-events: a linkage model", *Current Issues in Tourism*, 1(1), 47-57.

Hiller, H. H. (1995), "Conventions as mega-events", *Tourism Management*, 16 (5),. 375-379.

Holmes, R. and Shamsuddin, A. (1997), "Short- and long-term effects of World Exposition 1986 on US demand for British Columbia tourism", *Tourism Economics*, 3 (2), 137-160.

Jeong, G. H., (1999), "Residents' perceptions on the long-term impacts of the Seoul Olympics to the Chamsil area development in a tourism perspective", *The impact of mega events*, Andersson, T., Persson, C., Sahlberg, B. and Strom, L. (eds.), ETOUR, Ostersund, pp. 169-178.

Law, E. (2002) *Urban Tourism: the visitor economy and the growth of large cities*, 2nd ed, Continnum, London.

Mihalik, B. and Simonetta, L. (1999), "A midterm assessment of the host population's perceptions of the 1996 Summer Olympics: support, attendance, benefits and liabilities", *Journal of Travel Research*, 37:February, pp. 244-248.

Mossberg, L. (1997), "The mega-event market", *Annals of Tourism Research*, 24, pp. 748-751.

Mossberg, L., (1999), "Mega-events as image creators: techniques to evaluate changes in Destination Image Perceptions", *The impact of mega events*, Andersson, T., Persson, C. Sahlberg, B. and Strom, L. (eds.), ETOUR, Ostersund, pp. 57-68.

Mules, T. (1998), "Events tourism and economic development in Australia", *Managing Tourism in Cities*, Tyler, D., Guerrier, Y. and Robertson, M. (eds.), John Wiley, Chichester, pp. 195-214.

Parque das Nações (2002), http://www.parquedasnacoes.pt (17-06-02).

Parque EXPO'98 (1994), *O Projecto Global EXPO'98*, unpublished document.

Parque EXPO'98 (1999), *Relatório Final da Exposição Mundial EXPO'98 em Lisboa*, Lisboa: Parque EXPO'98.

Ritchie, J. R. B. (1984), "Assessing the impact of hallmark events: conceptual and research issues", *Journal of Travel Research*, 23 (1), 2-11.

Ritchie, J. R. B. and Smith, B. H., (1991), "The impact of a mega-event on host region awareness: a longitudinal study", *Journal of Travel Research*, 30 (1), 3-10.

Robertson, M. and Guerrier, Y. (1998), "Events as entrepreneurial displays: Seville, Barcelona and Madrid", *Managing Tourism in Cities*, Tyler, D., Guerrier, Y. and Robertson, M. (eds.), John Wiley, Chichester, pp. 215-228.

Roche, M. (1994), "Mega-events and urban policy", *Annals of Tourism Research*, 21, pp. 1-19.

Silva, J. S. (1999) "Tourism and the EXPO'98", *PowerPoint presentation for the Conference on The Impacts of EXPO'98 on tourism*, Estoril (Portugal), Escola Superior de Hotelaria e Turismo do Estoril, January.

Vaughan, D. R. (1977), *The economic impact of the Edinburgh Festival*, Scottish Tourism Board, Edinburgh.

Verdaguer, C. C. (1995), "Mega-events – local strategies and global tourist attractions", *European tourism: Regions, Spaces and Restructuring*, Montanari, A and Williams, A. M. (eds.), John Wiley, Chichester, pp. 193-205.

Index

© Centre for Tourism and Cultural Change and the Authors

ISBN 1 901888 34 7

First published 2004

Cover Design Julie Kwan

Published in Great Britain by
Business Education Publishers Limited
The Teleport
Doxford International
Sunderland
SR3 3XD

Tel: 0191 5252410
Fax: 0191 5201815

British Cataloguing-in-Publications Data
A catalogue record for this book is available from the British Library

Printed in Great Britain by Athenaeum Press, Gateshead.